MICHEL TREMBLAY

LES BELLES-SOEURS

EDITED WITH INTRODUCTION,
NOTES AND GLOSSARY
BY RACHEL KILLICK

PUBLISHED BY BRISTOL CLASSICAL PRESS
GENERAL EDITOR: JOHN H. BETTS
FRENCH TEXTS SERIES EDITOR: EDWARD FREEMAN

This impression 2002
First published in 2000 by
Bristol Classical Press
an imprint of
Gerald Duckworth & Co. Ltd.
61 Frith Street, London W1D 3JL
Tel: 020 7434 4242
Fax: 020 7434 4420
inquiries@duckworth-publishers.co.uk
www.ducknet.co.uk

A catalogue record for this book is available from the British Library

ISBN 1 85399 550 9

Cover: Costume illustration for *Les Belles-Soeurs:* reproduction of a sketch by Francois Barbeau. By kind permission of Michel Tremblay fonds/Fonds Michel Tremblay, National Library of Canada/Bibliothèque nationale du Canada.

CONTENTS

ACKNOWLEDGEMENTS

I should like to express my gratitude to the Canadian High Commission for the Faculty Teaching Award which enabled me to embark on this project and the Centre for Canadian Studies at the University of Leeds for the grant that allowed me to complete my documentation in Canada. Many people have helped me develop my interest in Quebec. I have particularly appreciated the advice and support of Emmanuel Kattan at the Quebec Delegation in London and Vivien Hughes of the Canadian High Commission, David Coward of the University of Leeds, Jacques Allard of the French Department of the University of Quebec in Montreal, Micheline Cambron, director of the Centre d'études québécoises of the University of Montreal, and Linda Hoad of the National Library of Canada in Ottawa. I should also like to give especial thanks to my husband John who took me to Canada in the first place and to the family here and in Canada for their interest and support. I am indebted to Dr. Richard Rastall of the Music Department of the University of Leeds for his kindness in providing camera-ready copy of 'O Canada'; to Marie-Anne Hintze of the French Department of the University of Leeds for her advice on the linguistic aspects of *joual*; to Edward Freeman for his encouragement and above all to Jean Scott, of BCP, for her helpful comments and careful editorial work.

INTRODUCTION

Contexts

On 28 August 1968, *Les Belles-Soeurs*,[1] a play by an unknown 26-year-old Québécois, Michel Tremblay, had its first performance at the Théâtre du Rideau Vert, one of Montreal's most respected theatres.[2] An immediate 'succès de scandale', it rivetted the attention of public and critics and decisively inaugurated a new phase in Quebec theatre. Reviews were violently mixed. Some heaped unequivocal praise on *Les Belles-Soeurs* for its no-holds-barred portrayal of working-class Quebec society in the raw. Some vehemently denounced its vulgarity, as revealed most notably in its abandonment of standard, 'educated' French in favour of *joual*, the earthily aggressive idiom of East End Montreal. Others, hedging their bets, acclaimed the accuracy of the social and psychological portrayal while deploring the crudeness of the language in which it was couched.[3] It was the start of five years of controversy, culminating first in an acrimonious argument (1972-3) over the financing of the play's first production in Paris and then, following its 1973 Paris success, in the acceptance by the purist hardliners of Quebec's cultural establishment, of the creative originality and sociological and theatrical importance of Tremblay's work.

Joual[4]

> *Si j'écris en joual, c'est pas pour me rendre intéressant ni pour scandaliser: c'est pour décrire un peuple.*
>
> (Tremblay, *Le Jour*, 2 July 1976)

The term *joual*, the Montreal pronunciation of *cheval*, had first been used in 1959 by the intellectual, writer, and politician, André Laurendeau, editor of the influential Montreal newspaper, *Le Devoir*, as a derogatory term to deplore the disadvantaged status of Quebec society and culture as revealed in its distortion of the French language. The coining became headline news with the publication, first in *Le Devoir* and then in volume form as *Les Insolences du Frère Untel* (1960), of a series of letters, in response to Laurendeau's observations. Published anonymously at first, these were the work of Jean-Paul Desbiens, in religion the Marist teaching priest Pierre-Jérôme.[5] Reinforcing Laurendeau's criticisms with extensive reference to his own experience both as a teacher and earlier as a philosophy student at Laval University, Desbiens developed a stinging condemnation of the obscurantism and the shambolic 'organisation' of the Catholic-controlled education system, by which, 'avec un retard de deux révolutions et demie: horloge d'Amérique, heure du Moyen Age' (*Insolences*, p. 28), a whole society had been trapped in backwardness and ignorance.[6] *Joual*, he argued, was the outward and visible sign of the debasement of Quebec society, defining an excluded community and perpetuating that exclusion in a vicious circle of linguistic inadequacy and low expectation:

> Cette absence de langue qu'est le joual est un cas de notre inexistence à nous, les Canadiens français. [...] Notre inaptitude à nous affirmer, notre refus de l'avenir, notre obsession du passé, tout cela se reflète dans le joual, qui est vraiment notre langue... (p. 32)

> Nous vivons joual par pauvreté d'âme et nous parlons joual par voie de conséquence. Je pose qu'il n'y a aucune différence substantielle entre la dégradation du langage et la désaffection vis-à-vis des libertés fondamentales. (p. 34)

The solution, Desbiens maintained, was a root and branch reform in education, including, notably, a proper training in the French language: 'On n'étudiera jamais assez le langage. Le langage est le lieu de toutes les significations' (p. 32). This should stress the need for proper grammatical structures and precise and clear enunciation and thus, in giving the francophone community the means to conceptualise and articulate its ideas effectively in both the private and the public arena, provide the impetus for a political initiative for an active defence of the French language in Quebec. Such urgings bore fruit in the two following decades in the development of a raft of language legislation aimed at protecting and promoting the use of French and led in 1977, under the first Parti Québécois government, to the adoption of the *Charte de la langue française*, otherwise known as Law 101.[7]

This call for the restoration of the dignity of the mother tongue provoked, however, a contrary reaction amongst a new 1960s generation of 'angry young' writers and singers, who adopted the reviled *joual* and turned it into a language of self-definition and self-affirmation. Before the 1960s, popular working-class speech, perceived by the elite as the language of the socially and culturally deprived in Quebec society, had scarcely figured in the written forms of serious literature. The new postwar urban novel, initiated by Gabrielle Roy's *Bonheur d'occasion* (1945), contained a few softened snatches within its dialogues. Meanwhile, in the serious theatre, where concepts of 'correct' language, suspended between written and oral usage, assume a more problematic status, the most prominent Quebec playwrights such as Gratien Gélinas or Marcel Dubé, conscious of the literary expectations of their bourgeois audiences, pursued a prudent course, giving a nod to the informalities of popular language whilst maintaining an overall framework of standard French.[8]

In the 1960s, however, in an atmosphere of social and artistic liberation, the nationalist Parti Pris group gave *joual* an important billing in their manifestos and the use of *joual* began to permeate serious literature.[9] Jacques Renaud's novel, *Le Cassé* (1964), adopted the oral forms of *joual*, though perhaps rather less extensively than its reputation suggests. Then, in the public space of the theatre, Eloi de Grandmont's 1967 adaptation of Shaw's *Pygmalion* mixed standard French (for the upper classes) with Eliza Doolittle's *joual* (as the Quebec equivalent of Cockney); but it was 1968 that was a breakthrough year for *joual* in public performance. *Osstidcho*, a musical spectacular, spearheaded by a group including the monologuist Yvon Deschamps, the singers Robert Charlebois, Mouffe and Louise Forestier, and the musicians of Le Jazz libre du Québec, broke with the 'chansonnier' tradition established by Félix Leclerc, and combined *joual* and rock in a striking cultural 'happening'.[10] Réjean Ducharme's play *Le Cid maghané* used an amalgam of *joual* and burlesque French to send up Corneille's classic, thus encouraging through comic parody a reflection on the respective merits, for Quebec culture, of popular, local speech and literary metropolitan parlance.[11] But Ducharme's romp, even as it exploited the comic effects of the linguistic and cultural gap, continued to rely on a close knowledge of a canonic text of French literature and an appreciation of an elite French discourse. *Les Belles-Soeurs*, finally performed in August 1968 (though written in 1965), decisively cut the umbilical cord; Tremblay's whole-scale adoption of *joual* as the language of *Les Belles-Soeurs* uncompromisingly embodied an entire life-style, which it simultaneously and paradoxically defined, validated and condemned.

Tremblay rejected out-of-hand the fundamentally conformist approach to language of Gélinas and Dubé: 'Le joual vient, chez moi, d'une réaction contre un théâtre de compromis, à la Dubé, ni tout à fait français, ni tout à fait joual, mais entre les deux' (*Le Devoir*, 14 November 1969, p. 6). His assumption of his identity as a Québécois writer came with the sudden recognition of the linguistic falsity of early 60s Quebec cinema with its reliance, as a public medium, on standard French:

> Un jour, j'etais allé voir avec mon ami Brassard un film de Pierre Patry où jouait Guy Godin (*La Corde au cou*). En sortant du cinéma on se demandait ce qui clochait, pourquoi nous n'accrochions pas à l'histoire. A force d'en parler, l'hypothèse du langage artificiel des personnages s'est imposée. Et j'ai eu envie d'essayer d'écrire un dialogue où l'on parlerait vraiment comme dans la vie de tous les jours. Je suis parti avec deux vieilles dames qui revenaient du salon mortuaire et je me suis retrouvé avec 15 femmes dans une cuisine, invitées à un party de collage de timbres.
>
> (Tremblay to Martine Corrivault, *Le Soleil*, 8 December 1984, p. B 3)

Les Belles-Soeurs' introduction on stage of the strident vulgarities of *joual* caused an immediate uproar. The contrast with cherished beliefs about the 'voice' of Quebec was deliberately brutal ('une claque sur la gueule' as Tremblay put it to Fernand Doré, *Magazine Maclean*, June 1969, p. 10). Louis Hémon's *Maria Chapdelaine* (1913), a founding text of Quebec identity, had idealised the notion of a French Canadian 'mother tongue', deep-rooted in the language and songs of the Old World and blooming afresh in the New.[12] In the 1960s, as Tremblay created *Les Belles-Soeurs*, Gilles Vigneault from remote North Shore Natashquan continued to appeal to the same nostalgic vision of Quebec's rural past with songs such as 'Les gens de mon pays', which rapidly assumed the status of quasi-national hymns for the independence movement.[13] No less committed to the assertion of an independent identity for Quebec, Tremblay, the city boy, was less sentimental than Vigneault and more clear-sighted in his assessment of his community's contemporary limitations and modern specificity. For him, as for Laurendeau and Desbiens, *joual* was the true language of Quebec in that it expressed the alienated colonial mentality of a subject society. Unlike them, however, he also saw the public exhibition of *joual* as the means of forcing a general recognition of this unpalatable fact and thus of opening up a way out of insularity and frustration.

Tremblay was at pains from the beginning to stress that his own use of *joual* in *Les Belles-Soeurs* was not a matter of linguistic incompetence or carelessness nor a dogmatic attempt to promote a wider use of *joual*.[14] *Le Train* (1964), his first play, his collection of stories, *Contes pour buveurs attardés* (1965), and his adaptation of Aristophanes' *Lysistra* (1969) were all written in standard French. The choice of *joual* for *Les Belles-Soeurs* corresponds to a specific reality and a specific artistic vision and entails a two-fold artistic challenge: first, the imaginative reconstruction of the thought-process out of which the dialogue is born:

> Ce qu'on ne sait pas, c'est qu'écrire en joual est aussi difficile qu'écrire en français. Pour écrire une phrase en joual, je peux la recommencer dix fois avant de retrouver la structure de pensée d'une Québécoise.[15]

secondly, the creative highlighting by which the dialogue, transcending its apparent mediocrity or banality, achieves symbolic resonance.

The 1968 Quebec establishment was not, however, impressed by Tremblay's linguistic *tour de force* and strove to keep his 'family' piece and its linguistic dirty washing strictly 'within the family'. The two *directrices* of the bourgeois Théâtre du Rideau Vert agreed under pressure from the acting community to give the play its public performance (see below, p. x and n.28), but in 1972 the Quebec Ministry of Cultural Affairs was less amenable to the suggestion by the French actor/director Jean-Louis Barrault, that it should be performed in Paris as part of the Festival du Théâtre des Nations. The Minister, Claire Kirkland-Casgrain,[16] was adamant in refusing financial support, arguing that the play would be incomprehensible to a French audience and that a play in 'good' French should be sought instead. It was left to the Federal Government in 1973 to come up with the necessary subsidy. The success of the play in Paris and the ready acceptance there of *joual* not only as the appropriate medium for the portrayal of a disadvantaged community, but as a version of French with its own richness and vigour,[17] decisively vindicated Tremblay's initiative. The debate continued nonetheless in such far-flung corners of *la francophonie* as Dakar, where the linguists assembled for the 1973 *cinquième biennale de la langue française* were moved to deplore the obsessiveness and parochial violence of the Quebec delegates, Robert Choquette, writer and member of the Académie canadienne française, and Jean-Marie Laurence, 'conseiller linguistique à Radio-Canada', in reaction to the favourable reviews and in particular the favourable linguistic comments emanating from Paris.[18] One year later, in contrast, back home in Quebec, dissenting voices were substantially quelled, if not completely silenced, by the decision of the nationalist Société Saint-Jean-Baptiste to award Tremblay its 1974 Victor Morin prize for services to Quebec culture.[19] Thus was the linguistic black sheep restored to the family fold. Numerous subsequent honours in Quebec and in France have confirmed Tremblay's high profile in Quebec and francophone culture but the debate over *joual* is not, even now, completely stilled, as was clear from the mixed reception given by the Quebec literary and educational worlds to the 1992 Robert *Dictionnaire québécois*.[20]

Michel Tremblay

> *Je décris le seul milieu que j'aie jamais connu, le milieu que j'aime, le milieu d'où je viens [...] Mon Dieu que je les aime ces gens-là.*[21]

Who was the author of *Les Belles-Soeurs* and what lay behind his choice of subject? Born on 25 June 1942, in a house on the corner of the rue Fabre and the rue Gilford, Michel Tremblay hailed like the characters in his play from the working-class East End of Montreal. His childhood, as subsequently described in three volumes of autobiographical reminiscences, *Les Vues animées*, *Douze coups de théâtre* and *Un Ange cornu avec des ailes de tôle*, and as reflected in the novel cycle *Chroniques du Plateau Mont-Royal*, [22] combined the hurly-burly and constrictions of life in an extended family with the excitement and enjoyment of a vivid inner experience of the imagination.[23] His mother, in particular, provided a powerful stimulus to a mind preoccupied with fantasy and adventure, in part through her tales of her childhood with her Cree grandmother far away in the prairies of Sasketchewan, in part through her enjoyment of reading and her fascination with cinema, radio and television.[24] At the age of thirteen, Michel, a bright pupil, was among 31 boys chosen by the city of Montreal for a Quebec state bursary to the *école classique*.[25] But the snobbish atmosphere, isolating the schoolboys from their roots in the local community by its emphasis on their future status as members of the educated Quebec elite, was not to his taste, and after only three months he requested a transfer back to his local school.[26] On leaving full-time education he followed his father[27] and one of his elder brothers into the printing trade, though not without a sense of fatalistic misgiving:

> Cette décision, probablement celle d'un paresseux pour qui c'est la solution la plus facile, de suivre des cours à l'Institut des arts graphiques dans le but de devenir imprimeur comme mon père, me paraît encore aujourd'hui absurde; je n'étais pas fait pour ce métier-là, je le savais, tout le monde autour de moi le savait, et pourtant tout le monde m'a laissé faire; je me voyais travaillant comme linotypiste pour le reste de mes jours, perpétuel inadapté qui n'avait pas trouvé sa place dans le monde et qui commençait à douter de jamais le trouver. En un mot, vilain, hideux même, auquel j'étais encore incapable de faire face mais qui me trottait de plus en plus souvent par la tête: un raté. (DC, p. 255)

There followed two-and-a-half years as 'un ouvrier très bien payé, mais un être humain désespérément malheureux' on the night-shift at the Imprimerie judiciaire, type-setting the daily pages of the municipal court record. Yet the job gave him ample opportunity to write, either in the afternoons at home, or, having often despatched all his work by 10 p.m., on the shift itself:

> C'est ainsi que j'ai pondu *Les Belles-Soeurs* au complet entre dix heures du soir et une heure du matin, en août et septembre 1965, en volant du temps à l'Imprimerie judiciaire. (*AC*, p. 222)

In the same period Tremblay also wrote a large collection of fantastic tales, a selection of which he finally contrived to have published by Gérald Godin at the Éditions du Jour as *Contes pour buveurs attardés* (1965). Godin, much to his later chagrin, declined, however, to accept the commercial risk of publishing a play. Further rejections followed, this time from producers and actors unwilling to risk their reputation on a piece so clearly violating the linguistic and social norms of contemporary theatre. Then Tremblay's luck turned. A reading of the play took place on 4 March 1968, arranged, unbeknown to him, by his friend, the budding director André Brassard, under the auspices of the Centre des arts dramatiques; it met with an enthusiastic reception and led directly through pressure from the acting community to production at the Théâtre du Rideau Vert.[28] It was, in the words of the commentator Gilbert David, a 'Big Bang' event, that fundamentally reshaped theatre in Quebec and that reflected and moulded

Quebec consciousness at a critical moment in its evolution.[29] For Tremblay personally it was the beginning of an impressive and prolific writing career first in drama and later in the novel also, which is continuing into the new millennium.

Tremblay's Quebec 1942-1968

What was the cultural context of Tremblay's childhood and youth out of which *Les Belles-Soeurs* emerged? A convenient and appropriate way of finding out is through the autobiographical and semi-autobiographical accounts. *La Grosse Femme d'à côté est enceinte*, the first of the novel cycle *Chroniques du Plateau Mont-Royal*, focuses on a single day, 2 May, in 1942, the year of Tremblay's birth, and the activities of the various inhabitants of a street, closely resembling the rue Fabre, the street of Tremblay's own childhood.[30] The baby yet to be born is the writer to be, Tremblay's *alter ego*. The street is full of pregnant women, but their pregnancies, with the exception of that of 'la grosse femme', are ideologically dictated by the long-standing pro-natalist policies of church and state in Quebec, reinforced by the specificities of the conscription crisis of 1942.[31]

In 1917 Canadian conscription for the First World War had led to riots in Quebec. In the Second World War it had at first been ruled out in Canada by the federal government but then, in response to the gravity of the international situation, finally introduced by national plebiscite in 1942 though not fully implemented until 1944. Substantial hostility to it remained in Quebec, where the protected status of fathers of large families encouraged the additional reproductive surge reflected in Tremblay's novel. Tremblay's birth in the year of the conscription crisis locates him at a significant point in the development of Quebec's twentieth-century consciousness of itself as a society whose appartenance and aspirations were those neither of Anglophone Canada nor of France and Europe. On the one hand, the reluctance to accept the plebiscited decision of an anglophone federal majority was further fuelled by a sense of grievance and inferiority vis-à-vis France, the 'mother country', perceived as looking down on its North American offspring.[32] On the other, the severing of the 'cultural supply line'[33] from France suddenly isolated Quebec, projecting it temporarily into a new, potentially liberating role as a free-standing culture, with an independent specificity defined in the dual terms of its French language and North American geography.[34]

Despite this momentary glimpse of a possible high-profile role in the international francophone context, the post-war Quebec of Tremblay's childhood and youth remained in many respects a backward-looking and isolationist society, where narrow reactionary views in politics and religion, founded on a rural and small-town mentality, still contrived to hold sway.

Paying only limited attention to accelerating industrialisation and urbanisation, Maurice Duplessis and his ruling party, the conservative Union Nationale, continued to pursue a policy of provincial autonomy based on the old ideal of a self-sufficient, largely agricultural Quebec with a submissive, Catholic-controlled work-force. The hierarchy of the Catholic Church, in general sympathy with this vision which accorded closely with its perception of its own interests,[35] fell in with the demands of a regime run on the basis of favours performed and favours received and shared in attempts to muzzle political opposition and to limit democratic rights.

Tremblay, as a child, was naturally oblivious to the manoeuvrings and chicanery of the Quebec political and ecclesiastical establishment and *La Grosse femme d'à côté est enceinte*, his imaginative re-creation of Quebec 1942, gives primary stress to the domestic sphere. Political allusion is, for the most part, set at one remove, transposed from the human to the animal kingdom and literally displaced to the gutter as the cat Duplessis and the dog Godbout, each hell-bent on defending their territory of garbage cans, repeat the skirmishings of their two prime-ministerial namesakes.[36] His dawning consciousness of the nature of Quebec society is however captured entertainingly and with great sensitivity in the three volumes of reminiscences recounting the development of his cultural and literary self. His understanding of the displacement to the city of a rural population, ill-adapted to cope with urban life (the generation of Olivine Dubuc in *Les Belles-Soeurs*) comes to him through the experience of listening to his paternal grandmother with her tales of her childhood in Charlevoix, of:

> les quatre bateaux blancs qui partaient de La Malbaie pour remonter le Saguenay, le *Tadoussac*, le *Québec*, le *Saint-Laurent*, et le *Saguenay* [...] le lac Saint-Jean, tout au bout, mer intérieure toute noire et d'une si grande beauté qu'elle ne pouvait pas en parler sans sortir son mouchoir; la suffocation qui l'avait terrassée quand elle s'était vue obligée de déménager à Montréal, au début du siècle, pour suivre Télésphore Tremblay, qu'elle allait épouser [...] La misère, la misère noire des paysans de partout au Québec venus s'installer en ville pour devenir des ouvriers mal payés, le *cheap labor* des grandes compagnies anglaises, eux qui n'avaient jamais connu que le grand air. (*AC*, p. 106-7)

Later Gabrielle Roy's *Bonheur d'occasion*, memorably depicting the deprivation of the Montreal working-class in the early years of the Second World War, brings Tremblay, aged 14, to a critical awareness of the harsh realities of city life:

> C'était la première fois que je lisais un roman écrit dans ma ville où la vertu et le bon ordre ne régnaient pas en maîtres absolus, où la religion catholique ne répondait pas à toutes les questions, où Dieu n'était pas automatiquement au bout de chaque geste, et je n'en revenais pas. (*AC*, p. 158)

The suffering of the Lacasse family in the novel moves him to tears, tears shed not just over that one family, but

> pour la première fois de ma vie sur notre sort collectif de petit peuple perdu d'avance, abandonné, oublié dans l'indifférence générale, noyé dans la Grande Histoire des autres et dont on ne se rappelait que lorsqu'on avait besoin de chair à canon. (*AC*, p. 163)

Roy's book with its truths about Quebec and questioning of establishment myth, is, he suspects, from the point of view of the authorities, a 'livre athée'. As such, it rejoins those of almost all the great thinkers and writers of Metropolitan France, whose consignment to the Roman Catholic Index of prohibited books was still rigorously enforced in the Catholic-run schools of 1950s Quebec. Texts used for study in class were anodyne and always in extract form, unsupervised reading of a more substantial kind vigorously discouraged. For Brother Léon, one of Tremblay's teachers of French, even France's 'national' author, Victor Hugo, was anathema as a dangerous libertine and revolutionary:

> *Tout* Victor Hugo [...] *tout* Victor Hugo est à l'index! C'était un écrivain aux moeurs dissolues qui se prétendait près de Dieu mais qui pratiquait plus la révolution que la religion! N'approchez pas de ses livres, contentez-vous du court extrait des *Travailleurs de la mer* qu'on vous demande d'analyser dans vos cours de français. Ne lisez pas sa poésie! Ne lisez pas ses romans! Ce sont des oeuvres pernicieuses!' (*AC*, p. 183-4)

With such billing, as Tremblay dryly remarks, it is only because the class was part of a scientific stream that the whole group failed to turn instantly to Victor Hugo and his like! Tremblay's admission that he had already read *Notre-Dame de Paris*, his immediate despatch to the parish priest for confession of his 'sin', the priest's incredulity at the rigidity of the school's adherence to the Index, Tremblay's subsequent revenge (his deliberate reading in class of *Bug Jargal*, the one work by Hugo absent, though the teacher does not realise it, from the list of proscribed works) all add up to a hilarious episode, worthy of *Le Libraire* (1960), Gérard Bessette's comic classic of Catholic censorship in small-town Quebec. The comedy has, however, a bitter sting in the tail. The religious establishment cannot tolerate the public revelation of its ignorance and small-minded stupidity and metes out humiliating punishment to the boy who has dared to make a fool of it: 'L'humiliation systématique des élèves était la grande spécialité, la grande force des frères de l'Instruction chrétienne, j'en eus une fois de plus la preuve ce jour-là.' (*AC*, p. 191)[37]

The other major reality of Quebec gradually confronted in the autobiographical texts is the linguistic question and its socio-economic and political implications. At the age of five, Tremblay had his first lesson in the linguistic snobbery of social class through the lexical strictures

('Michel, on ne dit pas "un char", on dit "une voiture"' [*DC*, p. 19]) and the 'posh' speech habits of the mother of his friend, Jean Paradis:

> Madame Paradis était la première personne que je rencontrais dans ma vie qui utilisait les négations, j'étais donc très impressionné. En fait, elle parlait comme les actrices de la radio [...] Elle avait quelque chose d'irréel, presque d'un autre monde, parce qu'elle ne s'exprimait pas comme les femmes que je connaissais. Maman, qui était la personne qui parlait le mieux dans toute la famille avec mon frère Jacques, disait bien moi, toi, et ici, mais pour le reste c'était du bon vieux montréalais. (*DC*, p. 12)[38]

As the child grows into a teenager, he becomes increasingly aware of a deeper discriminatory rift, the gap between anglophone and francophone. His reading of the insipid, but published, fiction of a thirteen-year-old British schoolgirl highlights for him the weighting of the linguistic scales in Quebec against the aspirations of Quebec writers, including potentially himself.[39] Shopping in Eaton's, one of Montreal's large department stores, brings him into conflict with the rule that requires francophone shop assistants to speak in English to all customers, including francophone ones, and thus all customers, including francophone ones, to pose their questions in English to the assistants.[40] Going to the opera, he is humiliated to discover that the Quebec opera singers, the Simoneaus, are right pragmatically, if not in his view ideologically, in electing to use English, not French, for the dialogue in a performance of Mozart's *Il Seraglio* since the audience is almost entirely anglophone.[41] As far as work is concerned, his father advises him of the need to speak English if a job is to be readily obtained.[42]

The acquiescence of the 1950s Quebec population in these various forms of social and linguistic subjugation was however somewhat less monolithic than may appear retrospectively to have been the case. Looming large in a growing revolution in consciousness was television, starting up in Quebec in 1952. The new medium's demands for programme material and for personnel, the absence of regulations governing its activities and its social pervasiveness, particularly among the working class, were all nails in the coffin of the rear-guard restrictiveness of old-style Quebec. Tremblay recalls his father's early purchase of a large set which quickly became a focus of family life ('Comme tous les enfants de ma génération j'ai été élevé devant la télévision'[43]). What he records though, is his own imaginative development through exposure to the bi-weekly offerings of 'téléthéâtre'. Naturally, perhaps, given his age at the time, there is no mention of programmes of social and political debate such as *Prises de bec* or *Conférence de presse* but these were important catalysts in Quebec's awakening as a modern society.

With the ground thus prepared, Duplessis' death on 7 September 1959, rapidly and unexpectedly followed by that of Paul Sauvé, his successor as leader of the Union Nationale, finally cleared the way for the long-awaited modernising programme of Jean Lesage's Liberals, and then, emerging through the 1960s as a motivating force behind them, the separatist ambitions, violently articulated in the extremist activities of the Front de libération du Québec (FLQ, founded in 1963) and constitutionally advanced by the formation in 1968 of the Parti québécois (PQ) under the leadership of the TV journalist and erstwhile presenter of *Conférence de presse*, René Lévesque. Quebec writers reflected and furthered the desire for cultural self-expression and self-affirmation, increasingly identifying themselves with a separatist stance. Tremblay, established by *Les Belles-Soeurs* as a significant literary representative of an evolving new-style Québec, made clear his separatist sympathies by refusing to allow his play to be performed in English translation inside the province. He maintained this ban until the victory of Lévesque and the PQ in the provincial election of 1976 redrew the political map of Quebec, casting the anglophones for the first time in the role of political minority.

Women in Quebec

> *C'est à la femme canadienne-francaise que nous devons ce que nous avons de meilleur et ce que le voisin nous envie le plus: la famille, nombreuse, robuste, attachée au sol, fidèle à sa langue, à sa foi, et conservant le culte des aïeux, l'amour de la vieille patrie.*
> (Quebec Prime Minister Louis Alexandre Taschereau to the 1921 Congress of the Fédération Nationale Saint-Jean-Baptiste)[44]

Of all the aspects of twentieth-century Quebec society, it is arguably gender relations that most clearly exemplify the retrograde conservatism of the Duplessis regime. In the earliest days of the province, in the founding years of seventeenth-century New France, women enjoyed some flexibility of role and a measure of independence and freedom in the community's struggle for physical survival.[45] The British conquest of 1760 refocused francophone efforts on *cultural* survival, and with the Catholic Church as the single remaining source of francophone leadership, women were returned to a specifically familial role as the perpetuators and grass roots guardians of the francophone family.[46] This ethos, carried down the years, was emphatically renewed in the early decades of the twentieth century, against a background of economically provoked emigration and demographic loss. Arguing vigorously against calls for female suffrage, the influential Catholic politician Henri Bourassa stressed 'la sainte fécondité'[47] as women's crucial contribution to Quebec society and the message was consistently promulgated by the church-backed periodical, *L'Action catholique.* The Church's call for 'la revanche des berceaux'[48] still conditioned gender relationships in Quebec in the 1940s and 1950s, constraining individual potential and individual freedom within the supposedly immutable framework of a divinely pre-ordained design, that of Catholic and French survival in North America.

Men as well as women were losers in the arrangement, since the exaggerated promotion of the image of 'mère de famille', passing over the men, gave considerable power to the domestic partnership of women and parish priest,[49] a situation satirised by Roger Lemelin in his novel *La Famille Plouffe* (1948), adapted for television with huge success in the 1950s. But the emphasis on woman's social and moral duty as wife and especially mother and the desire to confine her to the domestic sphere constituted a more profound loss of individual choice and freedom. Furthermore, adding insult to injury, as Tremblay points out in a long and somewhat heavy-handed narratorial intervention in *La grosse femme d'à côté est enceinte*, the church's preoccupation with the sinfulness of sex coloured its pronatalist enthusiasm, making women ashamed of the very procreative function they were so insistently urged to fulfil:

> Ecrasées par cette religion monstrueuse qui défendait toute sorte de moyen de contraconception, cette religion fondée sur l'égoïsme des hommes, pour servir l'egoïsme des hommes, qui méprisait les femmes et en avait peur au point de faire de l'image de la Mère, la Vierge Marie, Mère de Dieu, une vierge intacte et pure, inhumaine créature sans volonté et surtout sans autonomie, qui s'était retrouvée un jour enceinte sans l'avoir désiré, par l'opération du Saint-Esprit (qu'on osait représenter sous la forme d'un oiseau! enceinte d'un oiseau, la Mère de Dieu!)[50] et qui avait enfanté sans avoir besoin de mettre au monde, insulte ultime faite au corps des femmes; gavées par les prêtres de phrases creuses autant que cruelles où les mots 'devoir' et 'obligations' et 'obéissance' prédominaient, ronflants, insultants, condescendants, les femmes canadiennes-françaises, surtout celles des villes, avaient fini par ressentir une honte maladive d'être enceintes, elles qui n'étaient pas dignes, comme l'autre, de mettre un enfant au monde sans qu'un homme, leur propriétaire et maître, leur passe dessus et qui, surtout, n'avaient pas le droit de se dérober à leur 'devoir', à leurs 'obligations' parce qu'elles devaient 'obéissance' à ce merveilleux outil du destin que leur avait fourni directement la Volonté de Dieu: leur mari. La religion catholique, en un mot, niait la beauté de l'enfantement et condamnait les femmes à n'être *jamais* dignes puisque la mère de leur Dieu, l'image consacrée de la Maternité, n'avait été qu'un entrepôt temporaire d'où l'Enfant n'était ni entré ni sorti. (*GF*, p. 229)

Humiliated thus in the very act of fulfilling their Catholic and 'national' duty, women remained subordinate and exploited members of the Quebec community. Though they had finally gained the vote in Quebec in 1940, their civil rights, as still determined by the Code of 1866, continued to be severely curtailed. The husband had legal control over every aspect of family life. A wife could not inherit or go to law in her own name, had no control of family finances, could not be employed without her husband's permission, had no right to live separately from her husband unless he had introduced a concubine into the home, could make no official decision over the upbringing of the children.

The liberalisation of Quebec society in the Quiet Revolution of the 1960s radically transformed the experience of women. The Church's rapid loss of influence, associated changes in women's legal rights and improvements in female education, created a new framework for women's aspirations consonant with that of other Western democracies. But *Les Belles-Soeurs* portrays the lives of the women born too early for these changes. Shaped and governed by the values of the Duplessis era, the world of Tremblay's growing up, they are untouched by the 1964 reforms to their civil status in law (Law 16),[51] still await a law permitting divorce (1969), have no easy access to contraception and, like women everywhere in Western society in the 1950s and early 60s, still have no general access to legal abortion (1968).[52]

Themes

Unhappy families

> *Quand tu t'appelles Tremblay, t'as des parents. Quand ta grand'mère Tremblay a épousé un gars qui s'appelait Tremblay, lui aussi, tu ne te rappelles plus avec qui t'es parent.*[53]

The title of the play identifies a key feature of Quebec experience, the ever-present extended family. As Tremblay explained to the journalist Claude Gingras:

> la pièce s'appelle les *Belles-Soeurs* parce qu'on ne peut rencontrer une Canadienne francaise sans qu'elle nous parle de 'sa belle-soeur Aline qui s'est cassé la jambe' ou de 'la belle-soeur d'une de ses belles-soeurs qui a eu un petit'. (*La Presse*, 16 August 1969, p. 26)

In the play itself there are, strictly speaking, only two sisters-in-law, Germaine Lauzon and her husband's sister, Thérèse Dubuc. However seven of the fifteen women are related and allusions to close and extended family are ubiquitous. The list, drawn up by André Brassard, Tremblay's *metteur en scène*, of 'personnages dont on parle, mais qu'on ne voit pas dans les *Belles-Soeurs*', contains 123 references to individuals. The greatest concentration of such references in the play is provided by Yvette Longpré's enumeration of those present at 'la fête de ma belle-soeur Fleur-Ange', a concatenation that simultaneously highlights the intricacies of family connexion that shape the *belles-soeurs*' world and the hollowness of such relationships, when they are based only on name and unsupported by any deeper bonds of personal attachment.

Indeed, if the Church's idealisation of family values, enshrined in the icon of 'la Sainte Famille', allowed the survival in Quebec first of a pioneering society, then of a minority culture, a counter-effect is shown to be the dysfunctionality of an inward-looking community, sinking beneath the weight of familial rivalries and oppressive mutual surveillance. The sticking bee provides a wonderfully appropriate metaphor for these contradictory tensions. Blood sisters, sisters-in-law, or sister members of the neighbourhood community, the women 'stick together' (both senses in French and in English) not through any true sisterly feeling but because they are 'stuck with' each other ('Arrête de coller après moé comme une sangsue', says Lise to Ginette, p. 45) and with their husbands and families ('Y est toujours après moé, collé après moé comme une sangsue', runs Rose's version of the refrain, p. 50) and each is determined that there shall be no escape for anyone while she herself remains entrapped.

To ensure that all shall continue, 'stuck', exactly where they are, strict social policing prevails. In a community where sisters can watch each other across the alley-way from apartment to apartment, as Rose and Germaine do, and where the outer staircases and balconies, characteristic of Montreal, provide an extension of domestic space that is nevertheless constantly open to public inspection, everything is seen and nothing overlooked, whether it is a suspiciously thickening waistline, the canoodling of a couple of teenagers, or the lack of underwear on a neighbour's clothes-line. Admonition and accusation reinforce the discipline of the ever-present 'family' gaze, closing off all exits to individual hopes and dreams. *Les Belles-Soeurs*, then, is above all an ironic title. Beautiful on neither the physical nor on the spiritual level and displaying little trace of an ethic of kinship, the women and the families of which they are the focus, testify not to supportive family feeling but to an implosion of familial relationships and to the collapse of an icon.[54]

A play about women

> *Jusqu'ici au théâtre, la mère canadienne française était effacée, reléguée à la cuisine. Elle n'avait pas droit à la parole, et dans la réalité, c'est le contraire, elle tient le premier rôle.*
>
> (Tremblay, *Le Devoir*, 14 November 1969)

> *Dans les 'Belles-Soeurs' je voulais vraiment donner le droit de parole aux femmes. Parce que l'art, surtout le théâtre au Québec, a toujours été un geste masculin.*
>
> (Tremblay, *Perspectives*, 26 April 1975, p. 2)

According to Tremblay the germ of the play was the conversation (pp. 29-32) between Rhéauna Bibeau and Angeline Sauvé, written in reaction to Quebec film-maker Pierre Patry's use of standard French in his films: 'J'ai eu l'idée d'écrire une pièce à deux personnes en joual. Deux femmes qui revenaient du salon mortuaire.'[55] The initial idea, a Quebec-style version of a well-worn musical-hall skit, the lachrymose one-up-(wo)man-ship of multiple operations and surgical excisions ('Dix-sept s'opérations! J'ai pus rien qu'un poumon, un rein, un sein...' [p. 30]), rapidly expands, however, into a much more ambitious and much more innovative project, both numerically ('De deux [femmes] je suis passé à quinze') and thematically: nothing less, in fact, using this caricatural presentation as a starting point, than the promotion of women's domestic space and woman's family voice to the public arena of theatre and the tragi-comic deconstruction of a central social myth of female fulfilment in devotion to the family.

The fifteen women of the play represent not so much fifteen individual psychologies as the female condition in Quebec,[56] three different generations 'from the nubile to the senile' (Murray Morgan, *Argus* [Seattle], 23 March 1979, p. 12) and a broad sweep of sexual and marital (in)experience. Seven are wives and mothers, most with large broods ranging from young adults down to children of only four years old. Three are spinsters at varying stages of middle to early old age, two of them definitively confirmed as old maids, one still hankering after a husband and married life. Three are young adults, two of them virgins, all still reluctantly tied to the family home. One lives in the shadow of her older sister, who has made the grade into one of the few socially acceptable professions for women in the Duplessis era, that variant on the mother as educator, the primary-school teacher. One works in a factory ('à shop') and is looking forward to marriage and settling down. The third, a waitress[57] made pregnant and deserted by her boyfriend, is faced with the prospect of stigmatisation as an unmarried mother. Finally at the extreme of the age-range, there is a 93-year-old senile grandmother, dragged from pillar to post, by a resentful daughter-in-law, and at the bottom of the respectability ratings, an 'ageing', thirty-year old nightclub 'hostess', thrown out by her pimp for whom she is no longer attractive enough to be useful.

Romance, marriage, sex

Le sujet de ma pièce c'est la frustration sexuelle
(Tremblay, *Le Devoir*, 14 November 1969)

The basic dream determining the lives of all these women is that of the fairy-tale wedding as the happy ending to a tale of romance. The wedding cake of Yvette Longpré's daughter with its miniature figures of bride and groom typifies a mentality that sees no further than the 'big day' where the 'happy couple' are reduced to pretty dolls in a social extravaganza designed to impress relatives and neighbours. As in Flaubert's celebrated description of Emma Bovary's wedding cake,[58] the cloying sugariness of the confection perfectly symbolises the unsustaining insubstantiality of this view of connubial bliss. Though the wedding cake with its romanticised representation of bride and groom may survive on display for a little time under its protective cover, as an image it has an inbuilt sell-by date, and very soon must be exposed to the real-life conditions of marriage. As described in the play, these bear little resemblance to the romantic dream. Would-be 'poetic' evocations of the dawn à la Romeo and Juliet (caricatured in Lisette de Courval's exaggerated 'Dès que le soleil a commencé à caresser de ses rayons les petites fleurs dans les champs et que les petits oiseaux ont ouvert leurs petits becs pour lancer des petits cris...' [p. 6]) wither fast under the pressure of family demands and in the economy of the play are immediately superseded by the 'quintette de la maudite vie plate' with its relentless detailing of the grinding round of thankless household chores, squabbling children, inconsiderate husbands and mandatory Sunday visits to the in-laws.

As Renate Usmiani points out, however, the list of tasks that the women are called upon to perform might be considered as bringing some sense of fulfilment if accomplished in an atmosphere of love and affection.[59] Unfortunately it is precisely this framework of mutual understanding and support between husband and wife that is missing from the *belles-soeurs*' world. The root cause, as Rose Ouimet's monologue on 'le mauvais cul' makes clear, is a woeful degree of sexual ignorance on the part of the women and hence, cause and effect perhaps, a (perceived?) unacceptably high level of sexual demand on the part of the men:

> J'arai jamais dû me marier! J'arais dû crier 'non' à pleins poumons, pis rester vieille fille! Au moins j'arais eu la paix! [...] ma Carmen, à s'f'ra pas poigner de même, ok? [...] a finira pas comme moé, à quarante-quatre ans, avec une p'tit gars de quatre ans sur les bras pis un écoeurant de mari qui veut rien comprendre, pis qui demande son dû deux fois par jour, trois cent soixante-cinq jours par année! (p. 50-1)

In such circumstances sexual adaptation between partners becomes impossible, plunging both of them, but especially the women, into a circle of hopelessness, frustration and resentment:

> Quand t'arrive à quarante ans pis que tu t'aparçois que t'as rien en arrière de toé, pis que t'as rien en avant de toé, ça te donne envie de toute crisser là, pis de toute recommencer en neuf! Mais les femmes, y peuvent pas faire ça... Les femmes, sont poignées à'gorge, pis y vont rester de même jusqu'au boute! (p. 51)

Though Rose and her generation may thus repent at leisure, sex and marriage remain the central issues for the women of the play. Indeed, with few other outlets for their dreams, the inadequacy of their sexual experiences, far from diminishing their interest in sexual matters, serves only to increase their obsession with them. Des-Neiges Verrette fantasises over a possible relationship with her 'gentleman caller', the door-to-door salesman, Henri Simard, enjoying his 'histoires cochonnes' as a substitute for the sexual experience that so far has always been denied her. Lisette de Courval, for all her 'respectability', is pleased to entertain the idea of shipboard dalliance and, home again in Quebec, whilst labouring ineffectively to maintain her distance from raucous vulgarity, willingly initiates sexual innuendo and malicious gossip. As for Rose, her conversation is all the more coarse and all the more sexually explicit because of her own sexual difficulties. The next generation too seems fated to continue the cycle of dream and disappointment. Though daughters may argue with their mothers, the same patterns repeat themselves. Germaine, urging Linda towards a marriage with a good economic provider, at the same time is fascinated by the physical attractiveness of the man who delivers the stamps: 'J'pense que tu l'aurais aimé, Linda. En plein ton genre. Dans les vingt-deux, vingt-trois ans, les cheveux noirs, frisés, avec une petite moustache... Un vrai bel homme' (p. 2). Lise, in her ferocious attempt to 'devenir quelqu'un' has allowed herself to be seduced by expensive presents and is engaged on the treacherous path of Pierrette. Carmen, Rose's daughter, meanwhile, will be lucky not to sustain irreparable psychological damage from her mother's 'home-truths' about men, marriage and sex. Her likely path is again that of Pierrette, the only possible alternative being the reclusion of Manon, the warped man-hater of Tremblay's 1971 play, *A toi pour toujours, ta Marie-Lou*.

Religion

> *Les curés, les religieux, je les hais franchement[...]. Au lieu de nous expliquer la religion de l'intérieur, on nous l'imposait de force à coups de marteau. [...] Enfant, j'ai donc subi la religion comme une pénitence, une discipline inepte.* (*Lire* 90 [February 1983], pp. 95-6)

The wedding cake decoration includes not only the bride and groom , but also a priest and altar likewise 'tout en sucre'. The romantic picture of marriage is not just a product of school-girl imaginings based on romantic novelettes (such as the 'livres de Magali', p. 27) and women's magazines (such as *Châtelaine*, p. 18) but is vigorously promoted by the Catholic Church. Rose, in her monologue 'du maudit cul', bitterly attacks the church for misrepresenting the married state and persuading naïve and trusting young girls to exchange their youth and their freedom for a life of sexual subservience and domestic servitude ('j'étais ignorante dans ce temps-là pis je savais pas c'qui m'attendait! Moé, l'épaisse, j'pensais rien qu'à "la Sainte-Union du Marriage"!' p. 51). But, married or no, religion provides a rigid framework for the life of each one of the women, rigorously prescribing what social activities and individual behaviours are acceptable and ruthlessly proscribing all deviation from these norms.

Tremblay shows a society characterised by mechanical and self-serving religious observance where the tradition of communal family prayers has been replaced by the impersonality of rosaries recited over the radio and where the Christian ideals of love of God and love of one's neighbour have long since mutated into bigotry, social climbing and hypocrisy. Rhéauna Bibeau, incessantly preoccupied with ritual observance as the means to her own salvation, represents religious bigotry in its most unyielding and unforgiving form. Despite her religious pretentions, she condemns Pierrette, and those like her who have 'fait la vie', in the most unchristian terms and has no compunction in rejecting out of hand her long-standing friend and companion, Angéline Sauvé, for her 'sinful' visits to Pierrette's club. Lisette de Courval, meanwhile, views religion and its associated charitable work as an extension of social status. She relishes her close social contact with the local clerics as chairwoman of 'la Supplique à Notre-Dame de Perpétuel Secours' and enjoys her leading role in organising parish activities. She is, however, radically incapable of recognising a cry for help or responding to it, a point involuntarily underlined by Angéline Sauvé who sees only too clearly that the revelation of her visits to Pierrette's club puts her beyond the social pale in Lisette's eyes. Thérèse Dubuc, sanctimonious, self-advertised martyr to a cause, lauded by all, initially at least, for her self-sacrificing devotion to family duty, provides a third example of religious display and religious self-deception. Care of her senile mother-in-law can be exploited as a source of moral kudos, but her 'Christian charity' in reality consists of granny-bashing and of minimal grudging hand-outs, not of desperately needed money, but of unwanted cast-offs to relatives, poorer than herself.

If these three characters provide the clearest, comically exaggerated, examples of religious hypocrisy, the other women, as a result no doubt of their own personal disappointments, adopt singly and as a group a puritanical attitude that forbids all pleasures except those which the Church sanctions and provides. Parish concerts and parish bingo are welcomed as diversions, but restaurants and especially clubs are considered no-go places of perdition.[60] The most obvious victims here are Pierrette, viewed for the most part as the devil in person and decisively rejected by her sisters, and Lise, ripe for social stigmatisation as fallen woman, like the other unmarried mothers Manon Bélair (p. 43) and Monique Bergeron (pp. 48-9). In the large sense, however, all the women are victims and none more pathetically than Des-Neiges Verrette and Angéline Sauvé, brought up in the cheerless surroundings of 'les soubassements d'église' and 'les salles paroissiales' by nuns 'qui faisaient c'y'pouvaient mais qui connaissaient rien, les pauvres!' (p. 38-9) and who crave the love or even just 'le fun' that could, so they believe, transform their unsatisfactory lives.

Closed exits

> *Les femmes, sont poignées à'gorge, pis y vont rester de même jusqu'au boute!* (Rose Ouimet, p. 51)

Education

What means do these women have of transforming their lives? Competitions hold out the tantalising prospect of a fairy-tale change of material life-style but outlets to a real broadening and enhancement of personal and social experience are few and those that do exist, are refused, pass unrecognised or exceed the competence and the self-confidence of the individual concerned. Pierrette, the brightest of the Guérin sisters, lured by her feelings for 'le mauvais Johnny' and the desire to escape the restrictions of home, turns her back on education and chooses romance, 'le fun' and the money of the clubs. But had she accepted the educational route mapped out for her, it would almost certainly not have led her out of the narrow mind-set of her community. The educational opportunities available to working-class boys such as Raymond Jodoin (p. 14) (or Tremblay himself) through state-funded bursaries to the *école classique*, did not become available to girls until the educational reforms of the 1960s. Pierrette as a 'maîtresse d'école' would merely have relived her own narrow educational trajectory, transmitting to a new generation of children the ethos of family duty and individual sacrifice in the interests of the survival of a Catholic Quebec. Even for Raymond Jodoin, it will be an uphill struggle against ignorance, entrenched prejudice and the inverted snobbery of an educationally deprived community and the likely outcome, a betrayal of social class by the acceptance of an establishment position in a society whose fundamental attitudes remain unchanged.

Travel

Few of the *belles-soeurs* have the means to expand their horizons through travel, but no advantage is taken of the opportunity even when it does arise. Travel for Lisette de Courval serves a strictly domestic end: the enhancement of her social standing in Quebec. With no sense of her imprisonment, she carries with her to 'Urope' the cultural and behavioural baggage of the community she affects to despise ('Quand on a connu la vie de transatlantique pis qu'on se retrouve ici, ce n'est pas des farces! J'm'revois, là, étendue sur une chaise longue, un bon livre de Magali sur les genoux... Puis le lieutenant qui me faisait de l'oeil...' [p. 27]) and returns home to Quebec with her parochial prejudices intact ('En Urope, le monde se lavent pas!' [p. 9]); 'A Paris, tout le monde perle bien, c'est du vrai français partout...' [p. 27]). A similar pattern can be observed with Yvette Longpré's daughter Claudette and her new husband. A lucky win (Germaine's then is not the only one!) makes the Canary Islands honeymoon trip possible, but far from taking the opportunity to explore a different cultural environment or, more importantly perhaps in this case, to develop their emotional relationship with each other, the newly-weds quickly re-establish the *belles-soeurs*' pattern of Quebec life, meeting up in the Canaries with 'des couples qu'y connaissaient – des amies de filles de Claudette' (p. 10), and at the end of the trip returning stateside via New York in one big 'family' group. Meanwhile in Quebec itself, xenophobia is rife. The *belles-soeurs* keep ferociously to their own community; foreigners, notably the Italians, the largest immigrant group to Montreal in the 1950s and 1960s,[61] are viewed with mistrust and hostility. The reasons given are stereotypical: the alien group is dirty, smells and does not wear underclothes.[62]

Language

> *Les Québécois ne se parlent pas. Alors 75 p.cent des 'Belles-Soeurs' est fait de propos stupides et 25 p.cent de monologues et de choeurs. Les femmes sont si peu capables de se parler entre elles que lorsqu'elles pensent la même chose d'un même sujet, elles doivent le dire au public et en choeur. Si au lieu de dire leur vie 'plate' en quintette, elles se le disaient entre elles, peut-être réussiraient-elles à sortir de leur impasse. Mais cela est au-dessus de leur force.*
>
> (Tremblay, *Magazine Maclean*, September 1972, pp. 20-1)

Within the *belles-soeurs*' community poor communication skills reinforce the disempowerment of both the individual and the group. For all their surface volubility, the women are fundamentally inarticulate. Germaine, officially classified as 'ménagère' (p. 2), i.e. an inhabitant of purely domestic space, is reduced to stammering incoherence when faced on the doorstep by the outside world in the shape of the men delivering her trading stamps. Her linguistic incompetence establishes a persistent pattern for the rest of the play. The old grandmother, deprived of all syntax and reduced to a minimal, mindlessly repeated vocabulary of 'Coke!', 'Bingo', 'Timbres!', and 'O Canada!'[63] provides a caricatural example of linguistic aphasia while a more realistically presented spectacle of linguistic backwardness is offered by Yvette Longpré, constantly interrupted by the rest, always one step behind in the conversation, and never aspiring beyond simple description and enumeration. Though more dynamic and more vociferous, Rose, 'the life and soul' of the party ('on a toujours eu du fun dans les parties avec elle!' [p. 16]) never escapes the language of the coarse joke and has a faltering grip on more sophisticated vocabulary and word-games. At the upper end of the scale, Lisette de Courval, for all her pretentions to a linguistic sophistication not possessed by her neighbours, is as capable of malaproprisms as Rose, Des-Neiges Verrette, or Pierrette, and though aping more elevated diction, constantly relapses into the *joual* which confines them all within their cultural ghetto.

A frequent phrase, 'J'ai pour mon dire', defines the individual narrowness of thought and language that inhibits any meaningful articulation by the *belles-soeurs* of their predicament. Though the conversation at Germaine Lauzon's party touches on all the major periods of life and all the major life events (childhood and youth, marriage, parenthood, old-age and death), it remains on the level of 'filler' small-talk and tittle-tattle ('Jasez, en attendant, jasez!', enjoins Germaine to her guests, as they wait for her to get changed for her party [p. 8]) with the exchanges between Lise, Linda and Pierrette over Lise's pregnancy as the only exceptions. Eloquence in the play is confined to the monologues and some of the choruses, where the characters, in the secret space of their hearts and apart from the conversational flow, are able – with the indispensable assistance of the author – to articulate their resentments and disappointments. But this is a silent 'raising of voices' where each remains irremediably alone. The only external traces are the petty tale-telling treacheries and the quarrelsomeness by which each tries to affirm herself vis-à-vis the rest. Verbal aggressiveness, 'la chicane', not verbal finesse, is the defining characteristic of the *belles-soeurs*' public discourse and a measure of their linguistic inadequacy. When words fail them, physical violence fills the gap – Rose's chastisement of her grandchildren and threatened chastisement of Linda, Thérèse's 'pacification' of her mother-in-law, in which Germaine and Rose seem increasingly inclined to share, and, as the culmination of the women's accelerating inarticulate fury, the great fisticuffs of the finale, where exasperated family and neighbours join in a free-for-all to grab as much as possible of Germaine's 'undeserved' windfall.

In the cage

> *Nous vivons dans un pays sous cloche. Tous mes personnages vivent sous cloche.*
>
> (Tremblay, *Magazine Maclean*, September 1972, p. 20)

Images of enclosure provide a strong leitmotif in *Les Belles-Soeurs*: windows shut against draughts, excluding any fresh air, wedding cakes decaying under glass domes, caged birds let out to flutter around in the confinement of an apartment, fouling it as they do so. Rose's account of Manon's sparrows is an obvious fable for the situtation of the women. The cramped conditions of Germaine's overcrowded kitchen translate it readily into visible reality. In this hen party, the women are indeed like battery fowl, too tightly packed in their shed, their frustration rapidly translating into viciousness, as individually and jointly, they vigorously defend their place in the pecking order. As the dramatic interplay of dialogue, monologue and chorus makes plain, the women are united only in their impotence. Their individual needs, dreams, cries for help, silently repressed, cannot be shared with their neighbours and there is therefore no way forward for any of them to a better or more hopeful future. When, exceptionally, help is provided, it is an isolated and thus futile attempt to combat the emotional and social inadequacy of an entire community. At the end of the play Germaine, betrayed by her 'respectable' friends and relations, is incapable of responding to Pierrette's unlooked-for offer of support. Similarly Pierrette's attempt to help Lise by providing her with an address for a safe abortion cannot change the limited materialism of Lise's dreams. The abortion thus comes to signify both the failure of the traditional maternal ideal and the failure of the consumer life-style envisaged as its only alternative.[64]

Les Belles-Soeurs, though set in 1965, the year in which the play was written, harks back to the time before the changes of the Quiet Revolution. Retrospectively it can be seen as the death throes of the old society, the last reluctant submission of the women of Quebec to their subordinate status. To the critic Donald Smith Tremblay characterised his presentation thus:

> Dans *Les Belles-Soeurs*, chaque monologue est une espèce de tentative de révolution, de révolte, mais, malheureusement, ça se passe en 1965, puis la fin du monologue de Rose Ouimet est très explicite quand elle dit: 'Les femmes ne peuvent pas faire ça, les femmes vont rester pognées'. C'étaient des femmes qui auraient dû se révolter, mais il était encore trop tôt dans notre histoire. Elles savent pourquoi elles sont malheureuses; elles voudraient que ça change, mais elles n'ont pas encore les moyens de le faire. Tout ce qu'elles peuvent faire, c'est se soumettre encore une fois. D'ailleurs quand on remontera *Les Belles-Soeurs*, c'est ce qui va ressortir le plus, chose qui n'a pas tellement été remarquée jusqu'ici, parce qu'on était dedans. Pour la dernière fois, les femmes se soumettent dans *Les Belles-Soeurs*.[65]

A play without men

> *Je voulais faire une grosse pièce avec des femmes, seulement des femmes, parce que dans le milieu québécois les hommes sont très secondaires.*[66]

Men are explicitly excluded from the play. Germaine's husband is absent from the family kitchen because he works a night shift. Linda's boyfriend is not allowed to attend, even though it would normally be his night out with Linda, because this is a hen party, a specifically female occasion. The non-appearance of men on the stage does not necessarily mean, though, that their voice goes unheard. Indeed it could be perceived as pervasively present in the controlling discourses of religious observance and consumer capitalism that the media import directly into Germaine's kitchen. Similarly in sexual matters men apparently call the tune: boyfriends use and desert their partners, stepfathers interfere with their stepdaughters, and married men insist on their conjugal rights with scant regard for the emotional and physical well-being of their wives.

Yet male domination is far from constituting the whole truth. The absence of men from the stage also corresponds to a diminishing of their value as individuals, in which they, as much as the women, are victims of the patriachal myths they appear to embody. Viewed by the women at best with resignation, at worst with loathing and contempt, the men too are reified – as less than adequate economic providers or unsatisfactory sexual partners, or, in the shape of the celibate priest or the remote (foreign) film star, as inaccessible fantasy objects. Men as real-life husbands and fathers have little family standing. Sons, for their part, are either perceived as a threat (Raymond Jodoin, p. 14) or are the objects of maternal domination (Bernard Ouimet, p. 15). Rosaire Baril's premature death, brought about, it seems, by the uppitiness of his daughter, extends the earlier comically nonchalant mention of serious male injury (Monsieur Dubé's three-month hospitalisation as a result of the infant Daniel Robitaille's plunge on top of him from a second-floor window) and, though seen as the loss of 'un gros morceau', is considered, predictably, much less serious than the death of a mother ('Une mère, ça se remplace pas!' [p. 31]). This symbolic despatching of husband and father crystallises a masculine exclusion which re-emerges subsequently in Tremblay's work in an explicitly gay configuration in the homosexual transvestites of plays such as *La Duchesse de Langeais* (1970), *Hosanna* (1973) and *Sacrée Sandra, Damnée Manon* (1977). Though no men appear on stage in *Les Belles-Soeurs*, it could be argued that the play, as a play about gender, has much to say about men, that it is in a sense a 'closet' play where the insistence on the problems of women in Quebec society papers over a yet more profound anxiety over the positioning of Quebec male identity. In that perspective, and viewed in the context of Tremblay's global *oeuvre*, the vehemence of its denunciation of the heterosexual family acquires a socio-cultural and psycho-sexual resonance of considerably greater complexity than the title of the play and its all-female cast might initially seem to suggest.[67]

A political play

Mon théâtre suit l'actualité et c'est en cela qu'il est politique.
(*Tremblay, Magazine Maclean*, September 1972, p. 20)

> *Dans les années cinquante, les femmes québécoises commençaient à prendre conscience de certaines choses bien qu'elles n'aient pas les armes pour devenir féministes. Et les premiers êtres que j'ai entendu réagir contre la société, ce furent les femmes.*
> (Tremblay, *Lire* 90, February 1983, p. 90)

Tremblay is adamant that his plays are not *pièces à thèse* and has expressed his dislike of *théâtre engagé* in the Sartrean mould.[68] Nor does he offer a theatre like that of his québécois predecessors, Gélinas and Dubé, where the political and social questions that dominate the contemporary scene are explicitly discussed as such by the protagonists. Nevertheless *Les Belles-Soeurs* in particular amongst Tremblay's plays, has a strong political coloration, that was immediately evident at its first performance in 1968.[69] In the memorable concluding tableau Germaine stands to attention in the wreckage of her kitchen, gift stamps falling about her, and joins with those who have stripped her of her prize in the singing of the Canadian national anthem. To the critic Donald Smith Tremblay explained:

> Pour moi, le 'O Canada', en français, est un hymne à la soumission. C'était drôlement ironique de faire lever une femme qui s'était écroulée, à qui on a tout volé, et qui entonne avec tout le monde les deux derniers vers, 'Et ta valeur, de foi trempée, Protégera nos foyers et nos droits', alors qu'elle vient de se faire violer et son foyer et ses droits. C'était un geste politique que d'avoir une femme comme ça, complètement abattue, qui devrait se révolter (op.cit., p. 213).

In the context of the continuing conversation with Smith, the 'political gesture' concerns specifically the position of women in Quebec society. However the reference is just as capable of being reversed so that the subjugation of the women becomes a metaphor for the subjugation of Quebec itself. Tremblay's comments at the 'meet the author' meeting at the Centre culturel canadien in Paris in December 1973 clearly demonstrate the intertwining of a double dependency. The play, he is reported as saying, 'entend être une dénonciation de l'état de soumission des Québécoises en particulier et *du Québec en général*, état d'esprit qui culmine lorsque le choeur de tous les personnages des *Belles-Soeurs* entonne en apothéose finale l'hymne national'.[70]

Like Germaine at the close of the play, the people of Quebec have been robbed, robbed of what is rightfully theirs, robbed of their cultural specificity, robbed of their defining voice. Suspended between a French cultural heritage and an anglophone one, they are forced to 'speak white',[71] to accept as a ruling discourse a foreign tongue, which, though a nod may be given to bilingual equality ('O Canada', after all, has its French version, see pp. 75, 77), has already made its indelible imprint on the speech habits of *joualisant* Montreal.

Like Germaine and the rest of the *belles-soeurs*, the Québécois have moreover connived in their own dependency.[72] The official discourses of Quebec, those of the Church, those of politicians, have offered no challenge to anglophone hegemony. Supervising the life of the individual from the cradle to the grave, the Church has reinforced an attitude of obedience and passive supplication. In the conduct of social affairs too, the Church has determined a round of activities designed to maintain the inward-looking solidarity of the group. In return the women in the play, though they follow a centuries-old tradition in their enjoyment of scurrilous stories, born of popular scepticism, over the celibacy of nuns and priests, adopt without question the ecclesiastical rules and regulations which guarantee their own place in the community and protect that community from disruption from outside.

Significantly the concerns of the *belles-soeurs* are always purely domestic. Politics plays no part in their lives or conversation. The only other political allusion in the script beyond the final 'O Canada!' is to Maurice Duplessis, the dead hand of pre-1960s Quebec, who briefly resurfaces as a 'mystery voice' in a radio competition and who, typically, is identified not by Thérèse Dubuc but by her husband. But though the women take no interest in politics, this indifference is itself a political attitude. Silence means lack of questioning, silence means acquiescence by default. The women, in concert with their priests and thus with the political view supported by the church, are the dominant, if passive, voice of Quebec. In this perspective the absence of the men from the play corresponds not just to a social reality but also to a political one. The husbands and boyfriends, though physically and legally their role as master may seem assured, are as much as the women constrained by the political partnership of church and state. Identification *of* Duplessis' voice symbolises identification *with* Duplessis' policies. 'Il n' a pas d'homme au Québec',[73] because the men conform to a narrow, domestic vision of Quebec's political identity. The promoting of the insular voice of the kitchen to the public space of the stage makes explicit this political reality.

A universal play

> *Ce qui me permet d'aller ailleurs, c'est mon côté local ou régional. Autrement, on est de nulle part, on est rien.*
>
> (Tremblay, *Le Devoir,* 26 February 1977)

The controversial status of *Les Belles-Soeurs* in Quebec in the late 1960s and early 1970s is clearly linked with the political aspirations of a modernising Quebec. As the transposition of the play to the Paris stage in 1973 clearly revealed, however, and as a multiplicity of translations and performances across the world have also shown, the play is not limited to this domestic interpretation. The minority culture scenario fits the politics of numerous societies (see, for example, the Lowland Scots version of the play, *The Guid Sisters*[74]). But, more broadly than this, it fits the social politics of working-class marginalisation in a capitalist, consumerist society,[75] and then, beyond that again, the larger philosophical debate between humanist and materialist values.

Scrimping and spending

The men in *Les Belles-Soeurs* are wage-slaves, scraping a living which barely covers the needs of the families they rarely see or else, like the unemployed husband of Marie-Ange Brouillette, they are demoralised layabouts, staying late in bed, while their wives cope with the stress of the daily family routine. If by chance they do get a pay-rise, they are immediately caught in the classic poverty trap of clawback by the system. Thus the improvement in Monsieur Dubuc's wage has removed the family from the social security net, leaving them disastrously worse off financially if they leave the old grandmother in care, and disastrously worse off psychologically if they remove her from care and look after her themselves. Individual worth is measured solely in terms of earning power. Germaine criticises Linda's Robert because of his lack of financial prospects. Linda retorts that his boss has predicted an early promotion and pay-rise for him. In the absence of earning power, spending power becomes the crucial measure and here the trick is to create the appearance of affluence. The star performer is Lisette de Courval who flaunts her status-symbol mink and her European holidays, patronising her neighbours by attempting to sell on to them her cast-offs, while her husband, in Rose Ouimet's exasperated words, 'se fend le cul en quatre pour pouvoir emprunter de l'argent pour te payer des fourrures pis des voyages!' (p. 21). But for all the women, keeping up with the neighbours is a key preoccupation, tested out at each social gathering. Germaine's off-the-cuff party, run on a shoestring as far as refreshments are concerned, comes in for immediate criticism on that score from her sister Rose.

Weddings and funerals, the showpiece family gatherings, provide the ultimate test. How many are asked, what hospitality is on offer, what expense has been gone to, are all carefully scrutinised. Tremblay subsequently envisaged a film with Quebec director Gilles Carle (rather on the lines taken in Britain in the 1990s by *Four Weddings and a Funeral*) looking at the social mores of Quebec through these ceremonies. The film was to be:

> la description, dans ses moindres détails, d'un mariage canadien-français, québécois, si vous préférez: la mariée, le marié, les parents, les filles d'honneur, les garçons d'honneur, la bouquetière, la mère de la bouquetière, la tante sourde, la tante pas sourde, la tante soeur, la tante chanteuse, le 'mon

> oncle comique', la tante gênée, la femme dont la 'slip' dépasse sans arrêt ... j'ai ramassé tout ce qui peut se passer. Ce sont des gens qui ne connaissent pas l'étiquette mais qui veulent faire 'un grand mariage'.
>
> (Tremblay, *La Presse*, 16 August 1969, p. 26)

The film has never been made, but already in *Les Belles-Soeurs*, Yvette Longpré in her naïve detailing of her daughter's wedding cake with its sugar church, bride, bridegroom and priest, displays both the importance of the façade and the shifts necessary to achieve it: 'Le gâteau nous avait coûté assez cher, aussi! C'tait un gâteau à six étages, vous savez! C'tait pas toute du gâteau, par exemple. Ç'arait été ben que trop cher! Y avait juste les deux du bas en gâteau, le reste, c'tait du bois' (p. 19). The sartorial arrangements for Rosaire Baril's 'salon mortuaire', by contrast, fail to pass muster. The deceased's sister-in-law wears a green dress and the deceased himself, though his face has been well made-up, is laid out in a powder-blue suit! What were the family thinking of? After all, says Angéline Sauvé, even if the family is not well off, 'une habit noire, ça se loue!' (p. 31).[76]

Scooping the pool, selling one's soul

In such a society, getting a bargain or, even better, getting something for nothing, is a matter of extreme (self)-congratulation. Normally this takes the form of finding the same suit at a cheaper price (p. 44), getting the better of the butcher (p. 34) or a win at the monthly parish bingo session. Competitions (making up slogans, solving anagrams, guessing the mystery voice or the mystery object) attract with their illusory promise of easy rewards. Promoted to a central position in the economy of the play, they are used in obverse to signify the women's position as permanent losers in society, provoking on each mention from each women the disabused refrain: 'J'ai-tu l'air de quequ'un qui a déjà gagné quequ'chose?' Germaine's big win (and its echo in the free holiday in the Canaries) is the exception that proves the rule and perpetuates the system. The prospect of having every item in the catalogue, ('J'vas toute les avoir, madame Brouillette, toutes! Toute le cataloye!' [p. 5]) and for nothing ('j'vas toutes les avoir pour rien!' [p. 5]), and of stealing a march on her relatives and neighbours ('J'vas avoir des plats en verre soufflé[...]pareil come ceux de ta belle-soeur Aline! Pis même, j'pense qu'y sont encore plus beaux!'; 'J'vas avoir[...]des verres en verre taillé avec le motif "Caprice". Madame de Courval en a eu l'année passée. A disait qu'a l'avait payé ça cher sans bon sens... ' [p. 5]) transforms the acquisitiveness born of economic difficulty into mindless greed and Germaine into a thoughtless, ruthless exploiter of the labour of her less fortunate sisters. There is no suggestion of any sharing of the windfall, not even in return for their help in sticking stamps into booklets; they are called upon to work and admire from afar; all is to be used on the makeover of Germaine's apartment.

Meanwhile the prize winner is oblivious to the fact that making over the physical environment of one's home is not the same as radically redesigning one's inner self and the psychological dimensions of one's existence. The trashy objects of Germaine's 'cataloye', far from freeing her from the consumerist ethos, manifestly engage her even more deeply within it. Lise, at the end of the play, with her ambition to succeed at all costs ('Chus v'nue au monde par la porte d'en arrière, mais m'as donc sortir par la porte d'en avant! Pis y'a rien qui va m'en empêcher! Y'a rien qui va m'arrêter! [p. 44]) is the tragic face of that desperate attachment to material affluence as the only criterion of success.

Writing for the stage

'Les Belles-Soeurs' est une vraie pièce absurde. Ça n'est pas du tout la pièce réaliste qu'on a trop longtemps voulu y voir. A peu près rien dans l'action est vraiment réaliste, ou, si vous voulez, vérifiable dans la vraie vie, tout est sujet à transposition, à caricature.
(*Première*, 10,3, February-March 1984, p. 8)

Dès les 'Belles-Soeurs' j'empêche le spectateur d'être idiot en écrivant des pièces techniquement difficiles.[77]

At first glance the sociological content of Tremblay's play appears to be matched by an ultra-realistic handling of the three theatrical fundamentals, time, space and action. The time of the play's unfolding corresponds to the real time of the performance. The single set is a 1965 kitchen. The 'action' within the play itself is marked by a singular lack of progression, an absence of any defining crisis or cathartic release. The one unexpected incident, Pierrette's arrival at the party and its corollary, the revelation of Angéline Sauvé's 'sin', is quickly absorbed into the continuum of play by the repetition of the closing exchanges of Act I in a seamless overlap at the beginning of Act II. The dreariness of the starting material, the 'everyday life of city folk', insistently demands however an effort of the creative imagination whereby the comic and tragic potential of its human truths can be opened up for the entertainment and the reflection of the audience. Tremblay's innovative, highly 'theatrical' approach, drawing on such diverse traditions as popular revue, Brechtian *Verfremdung*, Ancient Greek theatre, contemporary American theatre, the tragi-comic absurdism of Beckett and Ionesco, provides the necessary dynamic. At the level of text, a keen sense of the absurd in the choice and handling of situation and character and an operatic conception of voice in the structuring of dialogue transform the mediocre and mundane into a bravura display of theatrical artifice, that brilliantly illuminates the wretched inadequacy of a whole society. In performance, inspired direction, notably by André Brassard, with particularly imaginative handling of sound and lighting effects and of set, costume and choreography, develops and expands the orientation and indications of Tremblay's script to produce a total theatrical experience, far exceeding the limited brief of sociological realism.

Situation: 'slice of life' or fairy-tale?

> *Aucune de mes pièces n'a d'histoire que tu peux raconter[...]. 'Les Belles-Soeurs' présente l'histoire d'une femme qui a gagné un million de timbres que ses voisines viennent lui voler, ce n'est pas cela.*[78]

Les Belles-Soeurs sets the pattern for all Tremblay's plays in its rejection of storyline as a focus of dramatic interest. Potentially the sensational stuff of tabloid newspapers, the story of Germaine's big win and her down-fall is not played for its inherent dramatic excitement. The point is rather that the the life of Germaine and her sisters cannot be changed from without, that grey drudgery confines them so completely that it corrodes and destroys every dream. This sociological realism is however radically transformed by Tremblay's inflated imaginings of Germaine's good fortune and the reactions of her circle. 'Real life' undergoes a carnivalesque metamorphosis, the anecdote providing the pretext for the revelation, blown up to grotesque proportions, of the tunnel vision of the participants. In a 1968 interview with Jean-Claude Germain Tremblay explained the different stages in the development of the idea:

> Pour faire *Les Belles-Soeurs* il me fallait trouver une situation absurde. Parce que je suis persuadé d'une chose: si on place une Québécoise dans une situation absurde, elle va immanquablement réagir d'une façon très réaliste, tout ce qu'il y a sous le vernis extérieur va sortir naturellement. Elle va lâcher son fou.[79]

The culture of puzzles and competitions proved a fertile source of comically absurd situations. Tremblay's attention was taken first by a Cadbury's competition involving counting the number of cows' heads in a chocolate advertisement. What interested him here may have been the comic disproportion between the derisoriness of the task and the inordinate degree of concentration involved in its accomplishment. However matters went no further, perhaps because the situation, motionless poring over an advertisement, seemed ill-suited for theatrical exploitation. When, however, Tremblay saw his aunt opening a drawer full of Gold Star trading stamps, the idea of Germaine's prize was born. The stamps have the advantage of fitting several formal and thematic desiderata. From the point of view of dramatic presentation they suppose a dynamic of barter and exchange. At the same time their status as substitutes for the material objects which they can be used to acquire allows a pointed comment on the inauthenticity of consumerist culture. Furthermore, complementing and exceeding both the dramatic requirement and the sociological reference, the tensions of accumulation and fragmentation which they embody allow a ready mutation from the realm of reality into that of fantasy. For Germaine's win, in Tremblay's hands, has the idiosyncrasy of fairy-tale. Not only is it subject to the excessively long odds that place any win on the pools or lottery at the very edge of normal possibility, but in addition, it has imposed upon it the singular condition that an enormous windfall be put together out of its minute component parts (the single stamps) before the beneficiary can actually profit from it. Like so many miller's daughters but with no Rumplestiltskin to magically transform their task, the *belles-soeurs*, in pursuit of Germaine's reward, confront a soul-destroying labour of gigantic proportions. Not only do their physical capacities seem likely to be taxed to breaking point ('Un million on rit plus', p. 2); even more severely challenged will be the fragile social face they present to the world and the profound emotional tensions it conceals.

Characters or caricatures

> *Les quinze personnages de la pièce, même si je m'en suis longtemps défendu, à tort d'ailleurs, sont des caricatures dans le bon sens du mot: ce sont des femmes plus grandes que nature, plus drôles et plus déchirantes.* (Tremblay, *Première*, 10,3, February-March, 1984, p. 8)

As noted earlier in the discussion of *Les Belles-Soeurs* as a play about women (p. xix), the characters are conceived not so much as individuals, but as types representing the range of female experience in Quebec. But as types they also fall within the stock typologies of popular theatre, 'the creaking-gate' (as in Rhéauna Bibeau's and Angéline's conversation following the 'salon mortuaire', one of the starting points of the play), the belly-aching housewife, the aggressive mother-in-law, the 'holier than thou' pillar of the church, the 'good-time girl fallen on hard times', the pushy snob, the 'take everything at its face value' simpleton. The 'absurd' situation of Germaine's win and its attendant conditions gives new bite and definition to these stereotypes, magnifying, now comically, now tragically, the clash of youth and age, of the pious and the prodigal, of no-hopers and social climbers, and transforming mother and daughter arguments, ructions between sisters and dissension between neighbours, from trivial, everyday happenings into monumental displays of aggressiveness, greed and envy, that are by turns 'furieusement et curieusement drôle[s]' (Martial Dassylva, *La Presse*, 5 April 1973). The final tableau provides a suitably carnivalesque conclusion to this evening of 'the world turned upside down'. Standing tearfully amidst a rain of falling stamps, the last tangible fragments of her dream, Germaine, Queen of Fools for just a single night, is returned decisively to her 'proper' place among her downtrodden sisters.

The fairy-tale is over, but Tremblay's 'absurd' magnification of the *belles-soeurs*' experience has laid bare in the meantime the essential absurdity of their 'ordinary' lives.

Structure: between classicism and cabaret

> *Pour moi une pièce de théâtre, c'est une suite de scènes dans lesquelles il n'y a rien qui se passe mais dans laquelle on parle des choses qui se sont passées ou qui vont se passer.* (*Voix et images*, 7 [1982], p. 214)

In its observance of the unities of time and space and its focus on a single 'action', *Les Belles-Soeurs* retains the tight overall cohesion of French classical theatre. But the emphasis on unchanging situation rather than on climactic progression and cathartic conclusion inhibits any full-scale adoption of the classical model or its derivatives and, moving away from the conventional framework of the 'well-made' play, *Les Belles-Soeurs* works to a structure more reminiscent of cabaret or music-hall.[80] The insignificant chatter and the unspoken feelings of these ordinary women are recast theatrically, not in a conventional format of scenes and acts marking out a plot-driven teleology, but as a series of moments given performative significance like numbers in a cabaret by the spotlighting of a face, the momentary foregrounding of a solo voice, or the introduction of a group routine. Though nominally split into two acts, *Les Belles-Soeurs* is in fact one continuous conversation where the inconsequential flow of everyday dialogue is interrupted, as J.P. Ryngaert has shown,[81] by fourteen different sequences, cunningly varied in form, tone and presentation, each of which is clearly announced by a change of lighting ('Projecteur sur Rose Ouimet', 'Blackout. Projecteur sur Yvette Longpré', etc.), a different style of performance ('Les cinq femmes se tournent vers le public', 'Blackout. Quand les lumières reviennent, les neuf femmes sont au bord de la scène') or even by the actual announcing of a title for a particular item ('Quintette de la maudite vie plate', 'Ode au bingo'). These different numbers (carefully balanced and juxtaposed for maximum comic, pathetic or tragic effect) each create a space, sometimes within, more often aside from the general conversation, where the banal, suddenly caught in the focus of the spotlight, is recreated as a telling fragment in a striking artistic fresco of empty lives and disappointed hopes.

Monologues

> *Nothing much happens in the dialogues, but lots of important things happen in the monologues.*
> (Tremblay to Renate Usmiani, *Canadian Theatre Review* 24 [Fall 1979] p. 27)

The basic dramatic building-block of *Les Belles-Soeurs*, it could thus be argued, is not the Scene or the Act, but the monologue, exploited by Tremblay in ways that interestingly combine the techniques of both popular and serious theatre. At one extreme the virtuoso solos like those of the music-hall (Germaine's enumeration of catalogue items, Yvette's list of names) provide moments of high comedy and, as pieces of performative brio, focus the attention of the audience on the play as a specifically theatrical, rather than a 'realistic' spectacle. More frequently, set apart from the main conversation, the monologues, in accordance with a long-standing convention of serious as well as popular theatre, allow the audible expression of a character's private thoughts. Tremblay varies standard procedure in that these monologues are neither brief asides, nor separate scenes with the character alone on stage. Instead they acted out alongside, but in another dimension to the ongoing conversation.[82] Silent thoughts are brought centre stage, voiced and exposed to the limelight, while the small talk is momentarily arrested and the gossiping figures 'frozen' in a shadowy stillness. A further variant is provided by individual voices entwined in an unwitting counterpoint whose ironies are only perceptible to the audience, Lise and Pierrette, for example, echoing each other's despair: 'J'le sais pas c'que je vas de venir; j'le sais pas pantoute!' (p. 46), while each believes the other to be happier and more fortunate than herself. The monologues are thus the structural embodiment of a central thematic paradigm, giving tangible shape to the disabling disconnection between individual and group and between the public persona and the private one, and it is their accumulation through the play and their final resolution in the solitary figure of Germaine that provide the structural backbone to Tremblay's presentation.

Choruses

I am a freak for the Greek
(Tremblay to Ray Conlogue, *Globe and Mail*, 3 March 1978, p. 16)

Balancing the single voices, Tremblay adopts, from Ancient tragedy on the one hand, from music hall on the other, the communal voice of the chorus. In *Un Ange cornu avec des ailes de tôle* he describes the profound effect of his adolescent discovery of the theatre of the Ancient Greeks and in particular his fascination with their use of the Chorus as a means of enhancing the dramatic impact of their plays.[83] His own 'choruses', in *Les Belles-Soeurs*, differ from theirs, however, in that they are formed not from the anonymous crowd, bystanders on the sidelines reacting as a group to the central action, but from shifting combinations of characters within the main action, each individually engaged with private anguish and frustration. They operate in fact not as a contrast and complement to monologue, but as an extreme variant of it. Though the women may physically stand together on the stage, each remains isolated in herself, her words addressed, not to her neighbour, but to the black void behind the footlights that maps the black pit of her despair.

Nevertheless, from the point of view of theatrical effect, the variation provided by the group voice vis-à-vis the solos is of crucial importance as a structuring device. The show-stopper numbers, 'Quintette de la maudite vie plate' and 'Ode au bingo', constitute a welcome comic respite amidst the portrayal of individual misery, offering lively group performance as an antidote to solo lamentation. Similarly, on a smaller scale, the voice of the group, chorally sympathising with Thérèse Dubuc or chorally castigating 'le mauvais Johnny', provides helpful vocal contrast to the fragmentation of monologue and the diffuseness of conversation, and satiric highlighting to the depiction of 'pious' and 'moralising' cliché. Tremblay, 'un auditif', 'un sonore' according to his own description,[84] has artistically transformed the characters' experience of alienation and isolation by expressing it in an essentially 'musical' form, combining solo voices, voices in counter-point, small group ensembles and chorales. Reflecting his fascination with the possibilities of musical comedy and opera, the play as theatre has moved far beyond its sociological roots to become, as Jacques Cellard put it, stressing its tragic aspect (*Le Monde*, 25-6 November, 1973) 'un extraordinaire oratorio moderne (quelque chose comme la Passion du Québec)'.[85]

Language

A 'realistic' use of language?

> *J'parle comme que je peux, pis j'dis c'que j'ai à dire, c'est toute!*
> (Marie-Ange Brouillette, p. 8)

The emphasis on voice as a structuring principle points to the crucial importance of Tremblay's handling of language and to the artistic considerations that underline its mimetic appearance. Pronunciation and vulgar vocabulary focussed the attention of the first audiences and critics on the 'realistic' display of the language of the street, but as subsequent spectators, translators and commentators have realised, Tremblay's *joual* not only shows an ear finely attuned to popular speech habits, but an artistic ability to mould and polish popular idiom – beyond the the vision and the linguistic capacities of the characters themselves – to lay bare the comic and the tragic aspects of their condition.[86]

A comic use of language

> *J'ai pour mon dire, que quand c'est le temps de rire, allons-y gaiement! Même quand j'conte des histoires tristes, j'm'arrange toujours pour les rendre un peu comiques ...* (Rose Ouimet, p. 16)

In their speech Tremblay's characters, like those of any playwright, conform not so much to a norm of common usage as to the specific requirements of the particular play and the particular authorial vision. As a comic piece therefore *Les Belles-Soeurs* foregrounds the deviance of *joual*, firstly by giving it 'house-room' on the stage, but secondly by presenting it as more highly coloured and more abrasive than its real-life equivalent.[87] Its non- standard phonetics, already unexpected on stage, are given increased comic prominence by Lisette de Courval's misguided 'over-corrections' and frequent regressions to her 'family' tongue. It has a larger-than-life share of comic off-the-cuff repartee and also exploits an uninhibited naturalistic vocabulary incorporating oaths[88] and obscenities, notably in the latter case the farmyard imagery and scatological and sexual terminology of Marie-Ange Brouillette and Rose Ouimet. It also exaggerates the inadequacy of the *belles-soeurs'* purchase on the logical structures of language, competition word-games explicitly developing the motif of (lack of) linguistic control, which non-sequiturs, redundancies and malapropisms distributed through the text entertainingly extend and underscore. This carefully orchestrated display of phonetic divergence, linguistic exuberance, absence of lexical inhibition and lack of intellectual rigour, efficiently and effectively unites key thematic and formal concerns. Combining misdirected linguistic verve with impenetrable conversational impasse, it provides an outrageous representation of communication gone awry, a hilarious ring-side view of exchanges that are all cackle and no contact in a world on the verge of social collapse.

A 'poetic' use of language

> *Il y a, chez moi, une sorte de lyrisme naturel qui fait que je pars toujours d'un peu plus haut que la réalité dans le verbe.*
>
> (*Séquences* 88 [April 1977], p. 6)

Language in *Les Belles-Soeurs* does not operate solely in the mode of exaggeration as lexical, intellectual or phonetic caricature. In the set-piece monologues and choruses in particular, Tremblay, carefully developing rhythmic and phonetic features, transforms the uncouthness of *joual* into a 'poetic' statement of the insufficiencies or inadequacies of the *belles-soeurs'* experience. A number such as the 'Quintette de la mauvaise vie plate' is structured as five stanzas, that are introduced by a prologue, terminated by an epilogue and each concluded by the refrain 'Pis le soir, on regarde la télévision'. Within these stanzas, Alvina Ruprecht has pointed to the importance of extensive phonetic networks that imitate and sustain the constraining rhythms of the *belles-soeurs'* circumscribed existence.[89] In contrasting mood but using similar techniques of echo and refrain the Guerin sisters' nostalgic remembering of Pierrette's childhood (pp. 32-3) plays on the semantic and phonetic repetition of the imperfect tenses that underline the lost possibilities of youth. The solo performances similarly marry the procedures of literary rhetoric to lowly subject-matter. Germaine's 'wish-list' of items from her 'cataloye', a masterpiece of rhythmic pacing, and Yvette's enumeration of her acquaintance, cunningly constructed on complex linkages of alliteration and assonance, are two very clear examples of a rhetorical process constantly at work throughout the monologues of the play.

Tremblay's 'poetic' use of language is not confined either to set-piece choral or solo performance. More broadly across the play, the tragic aspects of the women's predicament are made clear by formal emphasising of their experience of unrelieved 'misère' (significantly the first word of the play). The grammatical dependence and phonetic profiling of the participles 'énarvées', écoeurées', 'pognées' resonate throughout the play in a long litany of passivity. Meanwhile a nexus of imagery and vocabulary, underpinned by phonetic association, highlights key themes of imprisonment and theft. Birds, flight, and travel are persistently evoked, only to be stripped of their potency. Sparrows flutter hopelessly around the apartment of Rose's daughter-in-law. The honeymoon trip of Yvette's daughter and her new husband, foolish 'sérins' never escaping their cage, leads straight to the Canary Islands! Meanwhile the oft-repeated Quebec expression, 'J'ai mon voyage', rendering turn by turn opposing emotions of stupefaction and resentment, pinpoints both the aspiration to escape and the frustration of those who never get away. The word 'vol' itself passes from an expression of freedom ('vol'='flight') to one of deprivation ('vol'='theft') in a universe ruled by theft from God at the top ('Y l'a dit lui-même: "Je viendrai comme un voleur"' [p. 31]) to the local butcher at the bottom ('Le gars qui me vend ma viande, à shop, c't'un vrai voleur!' [p. 34]). The phonetic and thematic link with 'le viol', the central word of Desneiges Verrette's 'histoire cochonne' about the nun, the unspoken word of Rose Ouimet's 'mauvais cul' monologue, confirms the intimacy of the assault on the women's freedom. 'Coller' as the other key element in this central thematic and phonetic network provides (see p. xviii) the overarching and permanent reminder of enforced immobility.

Tremblay's expansion of *joual* beyond its documentary status into an instrument of telling comic or tragic expression has the paradoxical effect of translating a sociolect indicative of cultural inadequacy into a model of sophisticated literary control. This 'raising up' of popular language constitutes vicariously the ultimate revenge and redemption of the *belles-soeurs* and their world. In subverting linguistic codes, Tremblay subverts the social and cultural hierarchies which they both figure and underpin, hence no doubt, as Lise Gauvin has argued, the 'scandal' provoked, among certain members of the Quebec elite, by the first performances of the play.[90]

Les Belles-Soeurs in Performance

> *Au théâtre j'accorde aux autres une part de création qui est égale à la mienne: au metteur en scène, aux acteurs, au décorateur, comme aux techniciens.[...] Le vrai théâtre c'est quand le monde s'asseoit et que le show commence.*
> (Tremblay to Jacques Larue-Langlois, *Le Devoir*, 12 April 1980, p. 19)

> *La beauté du théâtre c'est justement le mot interprète.*[91]

A play exists fully only in performance in the mouths and gestures of the cast and in the focus chosen for it by the director. Tremblay consistently stresses that theatre is a collaborative, open-ended, dynamic venture in which the playwright has much to learn from the rest of the team. Crucial to the success of *Les Belles-Soeurs* as to the rest of Tremblay's plays has been his long partnership with director André Brassard and the links formed in the 1960s with established performers such as Denise Filiatrault, newcomers such as Rita Lafontaine,[92] and set and costume designers such as François Laplante and François Barbeau.

'Le tandem Tremblay-Brassard'

> *Si je m'entends bien avec Brassard, c'est que les spectacles qu'il fait ont la grande qualité d'avoir l'air d'un 'show'. Tu ne peux jamais oublier que tu es au théâtre.*[93]

Tremblay's collaboration with André Brassard is a striking example of 'a providential encounter between a playwright and his director'.[94] Brassard was instrumental in finally getting *Les Belles-Soeurs* performed (see above p. x) and his staging of the play and of Tremblay's subsequent plays has been a major element in their success. In a speech made at the presentation of the Société Saint-Jean-Baptiste's 1987 Victor Morin prize to Brassard, Tremblay affectionately recalled their first meeting, following his winning of the Radio-Canada young author's prize for his first play, *Le Train*:

> Le toupet généreux lui tombant sur l'oeil, le regard sombre et perçant, le sourire presque moqueur, déjà, un tout jeune homme, un gringalet à la fois engoncé dans un pantalon trop étroit et perdu dans un chandail trop large, un adolescent au charme évident, m'arrête dans la rue pour me demander:
> – 'C'est toi qui as gagné au concours des jeunes auteurs , y'a quelques mois?'
> J'dis oui, que c'est bien moi. Il me répond:
> – 'As-tu écrit autre chose?'
> C'est là, je crois, la question la plus importante qu'on m'ait jamais posée dans ma vie. De cette question est née une amitié plus que précieuse, vitale

> et, aussi, une collaboration qui a la particularité de faire partie intégrante de cette amitié: j'ai souvent l'impression que notre amitié et notre collaboration sont une seule et même chose. C'est ça, je suppose, un tandem.
>
> (*Le Devoir*, 21 November 1987, p. C 1)

In Tremblay's view 'pour un auteur dramatique [...] André est le plus grand cadeau que le ciel lui puisse envoyer' (*ibid.*) because the director is always asking provocative questions of the playwright and of all those working on the play. As a result, hidden implications are teased out, new suggestions made, there are amplifications, compressions, switching around of the dialogue to enhance or clarify an idea. Brassard, as director, thus extends and expands the indications of Tremblay's script, an approach which Tremblay views as a valuable complement to his writing ('Ce que j'aime chez Brassard, c'est qu'il ajoute à ce que je fais' (*Séquences* 88 [April 1977], p. 15) and one where he is prepared to give Brassard his head:

> Je considère qu'André fait un travail aussi important que le mien. On a beaucoup de respect l'un pour l'autre. C'est pourquoi on ne s'est jamais engueulé en 10 ans de travail en commun. L'interprétation ne me regarde en rien, mais quand j'arrive aux dernières répétitions, André m'en a déjà tellement parlé de ce qu'il fait que j'en ai une bonne idée'.

Brassard, for his part, has described the working relationship as the pouring of boiling water over the tea-leaves, the two inputs fused in a perfect synthesis (to Martine Corrivault, *Le Soleil*, 2 March 1985, p. C 1).

The 1977 *Séquences* joint interview with Tremblay makes plain the similarities of outlook that permit this mutually sustaining partnership. The fundamental starting point for both is the emphasis on theatre as a transposition of reality. Brassard as the creator of dramatic works *on stage* lays particular stress on the essential theatricality of his enterprise and on the need to transmit this understanding to the audience ('Je n'ai jamais cru à la réalité en art. La réalité est un point de départ' (*Séquences* 88 [April 1977], p. 6); 'J'ai toujours trouvé qu'une réalité jouée était plus intéressante qu'une réalité réelle' (ibid., p. 12) and the experimental bias of Tremblay's writing for the theatre has certainly been enhanced, and may even in part derive from Brassard's own desire to exploit and expand the specific possibilities of his medium.[95]

The first practical result is a renewed down-playing in actual performance of the mechanics of plot, evident in the desire to restrict plot-driven action on stage. Brassard, like Tremblay, sees the narrative line as important only as a trace of what lies concealed beneath it: 'J'ai toujours eu l'impression que les anecdotes étaient les points de repère d'une réalité qui se cache derrière l'action' (*Séquences* 88 [April 1977], p. 6) Of much greater significance, he believes, is the strength of the text in terms of its language and ideas:

> What I like is to put on plays where the physical presence of the actors is reduced to a minimum, where voices are very important, but aside from that, which present one central static image and let the whole performance focus on that image. I think that if you have a good script, there is no need for a lot of movement, it's only good for hiding weaknesses in a script.
> (*Canadian Theatre Review* 24 [Fall 1979], p. 39)

The second result is a reinforcement of Tremblay's insistence on the importance of the play as an auditory experience. Brassard too is 'un sonore' and the human voice is a powerful determiner in the evolution of his staging:

> J'ai toujours senti, autant au théâtre qu'au cinéma que le son amenait l'image.[...] si une personne doit parler dans un coin, je demande à l'acteur de commencer à parler avant de l'éclairer. C'est un procédé, peut-être. Je trouve que ça coule mieux.
> (*Séquences* 88 [April 1977], p. 13)

Les Belles-Soeurs provided him with his first major opportunity to experiment with his ideas, the attraction lying in the 'absurd' choice of situation, the strong central image and the linguistic and formal challenges posed by the play:

> Le prétexte était merveilleux: les timbres-primes. J'avais aussi envie d'entendre parler ma langue, de plonger dans des problèmes, une dramaturgie, des affaires qui sont très près de moi. Et puis ça m'excitait pour mourir d'avoir des choeurs: ma frustration, sans doute, de ne pas avoir été chef d'orchestre. Des choeurs en joual! Et c'est une des rares fois où j'ai fait des petits dessins, de la mise en scène sur papier, des marques partout.
> (Brassard to André Pontaut, *Le Devoir*, 11 September 1971)

The sound recording of the 1973 production, deposited in the National Library of Canada in Ottawa, reveals the degree of innovation and sophistication that can be attained in pursuit of the 'musical' effect. Tremblay's incorporation in his text of religious chanting on the radio and of the Canadian national anthem is expanded by Brassard into a detailed musical and vocal orchestration of the entire play that transforms the rawness of *joual* into something approaching incantation. A jaunty opening is established by the early 1960s pop-song , 'There she was, just a-walking down the street'; next comes the vigorous beat of rap rhythms, punctuated by brief conversational passages, for Germaine's expatiations on her 'cataloye'; then contrapuntal syncopation of the 'Quintette de la maudite vie plate', picking up as an additional refrain 'Des toasts, du café, du bacon, des oeufs'; then, developing the intoning of the radio, Gregorian chanting of 'Mais elle ne se plaint pas' as comic backing to Thérèse Dubuc's self-advertising dedication to daughterly duty. The process continues throughout the play, spoon and triangle playing, finger-clicking, foot-tapping, traditional folksongs and reels providing a continuo while individual voices or voice ensembles isolate key words and key phrases in the text, embroidering upon them as 'musical' variations on the leitmotifs of Tremblay's composition.

Brassard's influence as director is not of course limited to auditory aspects but underpins a global vision of the whole play. Here, as Tremblay emphasises, Brassard, like Tremblay himself, welcomes all the individual inputs of the cast, the set designers and the costume designers, working with them collaboratively, not rigidly imposing a once-and -for-all *a priori* reading:

> Si les acteurs se battent presque littéralement pour travailler avec lui, c'est qu'il les nourrit autant qu'ils le nourrissent; si les décorateurs, les dessinateurs de costumes et d'éclairage rêvent du jour où il va leur téléphoner, c'est qu'il sait les questionner, eux aussi, les provoquer aussi, à l'intérieur même de leur métier.
>
> ('Brassard vu par Tremblay', *Le Devoir,* 21 November 1987, p. C 12)

Sets

> *Je ne suis pas du tout un visuel.*
>
> (Tremblay, *Cahiers du théâtre. Jeu* 47 [June 1988], p. 66)

> *'L'action se déroule en 1965. Cuisine. Quatre énormes caisses occupent le centre de la pièce.'* (Stage directions for *Les Belles-Soeurs*, p. 1)

These minimalist stage directions for *Les Belles-Soeurs* leave ample scope for the imagination of the director and the set designer. Reflecting the 'openness' of Tremblay's own approach to the staging of his work, Brassard's evolving style as director, and the varying tastes and sophistication of theatre audiences inside and outside Quebec, the play has attracted a variety of visual treatments, some interpreting it in the perspective of the 'kitchen-sink' mimeticism of plays such as Shelagh Delaney's *A Taste of Honey*,[96] others preferring a more symbolically orientated visual approach where the set is configured as a metaphor for central thematic elements in the play. Réal Ouellette's set for the 1968 production transposed 'reality' to the stage with gloomy paint, the inevitable religious statuettes perched prominently on top of the fridge and functioning kitchen taps for a sink in which Linda washed her hair. In the 1971 production Brassard had already begun seek a less directly descriptive effect:

> At the beginning, I was perhaps looking for a kind of picturesque exterior in order to remain close to the realistic style. Later I gave that up. Perhaps I was influenced to move away from realism by the actors and actresses with whom I worked like Monique Mercure and Michelle Rossignol who rejected surface realism. My approach to Tremblay really changed drastically in 1971 with the new production of *Les Belles-Soeurs* at the Rideau Vert. It was really a very beautiful experience as we all discovered together

> how much there was behind the surface realism and the joual. So that production used a totally different set from the first one. We played on an inclined plane and all the pieces of furniture had wheels so that the actresses could move them about, there was less clutter, etc.
> (*Canadian Theatre Review* 24 [Fall 1979], p. 40-1)

The fifth (1973) Paris production took the process further. Working to the needs of a French audience and using visual prompts to support a broader cultural message and to compensate for any difficulties arising out of the specificities of Quebec language and experience, Brassard modified the setting 'du cheap au kitsch, avec les meubles rose-nanane et autres nouveaux gadgets expressifs' (Adrien Gruslin, *Le Devoir*, 29 June 1974, p. 16), for example a rose-pink washing machine and a rose-pink telehone, emphasising less the drab circumstances of the *belles-soeurs*' Montreal surroundings than 'l'envahissant confort américain', the women's absence of taste and the sugary inauthenticity of their Bovaresque dreams. Ten years later, another Brassard production, this time in Toronto, developed a set 'qui suggérerait un trou, parce que c'est une société qui est dans le trou':

> une série de toits urbains encastrant l'aire de jeu et limitée à l'arrière par des façades de briques rouge bordant une rue. [...] Décor impressionnant, stylisé et envahissant, au milieu duquel la cuisine n'est que suggérée par la présence du frigo, mais qu'une longue table [...] traverse en occupant presque tout l'espace. (Jean-Cléo Godin, *Cahiers de théâtre. Jeu* 31 [1984], p. 128-9)

In the 1990s, moving still more comprehensively towards a symbolic presentation, Serge Denoncourt's 1991 production deliberately dispensed with 'les artefacts de l'imagerie culturelle québécoise', offering 'une vision épurée de tout naturalisme', susceptible of a variety of imaginative readings by an attentive audience. Jean-Louis Tremblay decoded this set as suggesting the wild expansiveness of Germaine's dreams:

> Point de frigo, de crucifix, de 'pantry'. Non. Seulement des tables de cuisine, des dizaines, empilées, et une autre, magnifique qui trône au centre de la scène, toute de chrome et d'arborite gris, tel qu'on peut en trouver encore chez les marchands de meubles d'occasion. Mais celle-ci, ne nous y trompons pas, a été commandée pour la circonstance: en effet, à mesure que la parenté et les voisines arriveront, elle s'allongera pour devenir immense, immense comme le rêve de Germaine Lauzon qui, lui, s'effondre peu à peu.
> (*Cahiers de théâtre. Jeu* 60 [1991], p. 195)

Jocelyne Richer, on the other hand, (*Le Devoir*, 9 March 1991, p. C 2) deciphered it as the visual figuration of claustrophobic confinement:

> La cuisine des Belles-Soeurs est plus dépouillée, plus surréaliste, et les murs de préfini ont été remplacés par une sorte de cage métallique, faite de dizaines de tables de cuisine superposées. Génial. Les belles-soeurs sont cloîtrées dans leur cuisine comme des bêtes dans leur cage.

It is clear then that the brevity of Tremblay's stage directions is particularly successful in eliciting from producers and set designers that strong imaginative response that Tremblay considers an essential part of theatre. His sense of its importance goes back to his early teens and to his first experience of live performance, Paul Buissoneau's staging of Guillaume Hannoteau's *La Tour Eiffel qui tue,* which gave him:

> l'une de mes plus grandes leçons de théâtre; il m'apprit la signification et la magie de la transposition[...] La machinerie théâtrale devenait un personnage essentiel aussi intéressant que les êtres humains qui déambulaient sur la scène. (*DC*, pp. 53, 54-5)

Costumes

The costumes in the play, in a similar manner, can serve both the needs of referentiality and the requirements of imaginative theatre, enhancing in particular the visual comedy of the play, as noted by Martial Dassylva (*La Presse*, 11 October 1973):

> Voyants, quétaines,[97] chromés d'un mauvais goût voulu poussé jusqu'à l'invraisemblance, les costumes de Barbeau et Laplante sont, comme on dit familièrement, 'dans le parfait' et brillent de tous leurs feux sur le rose fadasse du mobilier.

With a cast consisting of fifteen women they are also crucial in establishing the particular female stance each character represents. Contrasting colours provide a frame of symbolic reference. In Brassard's 1984 production, for example, 'the jealous one wears green, the churchgoers are stiff in black, the hot-head is in red' (Marianne Ackerman, *The Gazette*, 31 March 1984, p. C 9). Dressing 'up', dressing 'down', dressing 'anyhow', underline the different responses that make up the intertwined thematics of social conformism and domestic confinement, public façade and private disintegration. In the play Lisette de Courval, Angéline Sauvé and Rhéauna Bibeau provide a comically exaggerated version of the norms of public attire. Lisette has come 'slumming' to the party, but her more formal clothing including, 'tired' (*maganée)* though it may be, the famous 'étole de vison', emphasises her obsessional need to 'keep up appearances' and marks a fragile attempt to separate herself from her neighbours. Angéline and Rhéauna, returning, suitably clad in 'customary suits of solemn black' (*Hamlet*, Act I, Scene ii, l. 78) from the 'salon mortuaire' display automaton-like compliance with the vestimentary code covering the social display of grief. Comic highlighting of the stereotype is provided at first textually by Angéline's disquisition on the sartorial shortcomings not only of the deceased's family but also of the deceased, then visually by the *coup de théâtre* irruption on stage of the décolletée, gold-chained, over-made-up night-club 'hostess' Pierrette, who greets the so proper Angéline as a bosom friend.

In contrast to these examples of dress for public display, the other *belles-soeurs*, *ménagères* and *femmes d'intérieur*, retain their kitchen attire, 'slips trail[ing] below their hemlines the way their lives trail behind their hopes' (Sandy Perry, *Seattle Sun*, 18 March 1979), bobby socks and slippers on their feet, lank-haired or heads bristling with curlers, half-covered by those 'bonnets de nylon à fleurs tels qu'en portent encore sur nos plages certaines grosses dames de province prenant leur bain de mer' (Patrick de Rosbo, *Combat*, 27 November 1973, p. 12).

Rising in hilarious short-lived splendour against both social conventions of public dress and private *laisser-aller* is the figure of Germaine. The big winner, she is also ample in physical size, a point underlined in Tremblay's text, first in her exchange with her sister Rose over the wisdom of adding a bathing costume to her substantial wish-list of catalogue items and secondly, in the discussion in Act II, instituted for diversionary purposes by Gabrielle Jodoin, over the difficulty of finding a suitable corset. Though she starts the play in an elderly dressing-gown, she dresses up extravagantly for her party ('Bonyeu, tu t'es checquée! T'en vas-tu aux noces?' [p. 10]). In production big hair (in the 1984 production, for example, a large red wig) completes the pantomime 'ugly sister' or 'dame' effect of vestimentary exaggeration and corporeal bulk. Developing the visual contrast between Germaine and the rest, François Barbeau's costumes in 1984 offered further illustration of the imaginative possibilities of the play for the costume designer. On this occasion Germaine emerged from her bedroom clad in 'une somptueuse tenue qui la transform[ait] en une sorte de "Miss Universe" au large ruban croisé sur sa robe de gala et tiare sur la tête'. Meanwhile, facing this 'vision loufoque', the rest of the group, their crudely coloured clothes swathed for the sticking bee in grey hairdressers' 'bavettes en plastiques' that covered even Lisette de Courval's stole, 'form[ai]ent un groupe homogène et harmonieux où les individualités se fond[ai]ent dans l'opposition commune à la "reine"' (Jean-Cléo Godin, *Cahiers de Théâtre. Jeu* 31 [1984], p. 130).

Choreography

The visual aspect of the play has as its third element the gestures and movements of the cast and their deployment amongst the furniture of the set. In this respect, *Les Belles-Soeurs* offers a considerable challenge, the 'quatre énormes caisses', specified by Tremblay, sharing a crowded stage with fifteen people who are all present in Germaine's kitchen for most of the duration of the play. The structuring of the text around a series of solo and ensemble 'turns' provides a helpful starting point for the gestural and choreographic development of the comic or symbolic aspects of Tremblay's vision by director and cast. The skill and imagination of the actresses can be manifest in their smallest movements, in the nuances of facial expression or of bodily deportment. Adrien Gruslin, commenting on the 1974 Montreal production, notes, for example:

> Dès la présentation initiale [...] on connaît la timidité de la Des-Neiges Verrette de Rita Lafontaine, il aura suffi d'un sourire. Les costumes noirs des vieilles filles Angéline Sauvé et Rhéauna Bibeau les définissent bien (cela reste vrai pour toutes), le procédé est aisé mais leur mimique et leur allure le sont moins. Elles ont une façon de marcher, de s'asseoir qui les fait ressortir. (*Le Devoir*, 29 June 1974, p. 16)

Similarly the actresses in *The Guid Sisters*, Michael Boyd's 1992 Glasgow production of the Scots translation of Tremblay's play, were enthusiastically commended *(The Herald*, 18 August 1992) for their ability to provide fifteen different approaches to the apparent unremarkable act of sticking Green Shield stamps into a booklet. More rumbustiously Thérèse's violence towards her mother-in-law can assume the farcical quality of a Punch and Judy beating and limited space be cleverly exploited to accommodate the comic by-play of the old woman whirling unpredictably around the stage in her wheel-chair.[98] Handling of the large groups produces other ingenious ideas. Spot-lighted monologues are spoken against 'beautifully choreographed "freezes"' by the rest of the cast (*Edmonton Journal*, 17 May 1980), the different speakers perhaps brought forward into a separate area of the set. Mass movement of chairs around the stage at the end of Act I is skilfully managed to create maximum comic bustle; the corresponding movement of frantic mayhem at the end of Act II subsides into lonely stillness, as the stamps are made to flutter down in deliberate slow-motion from the ceiling. To these imaginative renderings of the author's explicit intentions, directors can bring their own choreographic and visual underlining of the play's central themes. Thus, for example, in the 1973 production, Brassard developed group activity on stage to underline Tremblay's critique of Catholic influence in Quebec. The rosary has everyone on their knees even as they continue to argue. Elsewhere 'the whole group eat potato chips as if they were taking communion', or 'a squabble over seating arrangements freezes momentarily into a tableau of da Vinci's Last Supper' (Jack Kapica, *The Gazette*, 11 October, 1973, p. 36). With even greater panache Michael Boyd's 1992 Glasgow production incorporated some 'stunning visual flourishes', which were just as enthusiastically received when the production transferred to Montreal:

> At the mention of of hell-fire, smoke billows out [*sic*] the refrigerator door. During the we-love-bingo chorus, light bulbs framing the set flash off and

> on. The literally iconoclastic finale shows the entire loot-bearing gang bursting through a huge picture of the Virgin Mary while 'O Canada' is sung – in French.
> (Pat Donnelly, *The Gazette*, 30 October 1992, p. 14)

With dynamic interpretations and developments of his script such as these, Tremblay is amply repaid for his belief in the importance of the creative input of the performance team and for his 'sit-back and see' policy with regard to the production of his plays.

Les Belles-Soeurs: beyond 1968

The strength of Tremblay's theatrical imagination and the inventiveness of his theatrical collaborators has guaranteed and perpetuated the success of *Les Belles-Soeurs*. Since 1968 the play has been translated into a range of English language versions including North American English, Lowland Scots and Cockney,[99] and into many other languages, including German, Italian, Polish, Rumanian, Spanish and Yiddish. It has been performed outside Quebec in venues throughout Canada, including a televised CBC English language version in 1978.[100] Abroad it has been produced across the world in countries as various as Argentina, Australia, Chile, England, France, Germany, Italy, Rumania, Scotland, the United States and Zaire.

For Tremblay himself the success of the play stimulated the writing of ten further plays, to make up the eleven plays of the so-called *Belles-Soeurs* cycle.[101] In these works, Tremblay develops a portrayal both of a cramping domesticity that is quite literally soul-destroying and of illusory 'escape' to the seedy clubs and tawdry 'freedoms' of the Main (Montreal's rue Saint Laurent)[102] with its fringe population of prostitutes, transvestites and homosexuals. Alienation is the common thread binding the two ostensibly opposed milieux and the tone, leaving behind the slapstick elements in *Les Belles-Soeurs*, is increasingly one of tragic rage and despair as the protagonists, like rats in a trap, confront the hopelessness of their situation. Compensating the gloom of this vision, constant formal innovation establishes a freshness and liveliness that ensures the audience's interest and attention.[103]

In 1977 Tremblay renewed his material by turning to the novel.[104] The volumes of the *Chroniques du Plateau Mont-Royal* take the reader back to a starting point in 1942 Montreal, when the *belles-soeurs* are young women just starting out on their marriages and their families and the youngest Guérin sister, Pierrette, is still a 10 or 11 year old school-girl on the brink of adolescence. The women thus acquire retrospectively a more individualised history, the reader of the novels gaining a wider access to their external and family environments and also being privy to an ongoing narratorial reflection on their inner, psychological experience.[105]

However the novels themselves provoked further theatrical developments and experimentation. Thus *La Grosse femme d'à côté est enceinte* (1978) and *Thérèse et Pierrette à l'école des Saints-Anges* (1980) stimulated a triumphant return to the theatre with *Albertine en cinq temps* (1984) where Tremblay, expanding the theatrical inventiveness of *Les Belles-Soeurs* and the plays of the 1970s, explores in depth the psychological development of a single personage from the novels by disaggregating the stages of her evolution from 30 to 70 years old into five different characters on stage. Other plays have followed, notably *Le Vrai Monde?* (1987), *La Maison suspendue* (1990), *Marcel poursuivi par les chiens* (1992) and *Messe solennelle pour une pleine lune d'été* (1996) that similarly combine themes of family, personal, and also artistic development with further imaginative variations on theatrical form.[106]

Through his plays and his novels Tremblay has created a parallel and still expanding society alongside that of the 'real' Montreal. In 1996 his 'comédie humaine' received the ultimate accolade of its own *Who's Who*, Jean-Marc Barrette's *L'Univers de Michel Tremblay. Dictionnaire des personnages* (Montréal: Presses de l'Université de Montréal). The bombshell of 1968 has become a classic of Quebec literature and a canonic reference point for modern Quebec theatre, and the youthful iconoclast of the rue Fabre has taken on the aspect of a Quebec Balzac, both 'historien' and 'secrétaire de son temps' and visionary inaugurator of new modes of imaginative representation and expression.

NOTES TO INTRODUCTION

1. Written in 1965 and first performed in 1968, *Les Belles-Soeurs* can be located within the dual perspective of the increasingly tense political situation in Quebec, where terrorist bombings and kidnappings by the Front de libération du Québec were to culminate in the declaration of a state of emergency in October 1970, but also, more broadly, in the general turbulence of Western youth, finally articulated in the upheavals of 1968.

2. Le Théâtre du Rideau Vert, founded in 1948, was Montreal's first permanent home for serious theatre. 'Le théâtre le plus bourgeois de la ville', the so-called 'théâtre des grosses madames' (Robert Lévesque, *Le Devoir*, 27 August 1968, p. C 2), the theatre 'des toques de vison' (Jocelyne Lepage, *La Presse*, 27 August 1988, p. E 3), it was an unlikely venue for the staging of Tremblay's controversial, working-class play. It seems probable that the eagerness of Denise Filiatrault, an established Quebec star, to play the role of Rose Ouimet, may have been a decisive factor in the acceptance of Tremblay's play by the theatre management, Yvette Brind'Amour and Mercédès Palomino. For further details see below, n.28.

3. The Leméac edition of *Les Belles-Soeurs* (Montréal, 1972) reproduces a number of these reviews and comments. There are also two *dossiers de presse* of Tremblay's work, compiled by the Bibliothèque du Séminaire de Sherbrooke (Sherbrooke, Quebec), vol. 1: *1966-1981* (226 pp.); vol. 2: *1974-1987* (174 pp.). An extensive collection of review cuttings is held and updated by the Centre d'études québécoises (CETUQ) in the University of Montreal. Information can be obtained through e-mail: cetuq@ere.umontreal.ca

4. For a description of some key linguistic features of *joual*, see Appendix I, p. 63-73.

5. The 1988 edition of *Les Insolences du Frère Untel* (Montréal: Les Éditions de l'Homme) contains extensive annotations by the author and a substantial dossier of contextual material. Laurendeau's article (*Le Devoir*, 21 October 1959), responding to an item on television that claimed a constant improvement in the level of spoken French among the young, had complained that, on the contrary, all the young of his family and their acquaintance

> parlent JOUAL [...] Ça les prend dès qu'ils entrent à l'école [...] Les garçons vont plus loin; linguistiquement, ils arborent leur veste de cuir. Tout y passe: les syllabes mangées, le vocabulaire tronqué ou élargi toujours dans le même sens, les phrases qui boitent, la vulgarité virile, la voix qui fait de son mieux

> pour être canaille [...] Mais les filles emboîtent le pas et se hâtent. Une conversation de jeunes adolescents ressemble à des jappements gutturaux.
> (*Insolences*, pp. 151-3 [p. 151])

The edition also documents, through a number of letters between Desbiens, Laurendeau and others, first the attempts by Desbiens' religious order to prevent publication of his book and secondly the favourable reception of the book by the general public. Page references are to the 1988 edition.

6. The two revolutions are the American Revolution (1776) and the French Revolution (1789).

7. This language legislation includes: Law 63: *Loi pour promouvoir la langue française au Québec* (1969), a law aimed at curbing the increasing anglicisation of education in Quebec, brought about by immigrants chosing English over French as the medium of education for their children; Law 22: *Loi sur la langue officielle du Québec* (1974), a tougher set of measures making French the official language of Quebec, the language of communication for all provincial government business, and the official language of the workplace; Law 101 (1977), a comprehensive set of measures designed to enforce the use of French in the work-place, the use of French in education (with stronger limits on exceptions), and, most controversially, 'la francisation du paysage visible' (i.e. the mandatory use of French for, amongst other things, all shop signs). This law remains in force in Quebec, though various amendments required by the federal constitution, have slightly weakened the francophone requirements in education and 'le paysage visible'.

8. Use of popular language on stage was of course well-established in music-hall and variety shows. Serious theatre was another matter. Gratien Gélinas, despite his success in revue with his character Fridolin, was more circumspect in his serious plays. With regard to *Bousille et les Justes* (1960), for example, he outlined his precautions concerning the clarification of such canadianisms as *guidone* ('prostituée'), *bec* ('baiser'), *courir la galipote* ('courailler/fréquenter les lieux d'amusement'), *quêteux* ('quémandeur'), *comprenure* ('compréhension', 'intelligence'), etc. and the handling of pronunciation and of oral syntax: 'Les interprètes pourront se permettre de supprimer la particule négative *ne* comme on le fait souvent dans le parler populaire. Sans s'y complaire, ils en respecteront pourtant la prononciation', (reported by Martial Dassylva, *La Presse*, 16 June 1973, p. D 4).

9. The young Tremblay, working as a printer (see p. x) had, as one job, the setting of the *Parti Pris* texts, but, interestingly, soon found their doctrinaire approach to language unacceptable:

> c'est moi qui composais tous les textes du *Parti Pris*; au début, j'étais bien d'accord avec eux mais à la fin ça m'intéressait plus quand ça s'est compliqué pour rien. (*Chroniques* 22 [October 1976], p. 15)

10. *Osstidcho*, i.e. *hostie de show* ('a helluva show'), see the discussion of *les sacres* (religious swear-words) in Quebec, p.69. The production was described by Robert Lévesque (*Le Devoir*, 27 August 1988, p. C 2) as a 'déballage de folie, de musique, de bonheur et de conscience sociale'. In the latter perspective a notable contribution was Yvon Deschamps' monologue, 'Les Unions qu'Ossa donne?' (i.e. 'Les Unions, qu'est-ce que ça donne?'). Charlebois' role in establishing an international reputation for the 'pop' music of Quebec was enthusiastically recognised by Tremblay in conversation with Claude Gingras (*La Presse*, 16 August 1969, p. 26):

> J'aimerais bien qu'on sache combien j'admire Robert Charlebois. [...] Je lui baiserais les pieds pour avoir prouvé aux Français qu'on n'était pas des Français. [...] Ce seraient des gens bien gentils s'ils ne voulaient pas nous montrer à vivre, à manger, à parler.

11. The following exchange between Chimène and Don Rodrigue illustrates the mix:

> CHIMÈNE: Oh là! qu'ai-je devant les yeux? La main impitoyable qui poussait l'épée vengeresse qui est entrée sans frapper dans le ventre bien formé de mon père adoré et qui a failli sortir par l'autre côté! On peut dire que pour le moins que tu as du front tout autour de la tête! Je te chasse! Dehors! Je ne veux plus te revoir qu'en boulettes de steak haché!
> DON RODRIGUE: Pitié! Je ne veux plus vivre.
> CHIMÈNE (*elle s'effondre*): Tu vas me faire mourir.
> DON RODRIGUE: Règle-moi mon compte! Passe-moi au fil de cette épée.
> CHIMÈNE: Achale-moi pas! Sacre ton camp! Laisse moi brailler tranquille.
> (Extract taken from a cyclostyled typescript in the Centre d'études québécoises, University of Montreal. The play is still unpublished.)

12. At the end of Hémon's novel, Maria, faced with the choice of marrying Lorenzo Surprenant and moving to the United States to join him in the 'big city' or marrying Eutrope Gagnon and continuing to live a hard pioneering life in the Northern forests, hears three voices within her heart which will persuade her to remain:

> Maria se demandait encore: pourquoi rester là, et tant peiner, et tant souffrir. Pourquoi?... Et comme elle ne trouvait pas de réponse, voici que du silence de la nuit, des voix s'élévèrent. [...] Comme Maria songeait aux merveilles lointaines des cités, la première voix vint lui rappeler en chuchotant les cent douceurs méconnues du pays qu'elle voulait fuir [.../...] 'Ça doit être beau pourtant!' se dit-elle en songeant aux grandes cités américaines. Et une autre voix s'éleva comme une réponse. Là-bas, c'était l'étranger: des gens d'une autre race parlant d'autre chose dans une autre langue, chantant d'autres chansons [.../...] 'Tout de même ... c'est un pays dur icitte. Pourquoi rester?' / Alors une troisième voix plus grande que les autres s'éleva dans le silence; la voix du pays de Québec, qui était à moitié un chant de femme et à moitié

un sermon de prêtre. / [...] en vérité tout ce qui fait l'âme de la province tenait dans cette voix: la solennité du vieux culte, la douceur de la vieille langue jalousement gardée, la splendeur et la force du pays neuf, où une race ancienne a retrouvé son adolescence.

(*Maria Chapdelaine* [LGF, Bernard Grasset, 1954], p. 234-40)

13. Gilles Vigneault, 'Les gens de mon pays' (1965), *Le grand cerf-volant. Poèmes, contes et chansons* (Ottawa: Nouvelles Éditions de l'Arc, 1986), pp. 164-6:

Les gens de mon pays / Ce sont gens de paroles / Et gens de causerie / Qui parlent pour s'entendre [...//...] Voix noires, voix durcies / D'écorce et de cordage / Voix des pays plain-chant / Et voix des amoureux / Douces voix attendries / Des amours de village / Voix de beaux airs anciens / Dont on s'ennuie en ville [...//...] Est-ce vous que j'appelle / Ou vous qui m'appelez / Langage de mon père / Et patois dix-septième[...]

14. For example, to Claude Gingras (*La Presse*, 16 August 1969, p. 26): 'Je ne tiens pas à ce que le joual se propage' and to Jacques Larue-Langlois (*Perspectives*, 20 December 1969, p. 7): 'Je ne veux pas faire du joual un art, je veux le dénoncer.'

15. Tremblay to Jean-Claude Germain, 'Michel Tremblay: Le plus joual des auteurs ou vice versa' (*Digeste-éclair*, October 1968, p. 18).

16. Claire Kirkland-Casgrain's opposition has a paradoxical aspect to it in so far as the focus of the play is on the disadvantaged situation of women. As the first *députée* in the Quebec Parliament, she had introduced the bill for Law 16, which provided women with a range of civil rights from which they were excluded under the Code Civil of 1866. For further details, see p. xvi-xvii and note 51.

17. Thus, for example, Jacques Lafont (*Politique Hebdo*, 106 [5 December 1973]; quoted by Albert Brie, *Le Devoir*, 29 December 1973):

il faudrait[...] surtout dire les vertus de cette merveilleuse langue québécoise qui nous surprend d'abord et qui nous enchante ensuite par son pouvoir d'évocation, sa fraîcheur, sa justesse.

18. See the report on the Dakar conference, 'Le succès des *Belles-Soeurs* à Paris mécontente les adversaires du *joual*' (*La Presse*, 5 December 1973).

19. The Société Saint-Jean-Baptiste was founded in Quebec City in 1842 following the unification of anglophone Upper Canada and francophone Lower Canada with the motto 'Nos institutions, notre langue et nos lois' and has acted over the years as 'un lieu de rassemblement, de réflexion, d'action et de fraternité pour l'ensemble des Canadiens français et Canadiennes françaises' (its own description of its role in an article celebrating 150 years of its existence, *Cap-aux-Diamants*, 29 [Spring, 1992], p. 27). Saint John-the-Baptist had been informally adopted as the patron saint of the French Canadians in 1834 and was officially so named by Pope Pius X on 25 February 1908 (*Cap-aux-Diamants* [Summer 1991], p. 18). In 1977 the Parti Québécois government proclaimed his feast day, 24 June, the National Day of Quebec. The Victor Morin prize of $500 and a medal inscribed 'Bene merenti de patria' recognise the contribution of a figure from the world of the arts in Quebec.

20. Paule des Rivières' article, 'Deux camps autour du *Robert québécois*' (*Le Devoir*, 11 December 1992, p. B 4) notes the negative reaction of some writers and educationalists to the dictionary, especially to phrases such as 'Envoye [Vas-y], espèce de twit. On va pas rester amanchés [coincés] de même'. In contrast to this renewed concern for the maintenance of a standard French facilitating communication with the francophone world outside Quebec, Gilles Vigneault, in a short preface to the dictionary, describes it as a 'pépinière' and 'chacun de ses mots comme un lieu neuf d'enracinement dans l'humus du vrai pays'. Tremblay's linguistic view, as reported in the article, remains unchanged from the 1960s:

> Les opposants [au *Dictionnaire*] font beaucoup de bruit pour rien. Mais les tenants du bon parler français, qui à mon avis est éminemment bourgeois, ne lâchent pas prise. Ils ont peur lorsqu'ils voient un nouveau mot. Toute cette notion du bon français renvoie à une élite qui veut imposer la belle langue et ça me fait suer profondément.

However Tremblay's use of *joual* in work subsequent to *Les Belles-Soeurs* is in no way doctrinaire. Rather the whole range of discourse from *joual* to standard French is used depending on the requirements of the text in hand.

21. Quoted by Pascal Normand, 'Michel Tremblay and Robert Charlebois: l'émergence d'un parler québécois' (*Présence francophone* 32 [1988], p. 65).

22. Montreal: Leméac, 1990, 1992, and 1994 respectively. Subsequent references are given in the text as *VA*, *DC*, and *AC*. For *Douze coups de théâtre*, the paperback Babel edition (1997) has been used as the reference text.The five novels making up the *Chroniques du Plateau-Royal* are *La Grosse femme d'à côté est enceinte* (1978), *Thérèse et Pierrette à l'école des Saints-Anges* (1980), *La Duchesse et le Roturier* (1982), *Des Nouvelles d'Édouard* (1984), *Le Premier Quartier de la lune* (1989).

23. Tremblay to Claude Gingras (*La Presse*, 16 August 1969, p. 26): 'On était trois familles dans la même maison: treize dans sept pièces.' But Tremblay also stresses the happiness of his childhood:

> I've had an absolutely marvellous childhood. My childhood may have been hard on others, it wasn't hard on me. I lived in a poor milieu with people who were more or less unhappy, but for myself I was perfectly happy. (Renate Usmiani,'Where to begin the Accusation. Interview with Michel Tremblay', *Canadian Theatre Review* 24 [Fall 1979], p. 30)

24. *Un Ange cornu avec des ailes de tôle* opens with an affectionate portrait of Tremblay's mother including a brief account of her childhood:

> Les origines de ma mère sont compliquées et mystérieuses. Née à Providence, dans le Rhode Island, d'une mère *Cree* francophone de Saskatoon (Maria Desrosiers) mais qui parlait très mal le français, et d'un marin breton vite disparu dans l'abîme du souvenir (un dénommé Rathier dont je n'ai jamais su le prénom), elle fut élevée dans un petit village de Saskatchewan par sa grand-mère maternelle[...] Le Saskatchewan a toujours flotté dans l'appartement de la rue Fabre, puis celui de la rue Cartier, gigantesque fantôme aux couleurs de blé mûr et de ciel trop bleu. [...] Maman nous racontait les plaines sans commencement ni fin, les couchers de soleil fous sur l'océan de blé, les feux de broussailles qui se propageaient à la vitesse d'un cheval au galop, les chevaux, justement, qu'elle avait tant aimés, avec un petit tremblement dans la voix et les yeux tournés vers la fenêtre pour nous cacher la nostalgie qui les embuait. (pp. 15-16)

25. The *écoles classiques* grew out of the original college-seminaries of New France and up until the Quiet Revolution of the 1960s provided an elite humanist schooling and access to University education to the monied few or selected academic high-fliers. They disappeared in 1968 in the radical overhaul of the Quebec educational system and were absorbed with other types of school into the Collèges d'enseignement général et professionnel (CEGEPs).

26. Tremblay to Jacques Larue-Langlois (*Perspectives*, 20 December, 1969), p. 7:

> Je n'aimais pas les gens avec qui j'étais. On nous répétait sans cesse que nous étions l'élite, les 31 meilleurs élèves de Montreal et tout le tralala. Un jour, un de mes professeurs a voulu me donner une volée, j'ai foutu le camp pour ne jamais plus retourner.

27. Tremblay's autobiographical works give some affectionate and moving insights into his relationship with his his father, see especially *AC*, pp. 75-82 and *DC*, pp. 107-9, 121-34. The relationship is also reflected in that between Serge and his father in Tremblay's 1974 play *Bonjour, là, bonjour*.

28. There are varying accounts of how the play came to be accepted by the Théâtre du Rideau Vert. Robert Lévesque's article 'Le débarquement des *Belles-Soeurs*' (*Le Devoir*, 27 August 1988, pp. C 2 and C 4) incorporates most of the elements:

> C'est Denise Proulx, la comédienne qui allait créer le rôle principal des *Belles-Soeurs*, qui a fait une certaine ambassade dans l'affaire de la création. Connaissant Brassard et Tremblay, Denise Proulx avait lu la pièce dès 1966 ou 1967. Elle voulait à tout prix jouer Germaine Lauzon. Mais, me disait-elle la semaine dernière, je ne savais pas à quel théâtre cogner. 'Jacques Languirand avait voulu la programmer, à son Théâtre de la Bourse, l'actuel

Centaur), mais il fit faillite. On n'aurait jamais pensé au Théâtre du Nouveau Monde, ni au Rideau Vert, mais un jour Yvette Brind'Amour m'avait dit que la seule personne qui pouvait remplir un théâtre c'était Denise Filiatrault. Ça m'était resté dans la tête.' Le tout jeune Centre d'essai des auteurs dramatiques canadiens organisa une lecture au Théâtre d'Aujourd'hui. Denise Proulx, qui y lisait la partition de Germaine Lauzon, intéressa son mari à l'événement. Jean Saint-Jacques [son mari] était réalisateur aux affaires publiques de Radio-Canada. Résultat: on vit un soir, aux nouvelles, un topo sur une pièce mettant en scène 15 femmes de l'Est [de Montréal, i.e. the working-class francophone sector] qui parlaient *joual* en collant des timbres. L'effet fut saisissant. On fit entendre à Mme Brind'Amour l'enregistrement de la lecture. Yvette convainquit Mercédès, puisqu'il était question que Filitrault en soit! André Montmorency, Benoît Marleau, Filiatrault, qui avaient assisté à la fameuse lecture de la rue Papineau, avaient aidé les choses.

29. David's article, 'Tremblay explore le vertige de la vengeance', (*Le Devoir*, 30 May 1992), makes the most of the metaphor:

Michel Tremblay aura 50 ans le 25 juin prochain et dans un peu plus d'un an en 1993, il se sera passé 25 ans depuis la création des *Belles-Soeurs*. A partir du Big-Bang de 1968, le noyau compact de fiction dramatique de l'auteur né rue Fabre, en plein coeur du Plateau Mont-Royal, aura connu ainsi une irrépressible expansion, pour donner naissance à un univers aux multiples oeuvres, comme autant d'étoiles et de planètes piquées à jamais dans le ciel théâtral et littéraire du Québec.

30. *La Grosse Femme d' à côté est enceinte* (Montréal: Leméac, 1978). References, given in the text as *GF*, are to the paperback Bibliothèque québécoise 1990 edition. Tremblay has stressed the resemblance of the fictional characters to his own family: 'Actually in *La Grosse Femme*, the family I describe is exactly as my family was, the only character I've invented was Édouard' (interview with Renate Usmiani, *Canadian Theatre Review*, 24 [Fall 1979], p. 30). Similarly he commented to Marie-Lyne Piccione: 'Pour moi, la grosse femme est bien réelle, c'est ma mère telle que je la vois'.

31. Tremblay comments (*Lire* 90, February 1983, p. 90):

Jusqu'aux années soixante la majorité des Québécoises n'ont pas eu des enfants voulus et, même en ville, il était courant de voir des familles de quinze enfants. Or il se trouve que moi, j'ai été un enfant voulu, parce que, comme je le raconte, dans ma *Grosse Femme d'à côté est enceinte*, j'ai eu un frère et une soeur qui sont morts de la suite de la leucémie.

32. Québécois resentment towards France is vigorously expressed by Gabriel, the husband of 'la grosse femme': 'Sauver la France pour qu'on continue à nous chier sur la tête après, en riant de notre accent' (*GF*, p. 179).

33. Gérard Pelletier, *Years of Impatience 1950-1960*, trans. Alan Brown

(Methuen, 1984), p. 193 (first published as *Les Années d'Impatience 1950-1960* [Montréal: Stanké, 1983]). The repressive atmosphere of the Duplessis years is very readably evoked by Pelletier, a leading Quebec journalist, editor and politician, who in the 1950s was co-founder, with future Canadian Prime Minister Pierre Elliott Trudeau, of the small but influential review *Cité Libre*, that contested the anti-democratic practices of Duplessis' government and helped pave the way for the Quiet Revolution of the 1960s.

34. Interviewed by Marie-Lyne Piccione and J.M. Lacroix (*Études canadiennes* 10 [1981], p. 204) Tremblay notes:

> Malgré tout, mon roman se termine sur une image d'espoir. Les sept femmes enceintes bavardant sur un balcon se réunissent pour mettre un pays au monde. Leurs enfants auront 20 ans dans les années 60, au moment où le Québec entrera dans l'ère moderne.

35. In an interview with Léonce Catin and Alonzo Leblanc (*Québec français* 44 [December 1981], p. 40), Tremblay states categorically: 'La religion catholique est d'abord et avant tout une compagnie à but lucratif.'

36. Maurice Duplessis, Prime Minister of Quebec, 1936-9 and 1944-59 and Adélard Godbout, Prime Minister of Quebec, 1939-44.

37. *Thérèse et Pierrette à l'école des Saints-Anges* (Montréal: Leméac, 1980) opens with a similar account of the humiliation of one small schoolgirl by Mère Benoîte-des-Anges, the head of the school.

38. 'Moi, toi, ici', not the *joual* 'moé, toé, icitte', see Appendix I, p. 65.

39. See Tremblay's account (*AC*, p. 103):

> Le choc est tellement grand que je sursaute sur ma chaise. Ce livre, aussi ennuyant soit-il, a été écrit par une petite fille de treize ans. [...] Et son livre s'est rendu jusqu'à moi, à l'autre bout du monde, dans le fin fond du Canada français, là, où même les grands écrivains, selon mon frère Jacques qui a fait son cours classique et qui connaît tout, ont de la difficulté à se faire publier parce que ça coûte trop cher! On nous apprend, à l'école, que nous vivons dans le pays du papier et que les Européens, qui n'en ont presque pas, sont obligés de nous en acheter, mais on n'arrive pas à publier nos propres écrivains!

40. For a description of one such incident, see *VA*, pp. 140-1:

> Je savais que la politique du magasin voulait qu'on parle anglais, mais il n'y avait aucune chance pour que cette jeune fille-là soit anglaise, aucune! L'accent, la tête, la coiffure, les vêtements, la gomme à mâcher, tout provenait directement du Plateau Mont-Royal ou du faubourg à m'lasse [...]. Un quelconque gérant nous observait, près des escaliers mobiles, l'oeil soupçonneux, sans même cacher son pitoyable jeu d'espion mal payé pour prendre en flagrant délit des francophones qui communiquaient entre eux dans leur langue. Je compris tout en un instant: les incessantes humiliations,

le harassement, les petites et pitoyables capitulations. J'eus pitié d'elle. Et de moi.

41. See *DC*, pp. 231-2:

> Le spectacle [...] fut un mélange de ravissement et d'horreur; de ravissement quand mes idoles chantaient [...] d'horreur quand ils se mettaient à parler anglais [...] C'était absurde, ces quatre chanteurs francophones qui se parlaient anglais [...] sur leur propre scène! [...] Même devant un public en grande partie anglophone, c'était ridicule! C'était ma ville, j'étais chez moi, ces chanteurs avaient le français comme langue maternelle, pourquoi accepter ça?

42. 'When I was six years old my father took me on one side and said he had something very important to tell me. Something I should never forget. He said, "You have to speak English to get a job in Montreal"'. (Tremblay in conversation with James Quig, 'The *Joual* Revolution' [1977]).

43. Tremblay to Jean Royer, *Le Devoir*, 12 April 1980. For a succinct account of the impact of television on 1950s Quebec society, see Pelletier, *Years of Impatience*, Chapter 7, 'A Kind of Cultural Revolution', pp. 171-203.

44. The full text of Taschereau's speech, 'De l'influence de la femme sur nos destinées nationales' can be found in *Québécoises du 20e siècle*, ed. Michèle Jean (Montréal: Quinze, 1977), pp. 208-19. La Fédération nationale Saint-Jean-Baptiste, the female wing of the Société Saint-Jean-Baptiste, was founded in 1907 by Caroline Béïque and Marie Gérin-Lajoie. In its early years, alongside its charitable and social concerns, it championed female suffrage and equality of education for women. By the 1920s, however, its thinking had been reabsorbed into that of the ecclesiastical establishment and its feminist orientation had been dispelled.

45. See Jan Noel, 'New France: Les Femmes favorisées' in Veronica Strong-Boag and Anita Clair Fellman, eds. *Rethinking Canada. The Promise of Women's History* (Toronto: Copp Clark Pitman, 1986), pp. 23-44.

46. In his 1980 interview with Marie-Lyne Piccione and J.M. Lacroix (*Études canadiennes* 10 [1981], 204), Tremblay comments on the importance of this in his own family:

> Ce sont les femmes qui ont maintenu le Québec en parlant français avec les enfants. A la maison, ma mère parlait français; mais sans elle, nous serions devenus anglophones, car mon père, comme la plupart des Québécois, parlait anglais au travail.

As a child, out in Sasketchewan, Tremblay's mother had, however, experienced a largely anglophone upbringing. Her sister Bea remained anglophone. (See *AC*, pp. 17-22)

47. *Québécoises du 20e siècle*, p. 197. The book includes three Bourassa pieces attacking women's suffrage (pp. 193-207).

48. The phrase 'la revanche des berceaux' (more colloquially 'la revanche du ber') was first used in an article by Louis Lalande, PJ, *L'Action française* 2 (March 1918).

49. Tremblay, in conversation with to Jacques Larue-Langlois (*Perspectives*, 20 December 1969, p. 7) provides this summing up of the nexus of privation and compensation:

> Les femmes mènent chez nous parce qu'elles sont tellement frustrées sexuellement. Le contexte religieux a longtemps empêché les Québécoises de jouir; elles se soumettaient mais menaient la maison.'

50. The Holy Family with a hovering Holy Spirit in the form of a bird occurs as one of the subjects of the devotional cards circulated to the faithful by the Catholic Church. The image and its implications are even more strongly attacked in Denise Boucher's feminist play, *Les Fées ont soif* (Montréal: Éditions Intermède, 1978), 2nd edition (Montréal: Hexagone, 1989).

51. A list of the amendments introduced by Law 16 can be found in Collectif Clio, *L'histoire des femmes au Québec depuis quatre siècles* (Montréal: Le Jour, 1992), p. 444.

52. Divorce was only generally legalised in Canada in 1968 (previously it was a matter of individual application) and similar legislation introduced in Quebec in 1969. Birth control was illegal in Canada from 1892 until 1968 and, apart from the rhythm method, continues to be officially prohibited by the Catholic Church. The birth-rate in Quebec now runs, however, at well under two children per women. Abortion was legalised throughout Canada in 1968 though it continues to be prohibited by the Catholic Church. For discussion of these various points, see, *passim*, Collectif Clio, op. cit; John A. Dickinson and Brian Young, *A Short History of Quebec* (Toronto: Copp Clark Pitman; London: Longman, 1993); Mary F. Bishop, 'Vivian Dowding: Birth Control Activist 1892-') in Strong-Boag, Veronica, and Fellman, Anita Clair, op. cit., pp. 200-7.

53. Tremblay, reported by Jean-Claude Germain, *Digeste-éclair*, October 1968, p. 16. The Montreal telephone directory contains seven pages of Tremblays, including 4160 names of which 604 are M. Tremblay, and 35 Michel Tremblay. (I am indebted to Dominique Cambron and Catherine Scott for this information.)

54. Chapter 4 of Renate Usmiani's book, *Michel Tremblay* (Vancouver: Douglas & McIntyre, 1982) is entitled: 'Debunking the Myth. Tremblay's Unholy Families'.

55. The particular role of the 'salon mortuaire' in the Quebec imagination is highlighted by Tremblay in interview (*Séquences* 88 [1977], p. 14):

> *Interviewer*: Dans le cinéma québécois, je n'ai jamais vu une scène de résidence funéraire qui ne soit pas caricaturée, souvent à outrance. Est-il possible de montrer un 'salon' sans ridiculiser les gens qui s'y rendent?

MT: Je voulais donner une image du cinéma québécois comme mon père en avait une du cinéma français quand j'étais petit. Mon père disait: 'Ah! c'est une vue française, donc on va voir une femme en brassière!' L'équivalent de la femme en brassière pour nous, c'est le salon mortuaire.

56. Interviewed along with André Brassard (*Chroniques* 22 [October 1976], p. 25), Tremblay seeks to distance himself from a theatre focused solely on individual psychology:

Pour moi le théâtre psychologique c'est un théâtre à premier niveau seulement, c'est Williams. T'as juste à dire que Blanche Dubois, c'est Tennessee lui-même, c'est pas ce que je fais, du théâtre uniquement de confession.

57. Another avatar of woman's vocation to serve. The character Lise Paquette clearly owes much to Florentine, Gabrielle Roy's 'heroine' in *Bonheur d'occasion*, who is also a waitress. Florentine, however, unlike Lise, though 'v'nue au monde par la porte d'en arrière', contrives to 'sortir par la porte d'en avant', concealing her pregnancy by Jean by persuading her 'second string', the devoted Emmanuel, to marry her before he leaves to fight in the Second World War in Europe.

58. Gustave Flaubert, *Madame Bovary*, Part I, Chapter 4.

59. Renate Usmiani, *Michel Tremblay*, op.cit., pp. 41-2.

60. Parish bingo was a fund-raising activity for the Church and one of the few approved distractions.

61. The size of the Italian community in Quebec had increased dramatically by the beginning of the 1960s. In 1931, Italians constituted 4.6% of the non-francophone population of Quebec, in 1961 12.4%, the numbers rising from 24,845 (1931), 28,051 (1941), 34,165 (1951) to 108, 552 (1961). See Dickinson and Young, op. cit., p. 264.

62. 'Des Cannibales', Montaigne's celebrated essay on the New World, published in 1580, concludes with a notable example of this trope. Having extolled the native Brazilians as examples of virtue, Montaigne reproduces, as a satiric parting shot, the knee-jerk prejudices of the Europeans regarding 'primitive' peoples: 'Tout cela ne va pas trop mal: *mais quoy, ils ne portent point de haut de chausses*' (*Essais,* Book I, 31 [my italics]).

63. These four items summarise the multiple subjugations of Quebec: to American mass culture ('Coke'), to Church-inspired 'pie in the sky' (symbolised in the parish bingo sessions), to consumerism (figured by the 'timbres'), to Federal Canada ('O Canada').

64. Significantly the film *Il était une fois dans l'Est* based on a number of Tremblay's plays including *Les Belles-Soeurs*, concludes with the abortion and a double death, that of the foetus and that of Lise herself. Tremblay comments: 'La mort de Lise Paquette, c'est la mort d'une société' (*Séquences* 88 [1977], p. 12). Rita Lafontaine, the creator of the role, similarly sees Lise as 'déterminée, oui, de sortir par la porte d'en avant' but doomed, 'quelque chose en elle a été brisé et restera à jamais irréparable' (*Cahiers de théâtre. Jeu* [June 1988], p. 78).

65. Donald Smith, *L'Écrivain devant son oeuvre* (Montréal: Québec/Amérique, 1983), 'Michel Tremblay et la mémoire collective', pp. 213-4.

66. Tremblay, as reported by Jean-Claude Germain, 'Michel Tremblay: Le plus joual des auteurs et vice versa' (*Digeste-éclair*, October 1968, pp. 15-19 [p. 17]).

67. In *Lire* 90, February 1983 (p. 93), Tremblay stresses the advantage of theatre as a means of indirect communication with an audience:

> comme j'étais dans une société très fermée et non permissive et que j'étais homosexuel, ce qui était impossible à vivre ouvertement, le théâtre a été une façon détournée de dire mon mal de vivre en me cachant, en prétextant que ces problèmes-là, ceux des femmes, comme ceux de l'homosexualité, étaient vécus par d'autres et non par moi.

68. Tremblay: interview with Roch Turbide, 'Michel Tremblay: Du texte à la représentation', *Voix et images* 7 (1982), p. 223:

> Je trouve très prétentieux et très dangereux de dire qu'un auteur est là pour montrer la voie, surtout pas un auteur de théâtre. Un écrivain philosophique, d'accord. L'auteur de théâtre est là pour critiquer la société parallèlement à la société. Il n'est pas là pour donner des solutions [...] une pièce de théâtre, c'est une question que tu te poses et qui ensuite est reposée par d'autres personnes. Sinon, tu arrives au théâtre de Sartre et de Camus qui sont pour moi du mauvais théâtre.

69. 'C'est évident que quand on montre aux gens comment ils sont, c'est pour les changer.' Tremblay, as reported by Micheline Handfield (*Sept Jours* 26 [March 1970], p. 27).

70. My italics. See also, Tremblay to Charles Bolster (*Edmonton Journal*, 17 May 1980):

> The people of my country Quebec have always been a fringe of society in North America; when I wrote of the fifteen underprivileged women in *Les Belles-Soeurs*, I wrote, unwittingly, a political play. The microcosm of the frustrated women naturally suggests the greater macrocosm – Quebec.

Directors and critics have taken the analogy further. Serge Denoncourt, speaking of his 1991 production of *Les Belles-Soeurs*, sees the play as a comment on Quebec's constrained position vis-à-vis the other provinces of the Canadian Federation:

> Je ne peux pas m'empêcher de faire un rapprochement entre le Québec et cette femme qui allait vers son indépendance grâce à un million de timbres, et qui se fait posséder par son entourage qui ne veut pas le laisser partir (quoted by Jocelyne Richer, *Le Devoir*, 9 February 1991, p. E 7).

Similarly Jean-Louis Tremblay (*Cahiers du théâtre. Jeu* 60 (1991), pp. 195-6) suggests:

> Cette quête d'une vie meilleure – même par le biais des concours populaires – ne rappelle-t-il pas celle du Québec à la recherche de son autonomie? La dépossession de la grosse femme n'annonce-t-elle pas la nôtre au lendemain du rapatriement de la Constitution après l'échec du lac Meech?

71. The expression achieved a high public profile as the title of Michèle Lalonde's 1968 poem, 'Speak White', which was frequently recited in support of the movement for Quebec independence, notably at the 1970 Nuit de la Poésie.

72. Urjo Kareda (*Montreal Star*, 4 April 1973) reads the final shower of stamps from the ceiling as a further handout bestowed on a compliant victim of the political and social system: 'At the end Germaine weeps over the theft of her stamps, then picks herself together [*sic*] as she hears the chorus of "O Canada", to be rewarded by a shower of golden stamps from the establishment heaven (she sang the right song at the right moment).' Richard de Candole (*The Edmonton Sun*, 13 May 1980, p. 21) reports that Stephen Heatley, the director of an English-language production of the play in the city, sees the trading stamps as 'symbolic of monetary handouts from Ottawa that have attempted to pacify Quebec over many years'.

73. Tremblay, interviewed by Rachel Cloutier, Marie Laberge, Rodrigue Gignac, *Nord* 1 (Autumn 1971), p. 158. Tremblay has repeated the view several times subsequently, see, for example, his interview with Marie-Lyne Piccione and J.M. Lacroix, *Etudes canadiennes* 10 (1981), p. 204.

74. Translated by Martin A. Bowman and Bill Findlay. There have been three published editions of their translation: Toronto: Exile Editions, 1988; Glasgow: Tron Theatre (1989), London: Nick Hern Books, (1991). Dramatised readings of *The Guid Sisters* took place at the Lyceum Studio, Edinburgh, and Stirling University in 1987.The first full performance of *The Guid Sisters* was at the Tron Theatre, Glasgow, in 1989.

75. Receiving the Victor Morin prize in 1974, Tremblay emphasised that 'la culture d'un pays doit être une mosaïque de toutes les facettes de son peuple et non pas l'unique face de son élite.' His speech is printed in full in *Le Devoir*, 14 December, 1974, p. 65.

76. The apparent ludicrousness of this remark evaporates for anyone who has seen Claude Jutra's Quebec classic film, *Mon Oncle Antoine* (1971). Near the beginning, a sequence dealing with the archetypal Quebec event, a *salon mortuaire* (see note 55), shows the undertakers, immediately on the departure of the mourners, removing from the corpse the false suit-and-shirt front, which they had supplied for the occasion.

77. Roch Turbide, 'Michel Tremblay: Du texte à la représentation', *Voix et images* 7 (1982), p. 222.

78. Ibid., p. 213.

79. Jean-Claude-Germain, 'Michel Tremblay: le plus joual des auteurs et vice-versa', *Digeste-éclair*, October 1968, p. 17.

80. Jeannine Hiester, 'La structure classique des *Belles-Soeurs* de Michel Tremblay', *Incidences*, n.s. 6 (1982), 59-67, argues, however, a strong link with the classical theatre of the Ancients in respect of the 'alternance de passages dramatiques, ou épisodes, au cours desquels l'action progresse et se développe, et de passages lyriques - *stasima* ou odes chorales – pendant lesquels l'action reste en suspens' (p. 59).

81. J.-P. Ryngaert, 'Réalisme et théâtralité dans les *Belles-Soeurs*,' *Co-Incidences*, 1, no.3 (November 1971), 3-12.

82. Brassard highlights the formal importance of this effect: 'Ces monologues, je les explique comme la conscience qu'ont les personnages d'être des personnages de théâtre. Je ne sais pas si c'est voulu comme ça par Tremblay, mais, moi, c'est comme ça que je le prends' (Martial Dassylva, 'André Brassard et le message de *Hosanna*', *La Presse*, 12 May 1973).

83. 'Agamemnon. Eschyle', *AC*, pp. 165-78. See also Tremblay's comments in *Magazine Maclean*, September 1973, p. 20:

> J'ai découvert les choeurs en lisant le théâtre grec. C'est tellement extraordinaire un choeur parce qu'au lieu d'additionner, ça multiplie. Par exemple, dans les *Belles-Soeurs*, le fait que les femmes parlent en même temps, c'est comme si elles étaient cinq cents. Ce qui est encore plus extraordinaire, c'est de constater combien un choeur écrit en joual est musical. On peut s'imaginer l'effet qu'il produit lorsqu'en plus il est isolé par la musique.

84. *Cahiers de théâtre. Jeu* 47 (1988), p. 66.

85. Tremblay's enjoyment of opera and musical comedy is an important element in the reminiscences of *Douze coups de théâtre* and *Les Vues animées*. His reflections on *La Parade des soldats de bois*, a free Laurel and Hardy adaptation of Sigmund Romberg's operetta, *Babes in Toyland*, explain a fascination, first experienced in his youth:

> J'avais vu très peu de comédies musicales mais j'aimais beaucoup l'espèce d'absurdité qui envahissait l'écran quand les personnages, souvent des gens de la vie ordinaire, se mettaient à chanter et à danser au milieu de la conversation, en plein quotidien. (*VA*, p. 81)

86. The evolving reaction of Martial Dassylva, theatre critic of *La Presse*, is most instructive. In his generally positive review of the 1968 production of the play, he nevertheless wrote of the language: 'Je ne suis pas bigot de nature, mais je dois avouer que c'est la première fois de ma vie que j'entends autant de sacres, de jurons, de mots orduriers de toilette' (*La Presse*, 29 August, 1968, p. 50). Reviewing the production of 1971 he comments:

Au moment de la création en 1968, j'avais été pour ma part frappé et quelque peu blousé par l'usage du 'joual' dans les *Belles-Soeurs*. A trois ans de distance, disons que mon allergie a considérablement diminué, remplacée qu'elle a été par un réalisme légèrement teinté de défaitisme, surtout lorsque je nous écoute parler, lorsque je nous regarde écrire, et que j'entends les déclarations amphigouriques et dilatoires de nos politiques.

(*La Presse*, 25 May 1971, p. C 10)

Finally the review of the 1973 production reveals the context and scope of Dassylva's 'conversion':

En relisant ma critique de 1968, je me suis aperçu que tout en étant rebuté au plus haut point par le joual, par ses sacres et par ses pompes [...] et tout en le dénonçant avec la dernière vigueur, [...] j'ai tout de même écrit que la pièce [...] était une "mossus" de bonne pièce. [...] je dois avouer que mon texte a une autre valeur [...] en ce qu'y transpire le choc ressenti par un bon petit gars originaire de Charlevoix – une région où jusqu'à tout récemment encore on parlait avec le vocabulare et l'accent d'Henri IV – formé aux humanités gréco-latines dans la culture du *Devoir* de Bourassa, d'André Laurendeau et de Notre-Dame la Langue Française, et coiffé jusqu'aux mollets du bon usage, du Grévisse et de Laurence. /Et puis, je peux bien le dire: le premier choc passé, *les Belles-Soeurs* m'amenèrent à approfondir pour mon propre compte l'ensemble de la question du langage et à me renseigner sur les plus récentes découvertes en matière de linguistique./Et c'est ainsi que, le temps aidant, j'en suis venu à penser que les campagnes de bon parler et de francisation ne riment à rien, que l'usage ordinaire se moque en général éperdument du bon usage des pontifes et des académiciens, et surtout qu'une langue est un instrument de communication et non un absolu ou une fin. (*La Presse*, 16 June 1973, p. D 4)

87. Some of the comic effect of the language has been reduced over time as Tremblay noted in conversation with Renate Usmiani in 1980: 'Already today when you put on *Les Belles-Soeurs* in Montreal, nobody is shocked or laughing , and it's only been eleven years.' (*Canadian Theatre Review* 24 [Fall 1979], p. 32. Nevertheless, re-reading the play, Tremblay finds its language 'très transposé, plus juteux, que dans la vraie vie, plus structuré, plus clair, donc plus théâtral' (*Première* 10, 3 February-March, 1984).

88. On oaths as a feature of *joual*, see Appendix I, p. 69-70.

89. Alvina Ruprecht, 'Effets sonores et significations dans les *Belles-Soeurs* de Michel Tremblay', *Voix et Images* 36 (1967), 439-50, provides a detailed phonological and stylistic analysis of the 'Quintette de la maudite vie plate'. Speaking to Pierre Lavoie, Tremblay himself has stressed the centrality of rhythmic procedures: ' La structure musicale est toujours omniprésente, c'est-à-dire le rythme est prépondérant' (*Cahiers de théâtre. Jeu* 47 [June 1988], 65). In connection with their translations of Tremblay into

Lowland Scots, Martin Bowman and Bill Findlay also emphasise the importance of rhythm in Tremblay's dialogue.

90. Lise Gauvin, 'Le théâtre de la langue' in Gilbert David and Pierre Lavoie, eds, *Le Monde de Michel Tremblay* (Montréal: Cahiers de théâtre Jeu; Carnières: Éditions Lansman, 1993), pp. 346-7.

91. Roch Turbide, 'Michel Tremblay: Du texte à la représentation', *Voix et images* 7 (1982), p. 214.

92. The symbiotic relationship between playwright and performer is movingly expressed in an article quoting Tremblay and Rita Lafontaine: '"Tu m'as mise en mots", avoue la première; "Je sais qu'en écrivant ma prochaine pièce, j'entendrai ta voix", répond le second.' (*Spirale*, February 1995, p. 18)

93. Roch Turbide, 'Michel Tremblay: Du texte à la représentation', *Voix et images* 7 (1982), p. 217.

94. See Michel Beaulieu, *Le Jour*, 15 June 1974, p. 6: 'Cette rencontre providentielle entre un auteur et un metteur en scène équivaut dans l'absolu à d'autres rencontres similaires, entre Stanislavski et Tchékov, par exemple.'

95. See Rita Lafontaine, 'J'ai l'impression que tout l'aspect théâtral qui décolle de la réalité, relève beaucoup de Brassard, tient à sa façon de traiter l'oeuvre."(*Cahiers de théâtre. Jeu* 47 [June 1988], p. 81). Brassard notes that working with the actresses Monique Mercure and Michelle Rossignol on the 1971 production of *Les Belles-Soeurs* 'apporta une autre dimension à ma perception de la mise en scène. C'est aussi par la lecture d'un essai théâtral de Peter Brook, *Empty Space*, que je fus convaincu de donner à mes mises en scène une orientation plus théâtrale que réaliste'. (*Première*, 10, 3 [February-March 1984], p. 11.

96. For example, in *Sept-Jours*, 14 September 1968: 'la pièce de ce jeune dramaturge prend place d'emblée aux côtés des oeuvres sociales d'un Brecht: "Homme pour homme" ou d'un [*sic*] Shelagh Delaney: "Un goût de miel"'.

97. quétaine: 'Se dit de vêtements, d'ornements etc. voyants ou vieillots. Se dit de personnes qui ne sont pas à la mode de celui qui parle', Léandre Bergeron, *Dictionnaire de la langue québécoise.*

98. Marianne Ackerman, *The Gazette*, 12 October 1985, p. C 12, reports Tremblay's favourable attitude to imaginative revivals of his work and his mention, in particular, of 'a Seattle (Oregon) production of *Les Belles-Soeurs* by a feminist troupe where the setting was a three-ring circus, the style thoroughly slapstick'. James Quig, *International Herald Tribune*, 7 December 1973, sees the 1973 Paris production in somewhat similar vein as 'rather like a female minstrel show with granny presiding as the silent end-man.' The handling of the slapstick is, however, crucially important. Though the actresses playing Thérèse Dubuc and her mother-in-law in the 1979 Seattle production are praised by the local critics, Murray Morgan and Sandy Perry for their comic skills, McKenzie Porter noted in his review of the 1973 Toronto production: 'I felt uneasy when the audience roared at spectacles I considered too sad to be funny. I use as an example the slapping, as if she were a naughty child, of a senile, slobbering mother-in-law' (*Toronto Sun*, 4 April 1973).

99. Anglophone versions include the Canadian translation by John Van Burek and Bill Glassco (Vancouver: Talonbooks, 1991), the Scots translation, *The Guid Sisters* by Martin Bowman and Bill Findlay (see note 74) and its Yorkshire adaptation, *The Good Sisters*, by Noël Greig. The Fonds Michel Tremblay at the National Library of Canada also contains sample extracts of two futher English language translations, one entitled *Hen Party*, the other entitled *Jam*.

100. Produced by CBC (the Canadian Broadcasting Corporation) using the translation of John Van Burek and Bill Glassco and filmed in English in Montreal with Quebec actresses who had appeared in previous stagings of the play. A proposal by CBC to its French network, Radio Canada, for a francophone production to be filmed simultaneously was not taken up, as Tremblay recounted to Jean-Pierre Dunant, *TV Hebdo* XVIII, no. 33 (11-17 March 1978), p. 24.

101. The eleven plays are *Les Belles-Soeurs* (1968), *En pièces détachées* (1970*), La Duchesse de Langeais* (1970), *Trois petits tours* (1971), *A toi pour toujours, ta Marie-Lou* (1971*), Demain matin, Montréal m'attend* (1972), *Hosanna* (1973), *Bonjour, là, bonjour* (1974), *Sainte-Carmen de la Main* (1976), *Damnée Manon, Sacrée Sandra* (1977), *Surprise! Surprise!* (1977).

102. The Main (i.e. the main street) is the traditional dividing line between anglophone West and francophone East Montreal and has also been home to successive waves of immigrants.

103. For example the immobility on stage of the four characters, the double time dimension and the complex intercutting of conversations separated by ten years in *A toi pour toujours, ta Marie-Lou.*

104. Tremblay distinguishes thus between his aims in the theatre and in the novel: 'J'écris des pièces quand j'ai envie de crier des bêtises au monde et j'écris des romans quand j'ai envie de leur dire que je les aime' (*Cahiers de théâtre. Jeu* [June 1988], p. 63).

105. Interviewed in 1980 by Marie-Lyne Piccione and J.M. Lacroix and responding to their comment that in *La grosse femme d'à côté est enceinte* Gabrielle Jodoin at 20 is 'amoureuse, gaie et charmante', Tremblay explained:

> J'ai voulu montrer que certains de mes personnages avaient des dispositions pour le bonheur. Mais dans le contexte des années qui ont précédé la révolution tranquille, sous la règle de DUPLESSIS, l'oppression de la société était telle que cette propension au bonheur était irrémédiablement étouffée.
>
> (*Etudes canadiennes* 10 [1981], p. 204)

106. Other novels too, including *Le Coeur découvert* (1986), *Le Premier Quartier de la lune* (1989), *Le Coeur éclaté* (1993).

SELECT BIBLIOGRAPHY

Studies

David, Gilbert et Lavoie, Pierre, eds, *Le Monde de Michel Tremblay* (Montréal; Carnières: Cahiers du Jeu; Lansman, 1993).

Dennis, Katherine M, *The Problem of Freedom in the Theater of Michel Tremblay* (Ph.D.: Michigan State University, 1989).

Usmiani, Renate, *Michel Tremblay* (Vancouver: Douglas & McIntyre, 1982).

Book chapters, articles, interviews

Antosh, Ruth, 'Interview avec Michel Tremblay', *Quebec Studies* 7 (1988), 145-9.

Camerlain, Lorraine, 'Au fil des ans et des textes. Entretien avec Rita Lafontaine', *Cahiers de théâtre. Jeu* 47 (1988), 75-89.

Cardy, Michael, 'Varieties of anger in some early plays of Michel Tremblay', *Romance Studies* 31 (Spring 1988), 5-17.

Chadbourne, Richard, 'Michel Tremblay's "Adult Fairy Tales": The Theater as Realistic Fantasy. Once Upon a Time, in East Montreal', *Quebec Studies* 10 (1990), 61-7.

Godin, Jean-Cléo et Mailhot, Laurent, 'Tremblay: marginaux en choeur' in Godin and Mailhot, *Théâtre québécois* (see below), vol. 2, ch. X, 165-84.

Hiester, Jeannine, 'La structure classique des *Belles-Soeurs* de Michel Tremblay', *Incidences*, nouv. série 6 (1982), 59-67.

Lavoie, Pierre, '"Par la porte d'en avant...". Entretien avec Michel Tremblay', *Cahiers de théâtre. Jeu*, 47 (1988), 57-74.

Mailhot, Laurent, '*Les Belles-Soeurs* ou l'enfer des femmes', *Études françaises* 6 (1970), 96-104. Also published in Godin et Mailhot, *Théâtre québéçois* (see below), vol. 1, ch. X, pp. 307-27.

Nord 1 (Autumn 1971), Issue devoted toTremblay.

Robinson. Christopher, 'Transvestism, identity and textuality in the work of Michel Tremblay, *Romance Studies* 32 (Autumn 1998), 69-79.

Ruprecht, Alvina, 'Effets sonores et signification dans *les Belles-Soeurs* de Michel Tremblay', *Voix et images* 36 (Spring 1987), 439-50.

Ryngaert, J.-P, 'Réalisme et théâtralité dans les *Belles-Soeurs*', *Co-Incidences* 1, no. 3 (November 1971), 3-12.

Saint-Martin, Lori, *Malaise et révolte des femmes dans la littérature québécoise* (Ph.D.: Laval University, 1989). Chapter II, 'La Révolte de l'Auteur: Michel Tremblay', pp. 121-81.

Smith, Donald, *L'Écrivain devant son oeuvre* (Montréal: Québec/Amérique, 1983) 'Michel Trembley et la mémoire collective', pp. 205-42.

Turbide, Roch, 'Michel Tremblay: Du texte à la représentation. Une interview', *Voix et images* 7, no. 2 (Winter 1982), 213-24.

Turcotte, André, 'Les "belles-soeurs" en révolte', *Voix et images du pays* 3 (1970), 183-99.

Usmiani, Renate, *Canadian Theatre Review* 24 (Fall 1979) *Michel Tremblay Casebook*, including 'The Tremblay Opus: Unity in Diversity' (pp. 12-25) and three interviews: 'Where To Begin the Accusation. Interview with Michel Tremblay' (pp. 26-37); 'André Brassard. Discovering the Nuances' (pp. 38-41); 'John Van Burek.Tremblay in Translation' (pp. 42-6).

Weiss, Jonathan, *French-Canadian Theater* (Twayne, 1986). Ch. 2: 'Towards a New Realism, pp. 27-49: 'Michel Tremblay'.

On Quebec theatre in general

Cotnam, Jacques, *Le Théâtre québécois. Instrument de contestation sociale et politique* (Montreal: Fides, 1976).

———'Aperçu thématique du théâtre québécois contemporain' in *Culture populaire et littérature au Québec*, ed. René Bouchard (Stanford, CA: ANMA Libri, 1980), pp. 171-221.

Godin, Jean-Cléo et Mailhot, Laurent, *Théâtre québécois*, 2 vols (Montréal: Bibliothèque québécoise, 1988).

On the history and society of Quebec

Dickinson, John and Young, Brian, *A Short History of Quebec*. 2nd edition (Toronto: Copp Clark Pitman; London: Longman, 1993).

Provencher, Jean, *Chronologie du Québec* (Montréal: Bibliothèque québécoise, 1970).

Tétu de Labsade, Françoise, *Le Québec, un pays, une culture* (Montréal: Boréal, 1990).

On Quebec French and *joual*

See Appendix I: 'The Language of the Play', p. 70-3.

Les Belles-Soeurs

Personnages

GERMAINE LAUZON
LINDA LAUZON
ROSE OUIMET
GABRIELLE JODOIN
LISETTE DE COURVAL
MARIE-ANGE BROUILLETTE
YVETTE LONGPRE
DES-NEIGES VERRETTE
THERESE DUBUC
OLIVINE DUBUC
ANGELINE SAUVE
RHEAUNA BIBEAU
LISE PAQUETTE
GINETTE MENARD
PIERRETTE GUERIN

L'action se déroule en 1965.

Cuisine. Quatre énormes caisses occupent le centre de la pièce.[1]

ACTE PREMIER

(Entre LINDA LAUZON. *Elle aperçoit les quatre caisses posées au centre de la cuisine.)*

LINDA LAUZON: Misère, que c'est ça? Moman![2]

GERMAINE LAUZON, *dans une autre pièce*: C'est toé, Linda?

LINDA LAUZON: Oui. Que c'est ça, les caisses qui traînent dans'cuisine?

GERMAINE LAUZON: C'est mes timbres!

LINDA LAUZON: Sont déjà arrivés? Ben, j'ai mon voyage! Ç'a pas pris de temps!

(Entre Germaine Lauzon.)

GERMAINE LAUZON: Ben non, hein? Moé aussi j'ai resté surpris! Tu v'nais juste de partir, à matin, quand ça sonné à'porte! J'vas répondre. C'tait un espèce de grand gars. J'pense que tu l'aurais aimé, Linda. En plein ton genre. Dans les vingt-deux, vingt-trois ans, les cheveux noirs, frisés, avec une petite moustache... Un vrai bel homme. Y m'demande, comme ça, si chus madame Germaine Lauzon, ménagère. J'dis qu'oui, que c'est ben moé. Y m'dit que c'est mes timbres. Me v'là toute énarvée, tu comprends. J'savais pas que c'est dire... Deux gars sont v'nus les porter dans'maison pis l'autre gars m'a faite un espèce de discours... Y parlait ben en s'il-vous-plait! Pis y'avait l'air fin! Chus certaine que tu l'aurais trouvé de ton goût, Linda...

LINDA LAUZON: Que c'est qu'y disait, toujours?

GERMAINE LAUZON: J'sais pus trop... J'étais assez énarvée... Y m'a dit que la compagnie pour qui qu'y travaillait était ben contente que j'aye gagné le million de timbres-primes...que j'étais ben chanceuse... Moé, j'savais pas que c'est dire... J'aurais aimé que ton père soye là...y'aurait pu y parler, lui... J'sais même pas si j'y ai dit marci!

LINDA LAUZON: Ça va en faire des timbres à coller, ça! Quatre caisses! Un million de timbres, on rit pus!

GERMAINE LAUZON: Y'en a juste trois caisses. La quatrième, c'est pour les livrets. Mais j'ai eu une idée, Linda. On n'est pas pour coller ça tu-seules! Sors-tu, à soir?

LINDA LAUZON: Oui, Robert est supposé de m'appeler...

GERMAINE LAUZON: Tu pourrais pas r'mettre ça à demain? J'ai eu une idée, 'coute ben... A midi, j'ai téléphoné à mes soeurs, à la soeur de ton pére, pis chus t'allée voir les voisines. J'les ai toutes invitées à v'nir coller des timbres, à soir. J'vas faire un party de collage de timbres! C't'une vraie bonne idée, ça, hein? J'ai acheté des pinottes, du chocolat, le p'tit a été chercher des liqueurs...

LINDA LAUZON: Moman, vous savez ben que j'sors toujours, le jeudi soir! C'est not'soir! On voulait aller aux vues...

GERMAINE LAUZON: Tu peux pas me laisser tu-seule un soir pareil! On va être quasiment quinze!

LINDA LAUZON: Vous êtes pas folle! On rentre jamais quinze dans'cuisine! Pis vous savez ben qu'on peut pas recevoir dans le restant de la maison parce qu'on peinture![3] Misère, moman, que vous avez donc pas d'allure, des fois!

GERMAINE LAUZON: C'est ça, méprise-moé! Bon, c'est correct, sors, fais à ta tête! Tu fais toujours à ta tête, c'est pas ben ben mêlant! Maudite vie! J'peux même pas avoir une p'tite joie, y faut toujours que quelqu'un vienne toute gâter! Vas-y aux vues, Linda, vas-y, sors à'soir, fais à ta tête! Maudit verrat de bâtard que chus donc tannée!

LINDA LAUZON: Comprenez donc, moman...

GERMAINE LAUZON: J'comprends rien pantoute pis j'veux rien savoir! Parle-moé pus... Désâmez-vous pour élever ça, pis que c'est que ça vous rapporte? Rien! Rien pantoute! C'est même pas capable de vous rendre un p'tit sarvice! J't'avertis, Linda, j'commence à en avoir plein le casque de vous servir, toé pis les autres! Chus pas une sarvante, moé, icitte! J'ai un million de timbres à coller pis chus pas pour les coller tu-seule! Après toute, ces timbres-là, y vont servir à tout le monde ! Faudrait que tout le monde fasse sa part, dans'maison!... Ton père travaille de nuit, pis si on n'a pas fini de coller ça demain, y va continuer dans'journée, y me l'a dit! J'demande pas la lune! Aide-moé donc, pour une fois, au lieu d'aller niaiser avec c'te niaiseux-là!

LINDA LAUZON: C'est pas un niaiseux, vous saurez!

GERMAINE LAUZON: Ah ben, j'ai mon voyage! J'savais que t'étais nounoune, mais pas à ce point-là! Tu t'es pas encore aperçue que ton Robert c't'un bon-rien? Y gagne même pas soixante piasses par semaine! Pis tout c'qu'y peut te payer, c'est le théâtre Amherst,[4] le jeudi soir! C'est moé qui te le dis, Linda, prends le conseil d'une mére, si tu continues à le fréquenter, tu vas devenir une bonrienne comme lui ! T'as quand même pas envie de marier un colleur de semelles pis de rester strapeuse toute ta vie![5]

LINDA LAUZON: Farmez-vous donc, moman, quand vous êtes fâchée, vous savez pus c'que vous dites! C'est correct, j'vas rester, à soir, mais arrêtez de chiâler, pour l'amour! D'abord, Robert, là, y va avoir une augmentation ben vite, pis y va gagner pas mal plus cher! Y'est pas si nono que ça, vous savez! Le boss m'a même dit qu'y pourrait embarquer dans les grosses payes, ben vite, pis devenir p'tit boss! Quand t'arrives dans les quatre-vingts piasses par semaine, c'est pus des farces![6] Entéka! J'vas y téléphoner, là... J'vas y dire que j'peux pas aller aux vues, à soir... J'peux-tu y dire de v'nir coller des timbres avec nous autres?

GERMAINE LAUZON: Tiens, r'gard-la! J'viens d'y dire que j'peux pas le sentir, pis a veut l'inviter à soir! Ma grand-foi du bon Dieu, t'as pas de tête su'es épaules, ma pauv'fille! Que c'est que j'ai ben pu faire au bon Dieu du ciel pour qu'y m'envoye des enfants bouchés pareils! Encore, à midi, j'demande au p'tit d'aller me chercher une livre d'oignons, pis y me revient avec deux pintes de lait! Ç'a pas de saint grand bon sens! Y faudrait toute répéter vingt fois, ici-dedans! J'peux ben pardre patience! J't'ai dit que je faisais un party de femmes, Linda, rien que des femmes! C'est pas un fifi, ton Robert!

LINDA LAUZON: C'est correct, v'nez pas folle, la mère, j'vas y dire de pas v'nir, c'est toute! J'ai mon voyage! On n'est même pas capable de rien faire icitte! Voir si j'ai envie de coller des timbres après ma journée à shop![7] Pis allez épousseter dans le salon, un peu! Vous êtes pas obligée de tout entendre c'que j'vas dire! *(Elle compose un numéro de téléphone.)* Allô ! Robert, s'il-vous-plaît... Quand c'est que vous l'attendez? Bon, vous y direz que c'est Linda qui a appelé... Oui, madame Bergeron, ça va bien, pis vous? Tant mieux! Bon ben c'est ça, hein, boujour! *(Elle raccroche. Le téléphone sonne aussitôt.)* Allô! Moman, c'est pour vous![8]

GERMAINE LAUZON, *entrant*: T'as vingt ans, pis tu sais pas encore qu'y faut dire 'un instant s'il-vous-plaît' quand on répond au téléphone!

LINDA LAUZON: C'est rien que ma tante Rose. J'sais pas pourquoi j's'rais polie avec elle !

GERMAINE LAUZON, *bouchant le récepteur*: Veux-tu ben te taire! D'un coup qu'a t'aurait entendue!

LINDA LAUZON: J'm'en sacre!

GERMAINE LAUZON: Allô! Ah! c'est toé, Rose... Ben oui, sont arrivés... C'est ben pour dire, hein? Un million! Sont devant moé, là, pis j'le crois pas encore! Un million! J'sais pas au juste combien ça fait, mais quand on dit un million, on rit pus! Oui, y m'ont donné un cataloye, avec. J'en avais déjà un, mais celui-là, c'est celui de ç't'année, ça fait que c'est ben mieux... L'autre était toute magané... Oui, y'a assez des belles affaires, tu devrais voir ça! C'est pas creyable! J'pense que j'vas pouvoir toute prendre c'qu'y'a d'dans! J'vas toute meubler ma maison en neuf! J'vas avoir un poêle, un frigidaire, un set de cuisine... J'pense que j'vas prendre le rouge avec des étoiles dorées. J'sais pas si tu l'as déjà vu... Y'est assez beau, aie! J'vas avoir des chaudrons, une coutellerie, un set de vaisselle, des salières, des poivrières, des verres en verre taillé avec le motif 'Caprice' là, t'sais si y sont beaux... Madame de Courval en a eu l'année passée. A disait qu'a l'avait payé ça cher sans bon sens... Moé, j'vas toute les avoir pour rien! A va être en beau verrat![9] Hein? Oui, a vient, à soir! J'ai vu des pots en fer chromé pour mettre le sel, le poivre. Le thé, le café, le sucre, pis toute la patente, là. Oui, j'vas toute prendre ça... J'vas avoir un set de chambre style colonial au grand complet avec accessoires. Des rideaux, des dessus de bureau, une affaire pour mettre à terre à côté du litte, d'la tapisserie neuve... Non, pas fleurie, ça donne mal à tête à Henri, quand y dort...[10] Ah! j'te dis, j'vas avoir une vraie belle chambre! Pour le salon, j'ai un set complet avec le stirio, la tv, le tapis de nylon synthétique, les cadres... Ah! Les vrais beaux cadres! T'sais, là, les cadres chinois avec du velours... C'tu assez beau, hein? Depuis le temps que j'en veux! Pis tiens-toé ben ma p'tite fille, j'vas avoir des plats en verre soufflé! Ben oui, pareil comme ceux de ta belle-soeur Aline! Pis même, j'pense qu'y sont encore plus beaux! J't'assez contente, aie! Y'a des cendriers, des lampes... j'pense que c'est pas mal toute pour le salon... Y'a un rasoir électrique pour Henri pour se raser, des rideaux de douche... Quoi? Ben, on va en faire poser une, y'en donnent avec les timbres! Un bain tombeau, un lavier neuf, chacun un costume de bain neuf... Non, non, non, chus pas trop grosse, commence pas avec ça! Pis j'vas toute meubler la chambre du p'tit. Tu devrais voir c'qu'y ont pour les chambres d'enfants, c'est de toute beauté de voir ça! Avec des Mickey Mouse partout ! Pour la chambre de Linda... O.K. c'est ça, tu r'garderas le cataloye, plutôt. Viens-t'en tu-suite, par exemple, les autres vont arriver! J'leur s'ai dit d'arriver de bonne heure! Tu comprends, ça va ben prendre pas mal de temps pour coller ça! *(Entre Marie-Ange Brouillette.)* Bon ben, j'vas te laisser, là, madame Brouillette vient d'arriver. C'est ça, oui... oui...bye!

MARIE-ANGE BROUILLETTE:[11] Moé, c'est ben simple, madame Lauzon, chus jalouse.

GERMAINE LAUZON: J'vous pense! C'est tout un événement! Mais vous allez m'excuser, madame Brouillette, chus pas encore prête. J'parlais à ma soeur Rose... J'la r'gardais par la fenêtre... On se voit de bord en bord de la ruelle, c'est commode...

MARIE-ANGE BROUILLETTE: A vient-tu elle itou?

GERMAINE LAUZON: Ben oui, a manquerait pas ça pour tout l'or au monde vous comprenez! Assisez-vous un peu, en attendant, pis regardez le cataloye! Vous allez voir les belles affaires qu'y'a d'dans! J'vas toutes les avoir, madame Brouillette, toutes! Toute le cataloye!

(Germaine Lauzon entre dans sa chambre.)

MARIE-ANGE BROUILLETTE: C'est pas moé qui aurais eu c'te chance-là! Pas de danger! Moé, j'mange d'la marde, pis j'vas en manger toute ma vie! Un million de timbres! Toute une maison! C'est ben simple, si j'me r'tenais pas, j'braillerais comme une vache! On peut dire que la chance tombe toujours sur les ceuses qui le méritent pas! Que c'est qu'a l'a tant faite, madame Lauzon, pour mériter ça, hein? Rien! Rien pantoute! Est pas plus belle, pis pas plus fine que moé! Ça devrait pas exister, ces concours-là! Monsieur le curé avait ben raison, l'aut'jour, quand y disait que ça devrait être embolie![12] Pour que c'est faire, qu'elle, a gagnerait un million de timbres, pis pas moé, hein, pour que c'est faire! C'est pas juste! Moé aussi, j'travaille, moé aussi j'les torche, mes enfants! Même que les miens sont plus propres que les siens! J'travaille comme une damnée, c'est pour ça que j'ai l'air d'un esquelette. Elle, est grosse comme une cochonne! Pis v'la rendu que j'vas être obligée de rester à côté d'elle pis de sa belle maison gratis! C'est ben simple, ça me brûle ! Ça me brûle! J'vas être obligée d'endurer ses sarcasses, à part de ça! Parce qu'a va s'enfler la tête, c'est le genre! La vraie maudite folle! On va entendre parler de ses timbres pendant des années! Maudit! J'ai raison d'être en maudit! J'veux pas crever dans la crasse pendant qu'elle, la grosse madame, a va se 'prélasser dans la soie et le velours'![13] C'est pas juste! Chus tannée de m'esquinter pour rien! Ma vie est plate! Plate! Pis par-dessus le marché, chus pauvre comme la gale! Chus tannée de vivre une maudite vie plate!

(Pendant ce monologue, Gabrielle Jodoin, Rose Ouimet, Yvette Longpré et Lisette de Courval ont fait leur entrée. Elles se sont installées dans la cuisine sans s'occuper de Marie-Ange. Les cinq femmes se lèvent et se tournent vers le public. L'éclairage change.)

LES CINQ FEMMES, *ensemble*: Quintette: Une maudite vie plate! Lundi!

LISETTE DE COURVAL:[14] Dès que le soleil a commencé à caresser de ses rayons les petites fleurs dans les champs et que les petits oiseaux ont ouvert leurs petits becs pour lancer vers le ciel leurs petits cris...

LES QUATRE AUTRES: J'me lève, pis j'prépare le déjeuner! Des toasts, du café, du bacon, des oeufs. J'ai d'la misère que l'yable à réveiller mon monde. Les enfants partent pour l'école, mon mari s'en va travailler.

MARIE-ANGE BROUILLETTE: Pas le mien, y'est chômeur. Y reste couché.

LES CINQ FEMMES: Là, là, j'travaille comme une enragée, jusqu'à midi. J'lave. Les robes, les jupes, les bas, les chandails, les pantalons, les canneçons, les brassières, tout y passe! Pis frotte, pis tord, pis refrotte, pis rince... C't'écoeurant, j'ai les mains rouges, je t'écoeurée. J'sacre. A midi, les enfants reviennent. Ça mange comme des cochons, ça revire la maison à l'envers, pis ça repart! L'après-midi, j'étends. Ça, c'est mortel! J'hais ça comme une bonne! Après, j'prépare le souper. Le monde reviennent, y'ont l'air bête, on se chicane! Pis le soir, on regarde la télévision! Mardi!

LISETTE DE COURVAL: Dès que le soleil...

LES QUATRE AUTRES FEMMES: J'me lève, pis j'prépare le déjeuner. Toujours la même maudite affaire! Des toasts, du café, des oeufs, du bacon...J'réveille le monde, j'les mets dehors. Là, c'est le repassage. J'travaille, j'travaille, j'travaille. Midi arrive sans que je le voye venir pis les enfants sont en maudit parce que j'ai rien préparé pour le dîner. J'leu fais des sandwichs au béloné. J'travaille toute l'après-midi, le souper arrive, on se chicane. Pis le soir, on regarde la télévision! Mercredi! C'est le jour du mégasinage! J'marche toute la journée, j'me donne un tour de rein à porter des paquets gros comme ça, j'reviens à la maison crevée! Y faut quand même que je fasse à manger. Quand le monde arrivent, j'ai l'air bête! Mon mari sacre, les enfants braillent... Pis le soir, on regarde la télévision! Le jeudi pis le vendredi, c'est la même chose! J'm'esquinte, j'me désâme, j'me tue pour ma gang de nonos! Le samedi, j'ai les enfants dans les jambes par-dessus le marché! Pis le soir, on regarde la télévision! Le dimanche, on sort en famille: on va souper chez la belle-mère en autobus. Y faut guetter les enfants toute la journée, endurer les farces plates du beau-père, pis manger la nourriture de la belle- mère qui est donc meilleure que la mienne au dire de tout le monde! Pis le soir, on regarde la télévision! Chus tannée de mener une maudite vie plate! Une maudite vie plate! Une maudite vie plate! Une maud...

(L'éclairage redevient normal. Elles se rassoient brusquement.)

LISETTE DE COURVAL: Moi, quand je suis t'allée en Urope...

ROSE OUIMET: La v'la qui recommence avec son Europe, elle! Ça va être beau! On n'a pour toute la soirée, certain! Quand a commence, a s'arrête pas! A s'monte, a s'monte, pis y'a pas moyen d'la décrinquer!

(Entre Des-Neige Verrette. Petits saluts discrets.)

LISETTE DE COURVAL: J'voulais seulement dire qu'ils n'ont pas de timbres, en Urope. C'est à dire qu'ils ont des timbres, mais pas des comme ceux-là. Juste des timbres pour timbrer les lettres.

DES-NEIGES VERRETTE:[15] Ça doit être plat vrai ! Y peuvent pas avoir de cadeaux comme nous autres? Ça doit être plat vrai, en Europe!

LISETTE DE COURVAL: Non, c'est bien beau quand même...

MARIE-ANGE BROUILLETTE: Moé, chus pas contre les timbres, c'est ben commode. Si y'avait pas de timbres, j'attendrais encore après ma patente pour hacher la viande. Mais chus contre les concours, par exemple!

LISETTE DE COURVAL: Pourquoi, donc? Ça rend une famille heureuse!

MARIE-ANGE BROUILLETTE: Peut-être, peut-être, mais ça fait chier les familles qui vivent alentour, par exemple!

LISETTE DE COURVAL: Mon Dieu, que vous êtes donc mal embouchée, madame Brouillette! Regardez, moi, j'perle bien, puis j'm'en sens pas plus mal!

MARIE-ANGE BROUILLETTE: J'parle comme que j'peux, pis j'dis c'que j'ai à dire, c'est toute! Chus pas t'allée en Urope, moé, chus pas t'obligée de me forcer pour bien perler!

ROSE OUIMET: Commencez donc pas à faire la chicane, vous deux, là ! On n'est pas venues icitte pour se chicaner! Si vous continuez, moé, je r'travarse la ruelle, pis j'rentre chez nous!

GABRIELLE JODOIN: Que c'est que Germaine fait, donc, qu'a l'arrive pas! Germaine!

GERMAINE LAUZON, *dans sa chambre*: Oui, ça s'ra pas long, là! J'ai d'la misère avec... Entéka, j'ai d'la misère... Linda es-tu là?

GABRIELLE JODOIN: Linda! Linda! Non, est pas là!

MARIE-ANGE BROUILLETTE: J'pense que j'l'ai vue sortir, t'à l'heure.

GERMAINE LAUZON: Dites-moé pas qu'a s'est sauvée, la p'tite bougraise!

GABRIELLE JODOIN: On peut-tu commencer à coller les timbres, en t'attendant?

GERMAINE LAUZON: Non! Attendez-moé, j'vas toute vous dire c'que vous avez à faire! Commencez pas tu-suite, attendez que je soye là! Jasez, en attendant, jasez!

GABRIELLE JODOIN: Jaser, jaser, c'est beau...

(Le téléphone sonne.)

ROSE OUIMET: Mon Dieu, que j'ai eu peur! Allô! Non, est pas là, mais si vous voulez attendre, ça s'ra pas ben long, a va r'venir d'une seconde à l'autre, j'pense. *(Elle pose le récepteur, sort sur la galerie et crie.)* Linda! Linda, téléphone!

LISETTE DE COURVAL: Et puis, madame Longpré, comment est-ce que votre fille Claudette aime ça, être mariée?

YVETTE LONGPRE:[16] Ah! a l'aime ben ça. A trouve ça ben l'fun. A m'a toute conté son voyage de noces, vous comprenez.

GABRIELLE JODOIN: Où c'est qu'y sont allés, donc?

YVETTE LONGPRE: Ben, lui y'avait gagné un voyage aux îles Canaries, hein, ça fait qu'y se sont dépêchés pour se marier...

ROSE OUIMET, *riant*: Les îles Canaries? Ça doit être plein de serins, par là![17]

GABRIELLE JODOIN: Voyons, Rose!

ROSE OUIMET: Ben quoi!

DES-NEIGES VERRETTE: C'est où ça, les îles Canaries?

LISETTE DE COURVAL: Nous sommes passés par là, moi et mon mari lors de notre dernier voyage en Urope... C'est un ben...bien beau pays. Les femmes portent seulement que des jupes.

ROSE OUIMET: Le vrai pays pour mon mari!

LISETTE DE COURVAL: Pis j'vous assure que c'est du monde qui sont pas ben propres! D'ailleurs, en Urope, le monde se lavent pas!

DES-NEIGES VERRETTE: Y'ont l'air assez sales, aussi! Prenez l'Italienne[18] à côté de chez nous, a pue c'te femme-là, c'est pas croyable!

(Les femmes éclatent de rire.)

LISETTE DE COURVAL, *insinuante*: Avez-vous déjà remarqué sa corde à linge, le lundi?

DES-NEIGES VERRETTE: Non, pourquoi?

LISETTE DE COURVAL: J'ai rien qu'une chose à vous dire: c'monde-là, ça porte pas de sous-vêtements!

MARIE-ANGE BROUILLETTE: Pas vrai!

ROSE OUIMET: Arrêtez donc, là, vous!

YVETTE LONGPRE: J'ai mon voyage!

LISETTE DE COURVAL: Vrai comme je suis là ! Vous remarquerez, lundi prochain, vous allez voir!

YVETTE LONGPRE: Y peuvent ben puer!

MARIE-ANGE BROUILLETTE: Peut-être qu'a l'aime mieux étendre ses sous-vêtements dans la maison...par pudeur![19]

(Toutes les autres rient.)

LISETTE DE COURVAL: La pudeur, y connaissent pas ça, les Uropéens! Vous avez qu'à regarder les films, à la télévision! C'est ben effrayant de voir ça! Ça s'embrasse à tour de bras au beau milieu d'la rue! C'est dans eux-autres, ils sont faits comme ça! Vous avez rien qu'à guetter la fille de l'Italienne quand elle reçoit ses chums...euh...ses amis de garçons... C't'effrayant c'qu'elle fait, cette fille-là! Une vraie honte! Ça me fait penser, madame Ouimet, j'ai vu votre Michel, l'autre jour...

ROSE OUIMET: Pas avec c'te puante-là, toujours!

LISETTE DE COURVAL: Oui, justement.

ROSE OUIMET: Vous avez dû vous tromper! Ça peut pas être lui!

LISETTE DE COURVAL: Bien voyons, c'est mes voisins à moi aussi, les Italiens! Ils étaient tous les deux sur le balcon d'en avant... Y pensaient que personne pouvait les voir, je suppose...

DES-NEIGES VERRETTE: C'est vrai, j'les ai vus, moé aussi, madame Ouimet. Pis j'vous dis que ça s'embrassait sur un vrai temps!

ROSE OUIMET: Le p'tit maudit, par exemple! Y'avait pas assez d'un cochon, dans'maison... Quand j'parle de cochon, là, j'parle de mon mari... Y peut pas voir une belle fille, à la télévision, là, y...y...vient fou raide! Maudit cul![20] Y'en ont jamais assez, les Ouimet! Sont toutes pareils, dans famille, y...

GABRIELLE JODOIN: Voyons, Rose, t'es pas obligée de conter ta vie de famille devant tout le monde...

LISETTE DE COURVAL: Bien, ça nous intéresse...

DES-NEIGES ET MARIE-ANGE: Oui, certain!

YVETTE LONGPRE: Pour en revenir au voyage de noces de ma fille...

(Entre Germaine Lauzon, toute endimanchée.)

ROSE OUIMET: Bonyeu, tu t'es checquée! T'en vas-tu aux noces?

GERMAINE LAUZON: Me v'là, les filles! *(Salutations, 'bonjour, comment ça va', etc.).* De quoi vous parliez, donc?

ROSE OUIMET: Ben, madame Longpré nous contait le voyage de noces de sa Claudette, justement...

GERMAINE LAUZON: Oui? Bonjour madame... Pis, que c'est qu'a disait?

ROSE OUIMET: Ça l'air que c'était un vrai beau voyage. Y'ont vu tu-sortes de monde. Sont allés en bateau. Tu comprends, c'est des îles qu'y'ont visitées. Les îles Canaries... A pêche, y'ont pris des poissons gros comme ça, y paraît! Y'ont rencontré des couples qu'y connaissaient...des amies de filles de Claudette... Y sont toutes revenus ensemble. Sont arrêtés à New York. Madame Longpré nous a conté des anecdoques...

YVETTE LONGPRE: Ben...

ROSE OUIMET: Hein, madame Longpré, c'est vrai, c'que j'dis là?

YVETTE LONGPRE: Ben, c't'à dire...

GERMAINE LAUZON: Vous direz à votre fille, madame Longpré, que j'y souhaite ben du bonheur. On n' pas été invités aux noces, mais on sait vivre pareil!

(Silence gêné.)

GABRIELLE JODOIN: Aïe, y'est quasiment sept heures! Le chapelet![21]

GERMAINE LAUZON: Mon doux, ma neuvaine[22] à sainte Thérèse! J'vas aller chercher le radio à Linda...

(Elle sort.)

ROSE OUIMET: Que c'est qu'a peut ben vouloir à sainte Thérèse, donc elle? Surtout après c'qu'a vient de gagner!

DES-NEIGES VERRETTE: C'est peut-être ses enfants qui y donnent du mal...

GABRIELLE JODOIN: J'pense pas, a me l'aurait dit...

GERMAINE LAUZON, *de la chambre de Linda*: Où c'est qu'a l'a fourré, c'te radio-là, donc!

ROSE OUIMET: Ben, j'sais pas, Gaby, est pas mal cachottière, des fois, not'soeur!

GABRIELLE JODOIN: A me conte toute, à moé. Toé, on sait ben, commère comme que t'es...

ROSE OUIMET: Comment ça, commère comme que chus. T'es pas ben ben gênée! Tu sauras que chus pas plus commère que toé, Gabrielle Jodoin!

GABRIELLE JODOIN: Voyons donc, tu sais ben que tu peux rien garder pour toé!

ROSE OUIMET: Ah ! ben là, par exemple... Si tu penses...

LISETTE DE COURVAL: C'est vous, madame Ouimet, qui disiez tout à l'heure qu'on n'est pas venues ici pour se quereller?

ROSE OUIMET: Vous, là, mêlez-vous de ce qui vous regarde! D'abord, j'ai pas dit quereller, j'ai dit chicaner!

(Germaine Lauzon revient avec un appareil de radio.)

GERMAINE LAUZON: Que c'est qui se passe donc, on vous entend crier à l'aut-boute d'la maison!

GABRIELLE JODOIN: Ah ben! c'est notre soeur, encore...

GERMAINE LAUZON: Reste donc tranquille, un peu, Rose! D'habitude, c'est toujours toé qui fait le fun dans les parties... Commence pas la chicane à soir!

ROSE OUIMET: Vous voyez, on dit chicane, dans la famille!

(Germaine Lauzon branche l'appareil de radio. On entend des bribes de chapelet. Toutes les femmes s'agenouillent. Après cinq ou six 'Ave Maria' on entend un vacarme épouvantable provenant de l'extérieur. Toutes les femmes crient, se lèvent et sortent de la maison en courant.)

GERMAINE LAUZON: Mon Dieu, la belle-mère de ma belle-soeur Thérèse qui vient de tomber en bas du troisième étage![23]

ROSE OUIMET: Vous êtes-vous fait mal, Madame Dubuc?

GABRIELLE JODOIN: Farme-toé donc, Rose. A doit être au moins morte!

THERESE DUBUC, *de très loin*: Etes-vous correcte, madame Dubuc? *(On entend une espèce de râle.)* Attendez, j'vas enlever la chaise roulante de par-dessus vous, là ! Etes-vous mieux comme ça? J'vas vous aider à r'monter dans votre chaise. Voyons, madame Dubuc, aidez-vous un peu, restez pas molle de même! Ayoye!

DES-NEIGES VERRETTE: J'vas aller vous aider, madame Dubuc.

THERESE DUBUC: Merci, mademoiselle Verrette, vous êtes ben bonne...

(Les autres femmes entrent dans la maison.)

ROSE OUIMET: Farme donc le radio, Germaine, chus toute énarvée!

GERMAINE LAUZON: Ben, pis ma neuvaine?

ROSE OUIMET: Où c'est que t'es rendue?

GERMAINE LAUZON: A sept.

ROSE OUIMET: Sept, c'est pas grave. Tu recommenceras demain, pis samedi prochain, ta neuvaine s'ra finie!

GERMAINE LAUZON: Oui, mais ma neuvaine, c'tait neuf semaines! *(Entrent Therèse Dubuc, Des-Neiges Verrette et Olivine Dubuc*[24] *dans sa chaise roulante.)* Mon Dieu, a pas eu trop de mal, toujours?

THERESE DUBUC: Ben non, ben non, est habituée. A tombe en bas de sa chaise roulante dix fois par jour! Ouf! Chus toute essoufflée! Tirer c'te chaise-là pendant trois étages, c'est pas des farces! Vous auriez pas quequ'chose à boire, Germaine?

GERMAINE LAUZON: Gaby, donne donc un verre d'eau à Thérèse! *(Elle s'approche d'Olivine Dubuc.)* Pis, comment ça va, ma bonne madame Dubuc?

THERESE DUBUC: Approchez pas trop, Germaine, a mord depuis quequ' temps!

(Olivine Dubuc essaie effectivement de lui mordre la main.)

GERMAINE LAUZON: M'as dire comme vous, Thérèse, est dangereuse! Ça fait longtemps qu'est comme ça?

THERESE DUBUC: Eteindez donc le radio, Germaine, ça me tombe sur les nerfs! Chus trop énarvée après c'qui vient d'arriver.

(Germaine Lauzon ferme la radio à contrecoeur.)

GERMAINE LAUZON: J'comprends, ma pauvre Thérèse, j'comprends!

THERESE DUBUC: C'est ben simple, chus rendue au boute! Au boute! vous savez pas la vie que je mène, depuis que j'ai ma belle-mère sur le dos! Ah! c'est pas que je ne l'aime pas, la pauvr'femme, a fait tellement pitié, mais est malade pis capricieuse sans bon sens! Y faut toujours la guetter!

DES-NEIGES VERRETTE: Comment ça se fait qu'est pus à l'hôpital?

THERESE DUBUC: Oh! Vous comprenez, mademoiselle Verrette, mon mari a eu une augmentation de salaire v'là trois mois, ça fait que le Bien-être social voulait pus payer pour sa mère. On aurait été obligés de payer l'hôpital au grand complet...

MARIE-ANGE BROUILLETTE: Mon doux!

YVETTE LONGPRE: C'tu effrayant!

DES-NEIGES VERRETTE: Lâchez-moé donc!

(Pendant le récit de Thérèse Dubuc, Germaine Lauzon ouvre les caisses et distribue livrets et timbres.)

THERESE DUBUC: On a été obligés de la retirer. C'est toute une croix, j'vous en passe un papier! A l'a quatre-vingt-treize ans, c'te femme-là, y faut pas l'oublier! Y faut en prendre soin comme un p'tit bébé! Chus t'obligée de l'habiller, d'la déshabiller, d'la laver...

DES-NEIGES VERRETTE: Doux Jésus!

YVETTE LONGPRE: Pauvre vous!

THERESE DUBUC: Ah! C'est pas drôle! T'nez, à matin, encore. J'dis à Paolo, mon plus jeune: 'Moman va aller mégasiner, là, garde memére, pis prends-en ben soin.' Ben bonyenne, quand chus r'venue, madame Dubuc avait toute renversé le pot de mnasse[25] sur elle pis a jouait d'dans comme une bonne. Naturellement, Paolo avait disparu! J'ai été obligée de nettoyer la table, le plancher, la chaise roulante...

GERMAINE LAUZON: Pis madame Dubuc, elle?

THERESE DUBUC: J'l'ai laissée de même une bonne partie de l'après-midi! Ça y'apprendra! A l'agit comme un bébé, on va la traiter comme un bébé, c'est toute! Tenez, c'est pas ben ben mêlant, chus t'obligée de la faire manger à p'tite cuiller!

GERMAINE LAUZON: Mon Dieu, Thérèse, que j'vous plains donc!

DES-NEIGES VERRETTE: Vous êtes trop bonne, Thérèse!

GABRIELLE JODOIN: C'est vrai, ça, vous êtes ben que trop bonne!

THERESE DUBUC: Que voulez-vous, y faut ben gagner son ciel![26]

MARIE-ANGE BROUILLETTE: On pourra dire que vous l'avez gagné, vot'ciel, vous!

THERESE DUBUC: Ah! Mais j'me plains pas! J'me dis que le bon Dieu est bon, pis qu'y va m'aider à passer à travers...

LISETTE DE COURVAL: C'est ben simple, vous m'émouvez jusqu'aux larmes!

THERESE DUBUC: Ben, voyons donc, madame de Courval, prenez sur vous!

DES-NEIGES VERRETTE: J'ai rien qu'une chose à vous dire, madame Dubuc, vous êtes une sainte femme!

GERMAINE LAUZON: Bon, ben astheur que les timbres pis les livrets sont distribués, là, j'vas aller chercher les plats d'eau, pis on va commencer, hein? On n'est pas icitte rien que pour placoter! *(Elle emplit quelques petits plats d'eau et les distribue. Les femmes commencent à coller les timbres.)* Si Linda s'rait là, aussi, a pourrait m'aider! *(Elle sort sur la galerie.)* Linda! Linda! Aie, Richard, as-tu vu Linda? Ben, par exemple! A l'a le coeur de téter des liqueurs pendant que j'me désâme! Veux-tu y dire de v'nir tu-suite icitte, mon trésor? Tu viendras voir madame Lauzon, demain, pis a va te donner des pinottes pis des bonbons si y'en reste! O.K.? Va, mon coeur, pis dis-y de v'nir tu-suite! *(Elle rentre.)* La p'tite maudite! A m'avait pourtant promis de rester.

MARIE-ANGE BROUILLETTE: C'est toujours de même, les enfants...

THERESE DUBUC: Ah! pour ça, c'est ben ingrat!

GABRIELLE JODOIN: Parlez-moé-s'en pas! C'est pus vivable, chez nous! Depuis qu'y'a commencé son cours classique,[27] là, mon p'tit Raymond, y'a changé c'est ben effrayant! On le r'connaît pus! Y lève quasiment le nez sur nous autres! V'la rendu qu'y nous parle latin à table! Y nous fait jouer d'la musique, à part de ça, mes chers enfants, que c'est pas écoutable! Du classique à coeur de jour! Pis quand on veut pas regarder l'heure du concert, y nous pique une crise! Pis si y'a une chose que j'peux pas endurer, c'est ben la musique classique!

ROSE OUIMET: Ouache, moé non plus!

THERESE DUBUC: C'est pas écoutable, vous avez ben raison. Beding par icitte, bedang par là...

GABRIELLE JODOIN: Raymond nous dit que c'est parce qu'on comprend rien! J'sais pas c'qu'on peut comprendre là-dedans! Parce qu'y'apprend toutes sortes de folleries au collège, là, y nous méprise! J'ai quasiment envie d'le retirer d'là, c'est pas mêlant!

TOUTES LES FEMMES: Que c'est donc ingrat, les enfants, que c'est donc ingrat!

GERMAINE LAUZON: Remplissez vos livrets, là, hein? Y faut qu'y'en aie partout!

ROSE OUIMET: Ben oui, Germaine, ben oui, on connaît ça, des timbres, c'est pas la première fois qu'on en colle!

YVETTE LONGPRE: Vous trouvez pas qu'y commence à faire pas mal chaud, icitte? On devrait ouvrir le châssis, un peu...

GERMAINE LAUZON: Non, non, non, ça ferait des courants d'air! J'ai peur à mes timbres!

ROSE OUIMET: Voyons donc, Germaine, c'est pas des moineaux, tes timbres, y s'envolleront pas! En parlant de moineaux,[28] ça me fait penser, j'ai été voir Bernard, mon plus vieux, dimanche passé... J'ai jamais vu tant d'oiseaux dans une maison! Une vraie cage à moineaux, c'maison-là! C'est de sa faute à elle, ça. Une maniaque des oiseaux! Pis a veut pas en tuer, a dit qu'a l'a le coeur trop tendre! J'veux ben croire qu'a l'a le coeur tendre, mais y'a toujours ben des émittes! Ecoutez ça, ça vaut la peine... *(Projecteur sur Rose Ouimet.)* J'vous dis c't'une vraie folle! J'ris, là, pis au fond, c'est pas drôle. Entéka... A Pâques, Bernard a acheté une cage à moineaux pour ses deux p'tits. C't'un gars à'taverne[29] qui avait besoin d'argent pis qui y'a vendu ça pas cher... Elle, quand a l'a vu ça, est v'nue folle tu-suite, est quasiment tombée en amour avec ses oiseaux! A en prenait plus soin que de ses enfants, c'est pas mêlant... Mais v'la-tu pas que les femelles oiseaux se mettent à pondre... Quand les p'tits oiseaux sont arrivés, Manon les trouvait ben cute, pis a s'est mis à dire qu'a l'avait pas le coeur des tuer ! Ça prend-tu une saprée folle! Ça fait qu'y'es ont toutes gardés! Toute la gang! J'sais pas combien y'en a, j'ai jamais essayé des compter... Moé, quand j'vas chez eux, là, j'manque de v'nir folle à chaque fois, c'est pas ben ben mêlant! Vers deux heures, là, a l'ouvre la cage, pis les oiseaux sortent. Y volent un peu partout dans maison, y se lâchent n'importe où, pis on est obligé de toute nettoyer... Pis là, là, quand vient le temps d'les faire rentrer dans leur cage, y veulent pus, ces oiseaux-là, c'est ben sûr! Là, Manon crie aux p'tits: 'Poignez les oiseaux, là, moman est fatiguée!' Là, les p'tits s'garrochent après les oiseaux... C't'un vrai charivari dans' maison! Moé, j'sors, c'est pas mêlant! J'm'en vas sur le balcon pis j'attends qui les aye toutes poignés! *(Les femmes rient.)* Pis ces enfants-là sont pas tenables! J'les aime ben, c'est mes p'tits enfants, mais bonyeu qu'y sont tannants! Nos enfants étaient pas de même, nous autres! Vous direz c'que vous voudrez, les jeunes d'aujourd'hui savent pas élever leurs enfants!

GERMAINE LAUZON: Ça c'est vrai!

YVETTE LONGPRE: Certain!

ROSE OUIMET: Dans not'temps, on n'aurait pas laissé les enfants jouer dans la chambre de bain! Ben vous auriez dû voir ça dimanche! D'abord les enfants sont entrés dans la chambre de bain en faisant semblant de rien pis y'ont toute reviré à l'envers! Moé, j'osais pas parler, Manon dit toujours que j'parle trop! J'les entendais, pis j'fatiquais, vous comprenez! Là, y'ont pris le papier de toilette pis y l'ont toute déroulé. Manon a crié: 'Voyons, les enfants, moman va se fâcher, là!' Naturellement, c'était comme si a'vait rien dit ! Y'ont continué! J'les aurait étripés, les p'tits maudits! Y'avaient l'air d'avoir ben du fun, vous comprenez. Bruno, le plus jeune (c'tu effrayant appeler un enfant de même, moé, j'en r'viens pas encore!)[30] entéka... Bruno, le plus jeune, est monté dans le bain tout habillé avec le rouleau de papier de toilette déroulé enroulé autour de lui, pis y'a ouvert l'eau... Y trouvait ca drôle à mort, c'est ben sûr! Y faisait des bateaux avec le papier mouillé, pis l'eau coulait partout! Le vrai dégât, là! J'ai été obligée de m'en mêler! J'leu' s'ai donné chacun une bonne fessée sur les fesses pis j'les ai envoyés se coucher!

YVETTE LONGPRE: Vous avez ben faite!

ROSE OUIMET: C'a faite toute une histoire, mais écoutez donc! J'étais pas pour les laisser continuer comme ça! Elle, la niaiseuse, a l'épluchait les pétates en écoutant le radio! Eh! qu'a l'est donc sans allure, c'te femme-là! Au fond, a doit être heureuse, a s'occupe de rien! J'vous dis, des fois, j'plains assez mon Bernard d'avoir marié ça! Y'aurait dû rester avec moé, y'était ben mieux...

(Elle éclate de rire. L'éclairage redevient normal.)

YVETTE LONGPRE: Est-tu folle, elle, hein? Est pas tenable dans les parties! A'donc le tour de nous faire rire!

GABRIELLE JODOIN: Ah! pour ça, on a toujours eu du fun dans les parties, avec elle!

ROSE OUIMET: J'ai pour mon dire, que quand c'est le temps de rire, allons-y gaiement! Même quand j'conte des histoires tristes, j'm'arrange toujours pour les rendre un peu comiques...

THERESE DUBUC: Vous êtes ben chanceuse de pouvoir dire ça, vous, madame Ouimet. C'est pas tout le monde...

DES-NEIGES VERRETTE: Vous, on comprend ça, vous devez pas avoir le goût de rire ben ben souvent... Vous êtes trop charitable, aussi! Vous vous occupez trop des autres...

ROSE OUIMET: Pensez donc à vous, des fois, madame Dubuc. Vous sortez jamais.

THERESE DUBUC: J'ai pas le temps! Quand c'est que vous voudriez que je sorte? J'ai pas le temps! Y faut que j'm'occupe d'elle... Ah! pis si y'avait rien que ça...

GERMAINE LAUZON: Quoi, donc, Thérèse, dites-moé pas qu'y'a d'aut'chose!

THERESE DUBUC: Parlez-moé s'en pas! Parce que mon mari fait un p'tit peu d'argent, là, on nous prend pour la banque de Jos Violon,[31] dans'famille! Encore hier, la belle-soeur d'une de mes belles-soeurs est venue pour quêter chez nous. Vous me connaissez, le coeur m'a fondu quand a m'a conté son histoire, ça fait que j'y ai donné du vieux linge que j'avais pu besoin... Ah! est-tait ben contente... A pleurait comme une Madeleine.[32] A m'a même embrassé les mains.

DES-NEIGES VERRETTE: J'comprends! Vous le méritiez ben!

MARIE-ANGE BROUILLETTE: Moé, madame Dubuc, j'vous admire!

THERESE DUBUC: Dites pas ça...

DES-NEIGES VERRETTE: Oui, oui, oui, vous le méritez!

LISETTE DE COURVAL: Certainement, madame Dubuc, vous méritez notre admiration! Je ne vous oublierai pas dans mes prières, je vous le dis!

THERESE DUBUC: Ah! J'ai pour mon dire que si le bon Dieu a mis des pauvres sur la terre, faut les encourager!

GERMAINE LAUZON: Quand vous aurez fini de remplir un livret, là, au lieu d'les entasser sur la table pour rien, j'pense qu'on s'rait mieux d'les mettre dans une des caisses... Rose, viens m'aider, on va vider la caisse des livrets pis on mettra les livrets pleins dedans...

ROSE OUIMET: Ç'a ben du bon sens! Bonyeu, y'en a, des livrets! Faut-tu toute coller ça à soir?

GERMAINE LAUZON: J'pense qu'on peut. D'abord, tout le monde est pas arrivé, hein, ça fait que...

DES-NEIGES VERRETTE: Qui c'est qui vient à part ça, donc, madame Lauzon?

GERMAINE LAUZON: Rhéauna Bibeau, pis Angéline Sauvé sont supposées de venir après le salon mortuaire. Le mari d'la fille d'une amie d'enfance de Mlle Bibeau est mort... Un dénommé monsieur... Baril, j'pense...

YVETTE LONGPRE: Pas Rosaire Baril, toujours!

GERMAINE LAUZON: Oui, y'm'semble que c'est ça...

YVETTE LONGPRE: Mais j'l'ai ben connu, lui! J'ai déjà sorti avec! C'est ben pour dire, hein, j's'rais veuve, aujourd'hui!

GABRIELLE JODOIN: Aie, les filles, imaginez-vous donc que j'ai trouvé les huit z'erreurs dans le journal d'la semaine passée... C'tait la première fois que ça m'arrivait... Ça fait que j'ai décidé de concourir...

YVETTE LONGPRE: Pis, avez-vous gagné quequ'chose, toujours?

GABRIELLE JODOIN: J'ai-tu l'air de quequ'un qui a déjà gagné quequ'chose!

THERESE DUBUC: Mais que c'est que vous allez faire avec tous ces timbres-là, donc Germaine?

GERMAINE LAUZON: J'vous ai pas conté ça? J'vas toute meubler ma maison en neuf! Attendez... Où c'est que j'ai mis le cataloye... Ah! le v'là! Regardez ça, Thérèse, j'vas toute avoir c'qu'y'a d'dans!

THERESE DUBUC: C'est pas creyable! Tout ça vous coûtera pas une cenne?

GERMAINE LAUZON: Pas une cenne! C'est une vraie belle chose, ces concours-là, vous savez!

LISETTE DE COURVAL: C'est pas c'que madame Brouillette disait tout à l'heure...

GERMAINE LAUZON: Comment ça?

MARIE-ANGE BROUILLETTE: Voyons, madame de Courval!

ROSE OUIMET: Ben quoi, y faut pas avoir peur de ses convictions, madame Brouillette! Vous disiez tout à l'heure, que vous étiez contre les concours parce que y'a rien qu'une famille qui en profite!

MARIE-ANGE BROUILLETTE: C'est vrai, aussi! Moé, toutes ces histoires de tirages de machines, de voyages, pis de timbres, chus contre!

GERMAINE LAUZON: C'est ben parce que vous avez jamais rien gagné!

MARIE-ANGE BROUILLETTE: Peut-être, peut-être, mais n'empêche que c'est pas justc pareil!

GERMAINE LAUZON: Comment ça, c'est pas juste? Vous dites ça parce que vous êtes jalouse, c'est toute! Vous l'avez dit vous-même, que vous étiez jalouse, quand vous êtes arrivée! J'aime pas les jaloux, moé, madame Brouillette, j'les aime pas pantoute, les jaloux! Pis si vous voulez le savoir, là, les jaloux, chus pas capable d'les endurer!

MARIE-ANGE BROUILLETTE: D'abord que c'est comme ça, j'm'en vas!

GERMAINE LAUZON: Ben non, ben non, allez-vous-en-pas, là! J'm'excuse... chus toute énarvée, à soir, pis j'sais pus c'que j'dis! On en parlera pus! Vous avez le droit de penser c'que vous voulez, après toute, c'est votre droit! Assisez-vous, là, pis collez...

ROSE OUIMET: A l'a peur de perdre une colleuse, hein, not'soeur!

GABRIELLE JODOIN: Chut, farme-toé, pis mêle-toé de tes affaires! T'as toujours le nez fourré où c'est que t'as pas d'affaire!

ROSE OUIMET: T'es ben bête, donc, toé! T'es pas parlable, à soir!

MARIE-ANGE BROUILLETTE: C'est correct, d'abord, j'vas rester. Mais chus contre pareil!

(A partir de ce moment-là, Marie-Ange Brouillette volera tous les livrets de timbres qu'elle remplira. Les autres la verront faire dès le début, sauf Germaine, évidemment, et décideront d'en faire autant.)

LISETTE DE COURVAL: J'ai découvert la charade mystérieuse dans le Châtelaine,[33] le mois dernier... C'était bien facile... Mon premier est un félin...

ROSE OUIMET: Un flim?

LISETTE DE COURVAL: Un félin...bien voyons...'chat'...

ROSE OUIMET: Un chat, c't'un félin...

LISETTE DE COURVAL: Bien...oui...

ROSE OUIMET, *en riant*: Ben tant pis pour lui!

LISETTE DE COURVAL: Mon second est un rongeur...bien...'rat'.

ROSE OUIMET: Mon mari aussi, c't'un rat, pis c'est pas un rongeur... Est-tu folle, elle, avec ses folleries!

LISETTE DE COURVAL: Mon troisième est une préposition.

DES-NEIGES VERRETTE: Une préposition d'amour?[34]

LISETTE DE COURVAL, *après un soupir*: Une préposition comme dans la grammaire...'de'. Mon tout est un jeu de société...

ROSE OUIMET: La bouteille!

GABRIELLE JODOIN: Farme-toé donc, Rose, tu comprends rien! *(A Lisette.)* Le Scrabble?

LISETTE DE COURVAL: C'est pourtant pas difficile... Chat-rat-de... Charade!

YVETTE LONGPRE: Ah...c'est quoi, ça, une charade?

LISETTE DE COURVAL: Je l'ai trouvée tout de suite...c'était tellement simple...

YVETTE LONGPRE: Pis, avez-vous gagné quequ'chose, toujours?

LISETTE DE COURVAL: Ah! j'ai pas envoyé ma réponse... J'ai pas besoin de ça, moi...c'était seulement pour le défi que je l'ai faite... J'ai-tu l'air de quelqu'un qui a de besoin de ces affaires-là, moé...euh, moi?

ROSE OUIMET: Moé, là, c'est les mots mystérieux, les mots inversés, les mots cachés, les mots croisés, les mots entrecroisés, pis toutes ces affaires-là que j'aime... Chus spécialiste là-dedans! J'envoye mes réponses partout... Ça me coûte quasiment deux piasses de timbres par semaines, c'est pas ben ben mêlant...

YVETTE LONGPRE: Pis, avez-vous déjà gagné quequ'chose, toujours?

ROSE OUIMET, *en regardant vers Germaine*: J'ai-tu l'air de quequ'un qui a déjà gagné quequ'chose?

THERESE DUBUC: Madame Dubuc, voulez-vous lâcher mon plat d'eau... Bon, ça y'est, a l'a toute renversée! Maudit que chus donc tannée!

(Elle flanque un coup de poing sur la tête de sa belle-mère qui se tranquillise un peu.)

GABRIELLE JODOIN: Bonyeu, vous y allez raide! Vous avez pas peur d'y faire mal?

THERESE DUBUC: Ben non, ben non, est habituée. Pis c'est le seul moyen d'la tranquilliser. C'est mon mari qui a découvert ça! On dirait que quand on y donne un bon coup de poing sur la tête, ça la paralyse pour quequ'menutes... A reste dans son coin pis on est tranquille...

(Noir. Projecteur sur Yvette Longpré.)

YVETTE LONGPRE: Ma fille Claudette m'a donné le premier étage de son gâteau de noces, quand est revenue de voyage de noces. Vous pensez si j'étais fière! C'est assez beau, aie! C'est fait comme un sanctuaire d'église, tout en sucre! Y'a un escalier en velours rouge, pis une plate-forme au boute. Là, y'a les mariés. Deux p'tites poupées ben cute, habillées en mariés pis toute. Y'a un prêtre aussi qui les bénit. En arrière de lui, y'a un autel. En sucre. C'est de toute beauté de voir ça! Le gâteau nous avait coûté assez cher, aussi! C'tait un gâteau à six étages, vous savez! C'tait pas toute du gâteau, par exemple. Ç'a'rait été ben que trop cher! Y'avait juste les deux du bas en gâteau, le reste, c'tait du bois. Mais ça paraissait pas, par exemple. Ma fille m'a donné l'étage du haut en dessous d'une cloche de verre, toujours. C'est ben beau, mais j'avais peur que le sucre se gâte, à la longue... Vous comprenez, sans air! Ça fait que j'ai pris le couteau de mon mari exiprès[35] pour couper la vitre, là, pis j'ai fait un trou dans le haut de la cloche. Comme ça, le gâteau va être aéré comme y faut, pis y'aura pas de danger qu'y pourisse![36]

DES-NEIGES VERRETTE: Moé aussi j'ai concouru à quequ'chose y'a pas longtemps... Le slogan-mystère que ça s'appelait... Y fallait trouver un slogan pour une librairie... La librairie Hachette... Ça fait que j'en ai trouvé une: 'Achète bien, qui achète chez Hachette!' C'est beau, hein?

YVETTE LONGPRE: Pis, avez-vous gagné quequ'chose, toujours?

DES-NEIGES VERRETTE: J'ai-tu l'air de quelqu'un qui a déjà gagné quequ'chose?

GERMAINE LAUZON: Ecoute donc, Rose, j't'ai vue couper ton gazon, à matin... Tu devrais t'acheter une tondeuse!

ROSE OUIMET: Ben non! Les ciseaux, c'est parfait pour moé. Ça m'aide à garder ma shape.

GERMAINE LAUZON: J'te voyais forcer comme une bonne...

ROSE OUIMET: Ça me fait du bien, j'te dis. Pis à part de ça, j'ai pas d'argent pour me payer une tondeuse! Si j'arais d'l'argent, y'a ben de quoi que j'achèterais avant ça!

GERMAINE LAUZON: Moé, j'vas en avoir, une tondeuse, avec mes timbres...

DES-NEIGES VERRETTE: A commence à me tomber sur les nerfs avec ses timbres, elle!

(Elle cache un livret de timbres dans son sac à main.)

ROSE OUIMET: Voyons donc, j'sais pas à quoi ça pourrait te servir, tu restes dans un troisième!

GERMAINE LAUZON: Ah! ça peut toujours servir! Pis on sait pas, on peut toujours déménager, hein?

DES-NEIGES VERRETTE: J'suppose qu'a va nous dire qu'y faudrait une nouvelle maison pour mettre tout c'qu'a va avoir avec ses verrats de timbres!

GERMAINE LAUZON: Tu comprends, y nous faudrait une plus grande maison pour mettre tout c'que j'vas avoir avec mes timbres! *(Des-Neiges Verrette, Marie-Ange Brouillette et Thérèse Dubuc cachent chacune deux ou trois livrets de timbres.)* Si tu veux, j't'la prêterai, ma tondeuse, Rose...

ROSE OUIMET: Jamais ! J'aurais ben qu'trop peur d'la casser! J's'rais obligée de ramasser des timbres pendant deux ans, après, pour te rembourser!

(Les femmes rient.)

GERMAINE LAUZON: T'es donc smatte!

MARIE-ANGE BROUILLETTE: Es-tu bonne, celle-là! Cré madame Ouimet, est pas battable!

THERESE DUBUC: J'ai découvert la voix mystérieuse, au radio, la semaine passée...c'tait la voix à Duplessis...[37] Une vieille voix... C'est mon mari qui l'a trouvée... Ça fait que j'ai envoyé vingt-cinq lettres, là, pis pour me porter chance, j'ai mis le nom de mon p'tit dernier... Paolo Dubuc...

YVETTE LONGPRE: Pis, avez-vous gagné quequ'chose, toujours?

THERESE DUBUC, *en regardant Germaine*: J'ai-tu l'air de quequ'un qui a déjà gagné quequ'chose?

GABRIELLE JODOIN: Vous savez pas c'que mon mari va m'acheter pour ma fête?

ROSE OUIMET: Deux paires de bas de nylon comme l'année passée, j'suppose?

GABRIELLE JODOIN: Ben non! Un manteau de fourrure! Enfin, pas d'la vraie fourrure, là, mais d'la synthétique. D'abord, moé, j'trouve que ça sert pus à rien d'acheter d'la vraie fourrure. Les imitations sont aussi belles aujourd'hui, pis même, des fois, sont plus belles!

LISETTE DE COURVAL: Moi, je ne trouve pas ça...

ROSE OUIMET: On sait ben, elle, a l'a la grosse étoile de vison![38]

LISETTE DE COURVAL: Moi, je dis qu'il n'y aura jamais rien pour remplacer la vraie fourrure véritable. D'ailleurs, j'vais changer mon étole de vison, l'automne prochaine. Ça fait trois ans que je l'ai, puis elle commence à être pas mal maganée... Ah! est encore bonne, mais...

ROSE OUIMET: Farme donc ta grande yueule, maudite menteuse! On le sait que ton mari se fend le cul en quatre pour pouvoir emprunter de l'argent pour te payer des fourrures pis des voyages! C'est pas plus riche que nous autres pis ça pète plus haut que son trou![39] J'ai mon verrat de voyage!

LISETTE DE COURVAL: Si votre mari serait intéressé d'acheter mon étole, madame Jodoin, je lui vendrais pas cher. Comme ça, vous auriez du vrai vison. J'ai pour mon dire qu'entre s'amis...

YVETTE LONGPRE: Moé, j'ai envoyé mes réponses aux 'objets grossis'... Ben, vous savez, là, les affaires qu'y posent de proche-proche-proche, là, pis qu'y faut deviner c'est quoi... Ben, j'les ai trouvés... Y'avait une avis, un tourne-avis...pis un grand crochet tout croche...[40]

LES AUTRES FEMMES: Pis...

(Yvette Longpré se contente de regarder Germaine et se rassoit.)

GERMAINE LAUZON: L'autre jour, Daniel, le p'tit de madame Robitaille, est tombé en bas du deuxième. Y s'est même pas faite une égratignure! C'est ben pour dire, hein?

MARIE-ANGE BROUILLETTE: Faut dire aussi qu'y'tombé dans le hamac de madame Dubé, pis que monsieur Dubé dormait dans le hamac quand le p'tit est tombé...

GERMAINE LAUZON: Eh oui, pis monsieur Dubé est à l'hôpital! Y'en a pour trois mois...

DES-NEIGES VERRETTE: Ça me fait penser à une histoire, en parlant d'accident...

ROSE OUIMET: Quelle, donc, mademoiselle Verrette?

DES-NEIGES VERRETTE: Ah ! est trop osée, j'oserais pas...

ROSE OUIMET: Envoyez donc, mademoiselle Verrette! D'abord, on le sait que vous en savez ben, des histoires sucrées.

DES-NEIGES VERRETTE: Non, ça me gêne, à soir, j'sais pas pourquoi...

GABRIELLE JODOIN: Voyons donc, mademoiselle Verrette, faites-vous pas prier pour rien, là... D'abord, vous savez ben que vous allez finir par nous la conter, vot'histoire...

DES-NEIGES VERRETTE: Bon...correct, d'abord... C't'ait une religieuse qui s'était faite violer dans une ruelle...

ROSE OUIMET: Ça commence ben!

DES-NEIGES VERRETTE: Ça fait que le lendemain, on la retrouve dans le fond d'une cour, toute éfouerrée, la robe r'montée par-dessus la tête... A gémissait sans bon sens, vous comprenez... Ça fait qu'y'a un journaliste qui s'approche pis qui y demande: 'Pourriez-vous, ma soeur, nous donner quelques impressions sur la chose horrible qui vient de vous arriver?'[41] Ça fait que la soeur ouvre les yeux pis murmure: 'Encore! Encore!'

(Toutes les femmes éclatent de rire, sauf Lisette de Courval qui semble scandalisée et Yvette Longpré qui ne comprend pas l'histoire.)

ROSE OUIMET: Ah! ben est bonne en écoeurant, celle-là! Ça fait longtemps que j'en avais pas entendu une bonne de même... C'est pas mêlant, j'en braille! Cré mademoiselle Verrette, j'me d'mande où c'est que vous prenez toute ça, ces histoires-là...

GABRIELLE JODOIN: Tu sais ben que c'est son commis voyageur.

DES-NEIGES VERRETTE: Madame Jodoin, j'vous en prie!

ROSE OUIMET: Ah! oui, c'est vrai, son commis voyageur...

LISETTE DE COURVAL: Je ne comprends pas.

GABRIELLE JODOIN: Y'a un commis voyageur qui vient vendre des brosses à mademoiselle Verrette tous les mois... J'pense qu'a le trouve de son goût...

DES-NEIGES VERRETTE: Madame Jodoin, franchement!

ROSE OUIMET: En tous les cas, on peut dire que mademoiselle Verrette est la mieux grayée en fait de brosses, dans la paroisse! J'l'ai justement vu, vot' commis voyageur, l'aut'jour, mademoiselle Verrette... Y'était au restaurant... Y'a ben dû aller vous voir?

DES-NEIGES VERRETTE: Oui, y'est venu... Mais j'vous assure qu'y'a rien entre moé pis lui, par exemple!

ROSE OUIMET: On dit ça...

DES-NEIGES VERRETTE: Hon! Mon Dieu, madame Ouimet, des fois, j'trouve que vous avez la tête assez croche! Vous voyez toujours du mal où c'est qu'y'en a pas! C't'un bon garçon, monsieur Simard!

ROSE OUIMET: Reste à savoir si vous, vous êtes une bonne fille! Ben non, ben non, mademoiselle Verrette, fâchez-vous pas, là! Vous savez ben que j'dis ça rien que vous étriver!

DES-NEIGES VERRETTE: Vous m'avez faite assez peur! Moé, une demoiselle si respectable! Henri...euh...monsieur Simard m'a justement parlé d'un projet quand y'est venu... J'ai une invitation à vous faire de sa part, à tout le monde... Y voudrait que j'organise une démonstration, la semaine prochaine... Y m'a choisie parce qu'y connaît ma maison... Ça s'rait pour dimanche en huit... Après le chapelet. Y faut que j'ramasse au moins dix personnes pour avoir mon cadeau... Vous savez, y donne des belles tasses fancies à celle qui fait la démonstration... Des vraies belles tasses de fantaisie... Vous devriez les voir, sont assez belles! C'est des souvenirs qu'y' rapportés des chutes Niagara... Y'a dû payer ça ben cher...

ROSE OUIMET: On va y aller certain! Hein, les filles? Moé, j'aime assez ça, des démonstrations! Y va-tu y avoir des prix de présence?

DES-NEIGES VERRETTE: Ben, j'sais pas, là. Mais y devrait. Y devrait... Pis j'vas faire un p'tit lunch...

ROSE OUIMET: Ça va être mieux qu'icitte! J'ai pas encore vu le bout du nez d'une bouteille de liqueur!

(Olivine Dubuc essaie de mordre sa belle-fille.)

THERESE DUBUC: Encore! Madame Dubuc, si vous continuez, j'vas vous enfermer dans les toilettes, pis vous allez rester là toute la soirée!

(Noir, Projecteur sur Des-Neiges Verrette.)

DES-NEIGES VERRETTE: La première fois que j'l'ai vu, j'l'ai trouvé ben laid... C'est vrai qu'y'est pas beau tu-suite! Quand y'a ouvert la porte, y'a enlevé son chapeau, pis y m'a dit: 'Seriez-vous intéressé pour acheter des brosses, ma bonne dame?' J'y ai fermé la porte au nez. J'laisse jamais rentrer d'homme dans la maison! On sait jamais c'qui peut arriver... Y'a rien que le p'tit gars de 'La Presse'[42] que j'laisse rentrer. Lui, y'est trop jeune, encore, y pense pas à mal. Un mois après, mon gars des brosses est revenu. Y faisait une tempête de neige à tout casser, ça fait que j'l'ai laissé rentrer dans le portique. Un coup qu'y'a été rendu dans'maison, j'ai eu peur, mais j'me sus dit qu'y'avait pas l'air méchant, même si y'était pas ben beau... Y'est toujours sur son trente-six,[43] pas un cheveu qui dépasse... Un vrai monsieur! Pis tellement ben élevé! Y m'a vendu deux-trois brosses, toujours, pis y m'a montré son cataloye. Y'en avait une qui m'intéressait, mais y l'avait pas avec lui, ça fait qu'y m'a dit que je pouvais donner une commande. Pis y'est r'venu chaque mois depuis c'temps-là. Des fois, j'achète rien. Y vient juste jaser quequ'menutes. Y'est tellement fin! Quand y parle, on oublie qu'y'est laid! Pis y sait tellement de choses intéressantes! Aie, y voyage à tous les coins d'la province, c't'homme-là! J'pense...j'pense que je l'aime... J'sais que ça pas d'allure, j'le vois rien qu'une fois par mois, mais on est si ben ensemble! Chus tellement heureuse quand y est là! C'est la première fois que ça m'arrive! C'est la première fois! Les hommes se sont jamais occupés de moé, avant. J'ai toujours été une demoiselle...seule. Lui, y m'raconte ses voyages, y m'raconte des histoires... Des fois, sont pas mal sales, mais sont tellement drôles! Pis y faut dire que j'ai toujours aimé les histoires un peu salées... J'trouve que ça fait du bien de conter des histoires cochonnes, des fois... Ah! sont pas toutes cochonnes, ses histoires, ah! non, y'en a des correctes! Des histoires osées, ça fait pas longtemps qu'y m'en conte... Des fois, sont tellement cochonnes, que j'rougis. La dernière fois qu'y'est v'nu, y m'a pris la main parce que j'avais rougi. J'ai manqué v'nir folle! Ça m'a toute revirée à l'envers de sentir sa grosse main su'a mienne! J'ai besoin de lui, astheur! J'voudrais pas qu'y s'en aille pour toujours... Des fois, j'rêve, mais pas souvent! J'rêve...qu'on est mariés. J'ai besoin qu'y vienne me voir! C'est le premier homme qui s'occupe de moé! J'veux pas le pardre! J'veux pas le pardre! Si y s'en va, j'vas rester encore tu-seule, pis j'ai besoin...d'aimer... *(Elle baisse les yeux et murmure.)* J'ai besoin d'un homme.

(Les projecteurs se rallument. Entrent Linda Lauzon, Ginette Ménard et Lise Paquette.)

GERMAINE LAUZON: Ah ! te v'là, toé! Y'est quasiment temps!

LINDA LAUZON: J'étais au restaurant...

GERMAINE LAUZON: Je les sais ben que trop ben, que t'étais au restaurant! Continue à fréquenter les restaurants du coin, ma p'tite fille, pis tu vas finir comme ta tante Pierrette: dans une maison mal farmée!

LINDA LAUZON: Voyons donc, moman, vous faites des drames avec rien!

GERMAINE LAUZON: J't'avais demandé de rester...

LINDA LAUZON: J'étais rien qu'allée chercher des cigarettes, mais j'ai rencontré Lise pis Ginette...

GERMAINE LAUZON: C'est pas une raison! Tu savais que j'recevais, à soir, pour que c'est faire que t'es pas revenue tu-suite? Tu fais exprès pour me faire damner, Linda, tu fais exprès pour me faire damner! Tu veux me faire sacrer devant le monde! Hein, c'est ça, tu veux me faire sacrer devant le monde? Ben crisse, tu vas avoir réussi! Mais t'as pas fini avec moé, ma p'tite fille! Tu perds rien pour attendre, Linda Lauzon, j't'en passe un papier!

ROSE OUIMET: C'est pas le temps d'la chicaner, Germaine!

GABRIELLE JODOIN: Toé, mêle-toé pas encore des affaires des autres!

LINDA LAUZON: Quand même que j's'rais un peu en r'tard, mon Dieu, c'est pas la fin du monde!

LISE PAQUETTE: C'est de not'faute, madame Lauzon!

GINETTE MENARD: Oui, c'est de not'faute!

GERMAINE LAUZON: Je le sais que c'est de vot'faute! J'y ai pourtant dit à Linda de pas fréquenter les coureuses de restaurants! Mais non, a fait toute pour me contrarier! C'est ben simple, des fois, j'l'étriperais!

ROSE OUIMET: Voyons, Germaine...

GABRIELLE JODOIN: Rose, j't'ai dit de te mêler de tes affaires! M'as-tu compris! Leurs affaires, ça te'r'garde pas!

ROSE OUIMET: T'es donc ben fatiquante, toé! Achalle-moi donc pas! On n'est pas pour laisser Germaine chicaner Linda pour rien!

GABRIELLE JODOIN: C'est pas de nos affaires!

LINDA LAUZON: Laissez-la donc me défendre, vous, ma tante!

GABRIELLE JODOIN: Linda, sois polie avec ta marraine si tu l'es pas avec ta mère!

GERMAINE LAUZON: Tu vois comment c'est qu'a l'est! C'est toujours de même, avec elle! C'est pourtant pas comme ça que je l'ai élevée!

ROSE OUIMET: Parlons-en d'la manière que t'élèves tes enfants!

GERMAINE LAUZON: Ah! ben, toé, par exemple, t'as rien à dire... Tes enfants...

LINDA LAUZON: Allez-y, ma tante, donnez-y, une fois pour toutes! Vous êtes capable d'y parler, à ma mère, vous!

GERMAINE LAUZON: Que c'est qui te prend, toé, tout d'un coup, de te mettre du côté de ta tante Rose? Que c'est que t'as dit, quand a l'a téléphoné, à soir, hein, que c'est que t'as dit? T'en rappelles-tu de que c'est que t'as dit?

LINDA LAUZON: C'tait pas pareil...

ROSE OUIMET: Quoi'que c'est qu'a l'a dit, donc?

GERMAINE LAUZON: Ben, c'est elle qui a répondu quand t'as téléphoné, hein? Pis a l'a pas dit 'Un instant s'il-vous-plaît', ça fait que j'y ai dit d'être plus polie avec toé...

LINDA LAUZON: Moman, voyons, taisez-vous donc! C'est pas nécessaire...

ROSE OUIMET: Je veux le savoir, de que c'est que t'as dit, Linda!

LINDA LAUZON: Ça comptait pas, ma tante, j'étais en maudit!

GERMAINE LAUZON: A l'a dit: 'C'est rien que ma tante Rose, j'sais pas pourquoi j's'rais polie avec elle!'

ROSE OUIMET: Ah! ben par exemple... J'ai mon voyage!

LINDA LAUZON: J'vous le dis, ma tante, j'tais en maudit!

ROSE OUIMET: J'te pensais pas de même, Linda! Tu me désappointes, tu me désappointes ben gros ma p'tite fille!

GABRIELLE JODOIN: Voyons donc, Rose, laisse-les donc se chicaner tu-seules!

ROSE OUIMET: Certain que j'vas les laisser se chicaner! Envoye, vas-y, Germaine, manque-la pas, ta fille! Es-tu mal élevée, c't'nfant-là, rien qu'un peu! M'as dire comme ta mère, tu vas finir comme ta tante Pierrette, si tu continues, ma fille! Si j'me r'tenais pas, j'y mettrais ma main dans'face!

GERMAINE LAUZON: J'voudrais ben voir ça! Que j'te voyes donc toucher à mes enfants! Moé, j'ai le droit de les fesser, mais y'a personne qui va leu'toucher, par exemple!

THERESE DUBUC: Arrêtez donc un peu de vous disputer, chus fatiquée, moé!

DES-NEIGES VERRETTE: Ben oui, c'est fatiquant!

THERESE DUBUC: Vous allez réveiller ma belle-mère, pis a va recommencer à nous achaler!

GERMAINE LAUZON: C'était d'la laisser chez vous, aussi, vot'belle-mère!

THERESE DUBUC: Germaine Lauzon!

GABRIELLE JODOIN: Ben quoi! A l'a raison! On va pas dans une veillée avec une vieille de quatre-vingt-treize ans!

LISETTE DE COURVAL: C'est vous, madame Jodoin, qui disiez à votre soeur de se mêler de ses affaires, tout à l'heure!

GABRIELLE JODOIN: Ah! ben, vous, par exemple, la pincée, lâchez-moé lousse! Collez vos timbres, pis farmez-la ben juste, parce que sans ça, m'en va vous la fermer ben juste, moé!

(Lisette de Courval se lève.)

LISETTE DE COURVAL: Gabrielle Jodoin!

(Olivine Dubuc, qui joue depuis quelques instants avec un plat d'eau, l'échappe par terre.)

THERESE DUBUC: Madame Dubuc, attention!

GERMAINE LAUZON: Maudite marde! Mon dessus de table!

ROSE OUIMET: A m'a toute arrosée, la vieille chipie!

THERESE DUBUC: C'est pas vrai! Vous étiez trop loin!

ROSE OUIMET: C't'aussi ben de me dire en pleine face que ch't'une maudite menteuse!

THERESE DUBUC: Oui, vous êtes rien qu'une maudite menteuse, Rose Ouimet!

GERMAINE LAUZON: Attention à votre belle-mère, a va tomber!

DES-NEIGES VERRETTE: Ça y'est, la v'là encore à terre!

THERESE DUBUC: V'nez m'aider, quelqu'un!

ROSE OUIMET: Pas moé, en tout cas!

GABRIELLE JODOIN: Ramassez-la tu-seule!

DES-NEIGES VERRETTE: J'vas vous aider, moé, madame Dubuc.

THERESE DUBUC: Merci, Mademoiselle Verrette...

GERMAINE LAUZON: Pis toé, Linda, t'as besoin de filer doux pour le restant d'la soirée...

LINDA LAUZON: J'ai ben envie de sacrer mon camp...

GERMAINE LAUZON: Fais ça, ma p'tite maudite, pis tu r'mettras pus jamais les pieds icitte!

LINDA LAUZON: On les connaît, vos menaces!

LISE PAQUETTE: Arrête donc, Linda...

THERESE DUBUC: T'nez-vous donc un peu, madame Dubuc, raidissez-vous! Faites pas exiprès pour vous tenir molle!

MARIE-ANGE BROUILLETTE: J'vas tirer la chaise...

THERESE DUBUC: Merci ben...

ROSE OUIMET: Moé, à sa place, j'pousserais la chaise pis...

GABRIELLE JODOIN: R'commence pas, Rose!

THERESE DUBUC: Eh! qu'on a d'la misère...

GABRIELLE JODOIN: R'garde la de Courval qui continue à coller ses timbres... La maudite pincée! A s'occupe de rien! On n'est pas assez intéressantes pour elle, j'suppose!

(Noir. Projecteur sur Lisette de Courval.)

LISETTE DE COURVAL: On se croirait dans une basse-cour! Léopold m'avait dit de ne pas venir ici, aussi! Ces gens-là sont pus de notre monde! Je regrette assez d'être venue! Quand on a connu la vie de transatlantique pis qu'on se retrouve ici, ce n'est pas des farces! J'me revois, là, étendue sur une chaise longue, un bon livre de Magali[44] sur les genoux... Pis le lieutenant qui me faisait de l'oeil... Mon mari disait que non, mais y'avait pas tout vu! Une bien belle pièce d'homme! J'aurais peut-être dû l'encourager un peu plus... Puis l'Urope! Le monde sont donc bien élevé par là! Sont bien plus polis qu'ici! On en rencontre pas des Germaine Lauzon, par là! Y'a juste du grand monde! A Paris, tout le monde perle bien, c'est du vrai français partout... C'est pas comme icitte... J'les méprise toutes! Je ne remettrai jamais les pieds ici! Léopold avait raison, c'monde-là, c'est du monde *cheap*, y faut pas les fréquenter, y faut même pas en parler, y faut les cacher! Y savent pas vivre! Nous autres on est sortis de là, pis on devrait pus jamais revenir! Mon Dieu que j'ai donc honte d'eux-autres!

(Les lumières se rallument.)

LINDA LAUZON: Bon, ben salut, j'm'en vas...

GERMAINE LAUZON: Tu le fais exiprès! J't'avertis, Linda...

LINDA LAUZON: 'J't'avertis, Linda', c'est toute c'que vous êtes capable de dire, ça, moman!

LISE PAQUETTE: Fais pas la folle, Linda!

GINETTE MENARD: Reste donc!

LINDA LAUZON: Non, j'm'en vas! J'ai pas envie qu'a continue à me crier des bêtises de même toute la soirée!

GERMAINE LAUZON: Linda, j't'ordonne de rester icitte!

VOIX D'UNE VOISINE: Allez-vous arrêter de crier, en haut? On s'entend pus!

(Rose Ouimet sort sur la galerie.)

ROSE OUIMET: Rentrez donc dans vot'maison, vous!

LA VOISINE: C'est pas à vous que j'parlais!

ROSE OUIMET: Oui, c't'à moé, j'crie aussi fort que les autres!

GABRIELLE JODOIN: Rentre donc, Rose!

DES-NEIGES VERRETTE: Occupez-vous-en donc pas!

LA VOISINE: J'vas appeler la police!

ROSE OUIMET: C'est ça, appelez-la, on manque justement d'hommes!

GERMAINE LAUZON: Rose Ouimet, rentre dans' maison ! Pis toé, Linda...

LINDA LAUZON: J'm'en vas. Salut!

(Elle sort avec Ginette et Lise.)

GERMAINE LAUZON: Est partie! Est partie! Ça se peux-tu? C'est pas possible! A veut me faire mourir! Y faut que j'casse quequ'chose! Y faut que j'casse quequ'chose!

ROSE OUIMET: Voyons, prends su-toé, Germaine!

GERMAINE LAUZON: Me faire honte de même devant tout le monde! *(Elle éclate en sanglots.)* C'est ben simple... j'ai assez honte...

GABRIELLE JODOIN: C'est pas si pire que ça, Germaine...

VOIX DE LINDA: Ah! ben, si c'est pas mademoiselle Sauvé. Allô!

VOIX D'ANGELINE SAUVE:[45] Bonsoir ma belle fille, comment ça va?

ROSE OUIMET: Les v'lon! Mouche-toé, Germaine!

VOIX DE LINDA LAUZON: Ça va pas mal...

VOIX DE RHEAUNA BIBEAU: Où c'est que vous allez, de même?

LINDA LAUZON: J'm'en allais au restaurant, mais astheur que vous êtes là, j'pense que j'vas rester!

(Entrent Linda, Ginette, Lise, Rhéauna et Angéline.)

ANGELINE SAUVE: Bonsoir tout le monde!

RHEAUNA BIBEAU: Bonsoir.

LES AUTRES: Bonsoir, bonsoir, comment ça va?

RHEAUNA BIBEAU: J'vous dis que vous restez haut vrai, madame Lauzon! Chus toute essoufflée!

GERMAINE LAUZON: Assisez-vous donc...

ROSE OUIMET: Vous êtes essoufflées? C'est pas ben grave... Vous allez voir ça, ma soeur, a va faire poser un élévateur avec ses timbres.

(Les femmes rient, sauf Rhéauna et Angéline qui ne savent pas comment prendre cette phrase.)

GERMAINE LAUZON: T'es donc drôle, Rose Ouimet! Linda, va chercher d'aut'chaises...

LINDA LAUZON: Où, ça? Y'en a pus!

GERMAINE LAUZON: Va demander à madame Bergeron si a pourrait pas nous en passer quequ's'unes...

LINDA LAUZON: V'nez, les filles...

GERMAINE LAUZON *bas à Linda*: On fait la paix pour à soir, mais attends que la visite soit partie...

LINDA LAUZON: Vous me faites pas peur! Si chus rev'nue, c'est parce que mademoiselle Sauvé pis mademoiselle Bibeau sont arrivées,[46] c'est pas parce que j'avais peur de vous!

(Linda sort avec Lise et Ginette.)

DES-NEIGES VERRETTE: Prenez ma chaise, mademoiselle Bibeau...

THERESE DUBUC: Ben oui, v'nez vous asseoir à côté de moé, un peu...

MARIE-ANGE BROUILLETTE: Assisez-vous icitte, mademoiselle Bibeau.

ANGELINE SAUVE ET RHEAUNA BIBEAU: Merci, merci bien.

RHEAUNA BIBEAU: Vous collez des timbres, à ce que je vois?

GERMAINE LAUZON: Ben oui. Y'en a un million!

RHEAUNA BIBEAU: Seigneur Dieu! Etes-vous rendues loin?

ROSE OUIMET: Pas mal, pas mal... Moé, j'ai la langue toute paralysée...

RHEAUNA BIBEAU: Vous collez ça avec vot'langue?

GABRIELLE JODOIN: Ben non, voyons, c'tait une farce plate!

ROSE OUIMET: A comprend toujours aussi vite, la Bibeau!

ANGELINE SAUVE: On va vous donner un p'tit coup de main...

ROSE OUIMET, *avec un rire gras*: J'ai eu peur, j'pensais qu'a voulait nous donner un coup de langue...

GABRIELLE JODOIN: T'es donc vulgaire, Rose!

GERMAINE LAUZON: Pis, toujours, le salon mortuaire?

(Noir. Projecteur sur Angéline Sauvé et Rhéauna Bibeau.)

RHEAUNA BIBEAU: Moé, c'est ben simple, ça m'a donné un coup...

ANGELINE SAUVE: Tu le connaissais pas tellement, pourtant!

RHEAUNA BIBEAU: J'ai ben connu sa mère! Toé aussi, tu t'en rappelles, on allait à l'école ensemble! J'l'ai vu grandir, c't'homme-là...

ANGELINE SAUVE: Et! oui. Pis tu vois, y'est parti. Pis nous autres, on est encore là...

RHEAUNA BIBEAU: Ah! mais ça s'ra pas long, par exemple...

ANGELINE SAUVE: Voyons, donc, Rhéauna...

RHEAUNA BIBEAU: J'sais c'que j'dis ! Ça se sent quand la fin vient! Après tout c'que j'ai enduré!

ANGELINE SAUVE: Ah! pour ça, on pourra dire qu'on a souffert, toutes les deux...

RHEAUNA BIBEAU: J'ai souffert ben plus que toé, Angéline! Dix-sept s'opérations! J'ai pus rien qu'un poumon, un rein, un sein... Ah! j'en ai-tu arraché, rien qu'un peu...

ANGELINE SAUVE: Moé, j'ai mon arthrite qui me lâche pas! Mais madame...comment c'est qu'à s'appelle, donc...entéka. La femme du mort, a m'a donné une recette...y parait que c'est merveilleux!

RHEAUNA BIBEAU: Tu sais ben que t'as toute essayé! Les docteurs t'ont dit quy'avait rien pour ça! Ça se guérit pas, l'arthrite!

ANGELINE SAUVE: Les docteurs, les docteurs, j'te dis que j'les ai loin, astheur! Ça pense rien qu'à la piasse, les docteurs! Ça égorge le pauvre monde, pis ça va passer l'hiver en Califournie! T'sais, Rhéauna, le docteur, y y'avait dit qu'y guérirait, à monsieur...c'est quoi, donc, son nom, au mort?

RHEAUNA BIBEAU: Monsieur Baril...

ANGELINE SAUVE: Ah! oui, j'm'en rappelle jamais! C'est pourtant pas compliqué! Bon, ben son docteur y'avait dit qu'y'avait pas besoin d'avoir peur, à monsieur Baril... Pis tu vois...à peine quarante ans...

RHEAUNA BIBEAU: Quarante ans! C'est jeune, pour mourir!

ANGELINE SAUVE: Y'est parti ben vite...

RHEAUNA BIBEAU: A m'a toute conté comment ça s'était passé. C'est assez triste!

ANGELINE SAUVE: Oui? J'étais pas là quand a t'a conté ça... Comment c'est arrivé, donc?

RHEAUNA BIBEAU: Quand y'est rentré de travailler, lundi soir, a l'a trouvé ben changé. A y'a demandé si y se sentait pas ben, y'était blanc comme un linge. Y'a dit que non. Y'ont commencé à souper... Les enfants se disputaient à table, ça fait que monsieur Baril s'est fâché pis y'a été obligé de punir sa Rolande... Y'était pas mal caduc après, tu comprends... Elle, a le regardait sans arrêter. A l'observait. A m'a dit que ça s'était passé tellement vite qu'a l'a pas eu le temps de rien faire. Y'a dit tout d'un coup qu'y se sentait drôle, pis y'est tombé le nez dans sa soupe. C'tait fini!

ANGELINE SAUVE: Doux Jésus! C'est donc effrayant! Si vite que ça! Moé, c'est ben simple, ça me donne la chair de poule! C'est donc effrayant!

RHEAUNA BIBEAU: Tu peux le dire! On le sait jamais quand est-ce que c'est que le bon Dieu va venir nous chercher! Y l'a dit lui-même: 'Je viendrai comme un voleur.'

ANGELINE SAUVE: Ça me fait assez peur, ces histoires-là! Moé, j'voudrais pas mourir de même! J'veux mourir dans mon lit... avoir le temps de me confesser...

RHEAUNA BIBEAU: Pour ça, non, j'voudrais pas mourir sans me confesser! Angéline, promets-moé que tu vas faire v'nir le prêtre quand j'vas me sentir mal ! Promets-moé-lé!

ANGELINE SAUVE: Ben oui, ben oui, ça fait cent fois que tu me le demandes! J'l'ai fait v'nir, le prêtre, la dernière fois que t'as eu une attaque! T'as communié pis toute!

RHEAUNA BIBEAU: J'ai tellement peur de mourir sans recevoir les derniers sacrements!

ANGELINE SAUVE: Pour les péchés que tu peux faire!

RHEAUNA BIBEAU: Dis pas ça, Angéline, dis pas ça! Y'a pas d'âge pour faire des péchés!

ANGELINE SAUVE: Moé, chus ben sûre que tu vas aller au paradis tout dret, Rhéanna. T'as pas besoin d'avoir peur! Hon! As-tu vu la fille du mort si a l'était changée? Une vraie morte!

RHEAUNA BIBEAU: J'comprends! Pauvre Rolande! A dit à tout le monde que c'est elle qui a tué son père! Tu comprends, c'est à cause d'elle si y s'est fâché, à table... A fait donc pitié... Pis sa mère, astheur! Ah! c'est un ben grand malheur! Ça va faire un grand trou! C't'un gros morceau qu'y perdent là!

ANGELINE SAUVE: J'comprends! Le père! R'marque que c'est moins pire que la mère, mais ça fait rien...

RHEAUNA BIBEAU: Oui, c'est vrai, une mère, c'est pire! Une mère, ça se remplace pas!

ANGELINE SAUVE: As-tu vu si y l'ont ben arrangé, le mort, hein? Y'avait l'air d'un vrai jeune homme! Y souriait... On aurait dit qu'y dormait. Mais au fond, y'est ben mieux ousqu'y'est là... M'as dire comme on dit, c'est les ceuses qui restent qui sont les plus à plaindre! Lui, y'est ben, astheur... Ah! mais j'en r'viens pas si y'était ben grimé! Y'avait l'air vivant.

RHEAUNA BIBEAU: Eh oui! Mais y l'était pas.

ANGELINE SAUVE: Mais j'sais pas pourquoi y y'avaient mis c't'habit-là, par exemple...

RHEAUNA BIBEAU: Comment ça?

ANGELINE SAUVE: T'as pas remarqué? Y'avait une habit bleue! Ça se fait pas! Un mort, c't'un mort! Une habit bleue, c'est ben que trop pâle! Si au moins a l'avait été bleu-marin, mais non, c't'ait quasiment bleu-pourde! Un mort, ça doit porter une habit noire!

RHEAUNA BIBEAU: Y'en avait peut-être pas! C'est pas du monde ben riche!

ANGELINE SAUVE: Mon Dieu-Seigneur, une habit noire, ça se loue! C'est comme la soeur de madame Baril! Une robe verte! En plein salon mortuaire! Pis a l'a-tu vieilli, rien qu'un peu! A'vait l'air ben plus vieille que sa soeur...

RHEAUNA BIBEAU: A l'est, aussi.

ANGELINE SAUVE: Voyons donc, Rhéauna, est ben plus jeune!

RHEAUNA BIBEAU: Ben non!

ANGELINE SAUVE: Ben oui, Rhéauna, écoute! Madame Baril a dans les trente-sept trente-huit ans, pis elle...

RHEAUNA BIBEAU: A l'a plus de quarante ans!

ANGELINE SAUVE: Voyons donc, Rhéauna!

RHEAUNA BIBEAU: Moé, j'y donnerais ben quarante-cinq ans...

ANGELINE SAUVE: C'est ça que j'te dis, a l'a vieilli, a l'a l'air plus vieille que son âge... Ecoute, ma belle-soeur Rose-Aimée a trente-six ans pis y'ont été à l'école ensemble...

RHEAUNA BIBEAU: Entéka, ça me surprend pas qu'a vieillisse si vite... Avec la vie qu'a mène...

ANGELINE SAUVE: J'sais pas si c'est ben vrai, toutes ces histoires-là...

RHEAUNA BIBEAU: Ça doit! Mme Baril, elle, a l'essaye de cacher ça, c'est sa soeur...mais tout finit par se savoir! C'est comme madame Lauzon, avec sa soeur Pierrette! Si y'a quelqu'un que j'peux pas sentir, c'est ben Pierrette Guérin! Une vraie dévergondée! Une vraie honte pour sa famille! J'te dis, Angéline, que j'voudrais pas voir son âme, elle! A doit être noire, rare!

ANGELINE SAUVE: Voyons, Rhéauna, au fond, Pierrette, c'est pas une mauvaise fille!

(Un projecteur s'allume sur Germaine Lauzon.)

GERMAINE LAUZON: Ma soeur Pierrette, ça fait longtemps que j'l'ai reniée! Après toute c'qu'a nous a faite! Est'tait si fine, quand est'tait p'tite! Pis belle! Quand on dit une vraie catin! Ah! on l'a ben aimée, moé, pis mes soeurs! On la gâtait sans bon sens! Mais pour que c'est faire... J'comprends pas! J'comprends pas! Le pére, à'maison, l'appelait sa p'tite pourrite! Y l'amait donc, sa Pierrette! Quand y'a prenait sur ses genoux, là on sentait qu'y'était heureux! Nous autres, on n'était pas jalouses...

ROSE OUIMET: On se disait: 'C'est la plus jeune. C'est toujours comme ça, c'est les plus jeunes qui sont les préférées...' Quand a l'a commencé à aller à l'école, on l'a habillée comme une princesse! J'étais déjà mariée, moé, j'm'en rappelle comme si c'était hier! Eh! qu'a l'était donc belle! Une vraie Shirley Temple![47] Pis a l'apprenait donc vite, à l'école! Ben plus vite que moé! moé, j'ai jamais été ben bonne à l'école... J'étais la grosse comique d'la classe, c'était toute c'que j'pouvais faire, de toute façon... Mais elle, la p'tite bougraisse, a vous-en a-tu décroché, des prix!

Prix de français, prix d'arithmétique, prix de religion... Oui, de religion! C'était pieux comme une bonne soeur, c't'enfant-là. C'est ben simple, les soeurs étaient folles d'elle! Quand on la voit, aujourd'hui... Mon Dieu, au fond, j'ai un peu pitié d'elle. A doit avoir de besoin d'aide, des fois... Pis a doit être ben tu-seule!

GABRIELLE JODOIN: Quand a l'a fini ses études primaires, on y'a demandé c'qu'a voulait faire. A voulait faire une maîtresse d'école. Est-tait pour commencer ses études... Mais y fallait qu'a rencontre son Johnny!

LES TROIS SOEURS: Le maudit Johnny! Un vrai démon sorti de l'enfer! C'est de sa faute si est devenue comme a l'est astheur! Maudit Johnny! Maudit Johnny!

RHEAUNA BIBEAU: Comment, pas une mauvaise fille! Pour faire c'qu'a fait, y faut être rendue ben bas! Hon! Tu sais pas c'que madame Longpré m'a conté à son sujet?

ANGELINE SAUVE: Non, quoi, donc?

THERESE DUBUC: Ayoye!

(Les lumières s'allument. Thérèse Dubuc donne un coup de poing sur la tête de sa belle-mère.)

GERMAINE LAUZON: Assommez-la pour de bon, faites quequ'chose, Thérèse!

THERESE DUBUC: Assommez-la, assommez-la, j'fais comme j'peux pour la tranquiliser! Chus quand même pas pour la tuer pour vous faire plaisir!

ROSE OUIMET: Moé, j'la maudirais en bas de la galerie...

THERESE DUBUC: Pardon? Répétez donc c'que vous v'nez de dire, Rose, j'ai pas compris!

ROSE OUIMET: J'parlais tu-seule!

THERESE DUBUC: Vous avez peur, hein?

ROSE OUIMET: Moé, peur?

THERESE DUBUC: Oui, vous avez peur!

MARIE-ANGE BROUILLETTE: Dites-moé pas qu'la chicane va r'poigner!

ANGELINE SAUVE: Y'a-tu eu une chicane?

RHEAUNA BIBEAU: Qui c'est qui s'est chicané, donc?

ANGELINE SAUVE: On aurait dû arriver avant!

THERESE DUBUC: Chus pas pour la laisser faire! A vient d'insulter ma belle-mère! La mère de mon mari!

LISETTE DE COURVAL: Les revoilà qui recommencent!

ROSE OUIMET: Est assez vieille! Est pus bonne à rien!

GERMAINE LAUZON: Rose!

GABRIELLE JODOIN: Rose! t'as pas honte de parler de même! Que t'as donc le coeur dur!

THERESE DUBUC: J'oublierai jamais c'que vous v'nez de dire là, Rose Ouimet! Je l'oublierai jamais!

ROSE OUIMET: Ah ! pis sacrez-moé donc patience!

ANGELINE SAUVE: Qui c'est qui s'est chicané, avant, donc?

ROSE OUIMET: Vous voudriez tout savoir, hein, mademoiselle Sauvé, vous voudriez qu'on vous explique toute en détails?

ANGELINE SAUVE: Mon Dieu, madame Ouimet...

ROSE OUIMET: Ensuite, vous pourriez aller tout colporter un peu partout, hein, c'est ça?

RHEAUNA BIBEAU: Rose Ouimet! J'me fâche pas souvent, mais j'vous permettrai pas d'insulter mon amie!

MARIE-ANGE BROUILLETTE, *en aparté*: J'vas toujours ben m'en prendre quequ'paquets pendant qu'y me voient pas!

GABRIELLE JODOIN, *qui l'a vue faire*: Que c'est que vous faites là, Mme Brouillette?

ROSE OUIMET: Oui, j'pense que chus mieux de m'la farmer!

MARIE-ANGE BROUILLETTE: Chut! Taisez-vous, prenez ça! *(Arrivent Linda, Ginette et Lise avec des chaises. Grand branle-bas. Toutes les femmes changent de place. On en profite pour voler quelques livrets et quelques paquets de timbres.)* Prenez-en, ayez pas peur!

DES-NEIGES VERRETTE: Faudrait quand même pas exagérer.

THERESE DUBUC: Cachez ça dans vot'poche, Mme Dubuc... Non! J'ai dis d'les cacher!

GERMAINE LAUZON: Le gars qui me vend ma viande, à shop, c't'un vrai voleur!

(La porte s'ouvre brusquement. Pierrette Guérin entre.)

PIERRETTE GUERIN: Salut tout le monde!

LES AUTRES: Pierrette!

LINDA LAUZON: Ma tante Pierrette, c'est le fun!

ANGELINE SAUVE: Mon Dieu, Pierrette!

GERMAINE LAUZON: Que c'est que tu fais icitte, toé? J't'ai déjà dit que j'voulais pus te voir!

PIERRETTE GUERIN: J'ai appris que ma grande soeur Germaine avait gagné un million de timbres, ça fait que j'ai décidé de v'nir voir ça! *(Elle aperçoit Angéline Sauvé.)* Ah'ben câlisse! Angéline! Que c'est que tu fais icitte, toé!

(Tout le monde regarde Angéline Sauvé.)

Rideau

ACTE DEUXIEME

(Le deuxième acte commence à l'entrée de Pierrette.
On refait donc les six dernières répliques
du premier acte avant d'enchaîner.)

(La porte s'ouvre brusquement. Pierrette Guérin entre.)

PIERRETTE GUERIN: Salut tout le monde!

LES AUTRES: Pierrette!

LINDA LAUZON: Ma tante Pierrette, c'est le fun!

ANGELINE SAUVE: Mon Dieu, Pierrette!

GERMAINE LAUZON: Que c'est que tu fais icitte, toé? J't'ai déjà dit que j'voulais pus te voir!

PIERRETTE GUERIN: J'ai appris que ma grande soeur Germaine avait gagné un million de timbres, ça fait que j'ai décidé de v'nir voir ça! *(Elle aperçoit Angéline Sauvé.)* Ah ! ben câlisse! Angéline! Que c'est que tu fais icitte, toé?

(Tout le monde regarde Angéline Sauvé.)

ANGELINE SAUVE: Mon Dieu! Ça y'est, chus poignée!

GERMAINE LAUZON: Comment ça, Angéline?

GABRIELLE JODOIN: Comment c'est que tu parles à mademoiselle Sauvé, donc, toé?

ROSE OUIMET: T'as pas honte!

PIERRETTE GUERIN: Ben quoi, on se connaît ben, nous deux, hein, 'Géline?

ANGELINE SAUVE: Ah! J'pense que j'vas tomber sans connaissance!

(Angéline fait semblant de perdre connaissance.)

RHEAUNA BIBEAU: Doux Jésus! Angéline!

ROSE OUIMET: Est morte!

RHEAUNA BIBEAU: Quoi?

GABRIELLE JODOIN: Ben non, ben non, est pas morte! T'exagères encore, Rose!

PIERRETTE GUERIN: Est même pas sans connaissance! Vous voyez ben qu'a fait semblant!

(Pierrette s'approche d'Angéline.)

GERMAINE LAUZON: Touches-y pas, toé!

PIERRETTE GUERIN: Laisse-moé donc tranquille, c'est mon amie!

RHEAUNA BIBEAU: Comment ça, vot'amie !

GERMAINE LAUZON: T'as toujours ben pas envie de nous faire accroire que mademoiselle Sauvé est ton amie!

PIERRETTE GUERIN: Ben tiens! A vient nous voir au club quasiment tous les vendredis soir!

TOUTES LES FEMMES: Quoi!

RHEAUNA BIBEAU: Ça se peut pas, voyons!

PIERRETTE GUERIN: Demandez-y! Hein, 'Géline, c'est vrai c'que j'dis là? Voyons, arrête de faire la folle, pis réponds! Angéline, on sait que t'es pas dans les pommes! Dis-leu' donc que c'est vrai que tu viens souvent au club!

ANGELINE SAUVE *après un silence*: Oui, c'est vrai!

RHEAUNA BIBEAU: Hon! Angéline! Angéline!

QUELQUES FEMMES: C'est ben effrayant!

QUELQUES AUTRES: C'est ben épouvantable!

LINDA, GINETTE, LISE: C'est le fun! *(Noir.)*

RHEAUNA BIBEAU: Angéline! Angéline! *(Projecteur sur Angéline et Rhéauna.)*

ANGELINE SAUVE: Rhéauna, y faut me comprendre...

RHEAUNA BIBEAU: Touche-moé pas! Recule!

LES FEMMES: Si j'arais pensé une chose pareille!

RHEAUNA BIBEAU: J'arais jamais pensé ça de toé, Angéline! Dans un club! Pis à tous les vendredis soir! C'est pas possible! Ça se peut pas!

ANGELINE SAUVE: J'fais rien de mal, Rhéauna! J'prends rien qu'un coke!

LES FEMMES: Dans un club!

GERMAINE LAUZON: Dieu sait c'qu'à fait là!

ROSE OUIMET: C'est peut-être une courailleuse!

ANGELINE SAUVE: Mais puisque que je vous dis que je fais rien de mal!

PIERRETTE GUERIN: C'est vrai qu'a fait rien de mal!

ROSE, GERMAINE, GABRIELLE: Toé, tais-toé, démonne!

RHEAUNA BIBEAU: T'es pus mon amie, Angéline. J'te connais pus!

ANGELINE SAUVE: Ecoute-moé, Rhéauna, y faut que tu m'écoutes! J'vas toute t'expliquer, pis tu vas comprendre!

ROSE, GERMAINE, GABRIELLE: Le club! Un vrai endroit de perdition!

TOUTES LES FEMMES, *sauf les jeunes*: Ah! endroit maudit, endroit maudit! C'est là qu'on perd son âme. Maudite boisson, maudite danse! C'est là que nos maris perdent la tête pis dépensent toutes leurs payes avec des femmes damnées!

GERMAINE, ROSE, GABRIELLE: Des femmes damnées comme toé, Pierrette!

TOUTES LES FEMMES, *sauf les quatre jeunes*: Vous avez pas honte, Angéline Sauvé, de fréquenter un endroit pareil?

RHEAUNA BIBEAU: Angéline! le club, mais c'est l'enfer!

PIERRETTE GUERIN, *en riant très fort*: Si l'enfer ressemble au club ousque j'travaille, ça m'fait rien pantoute d'aller passer mon éternité là, moé!

GERMAINE, ROSE, GABRIELLE: Farme-toé, Pierrette, c'est le diable qui parle par ta bouche!

LINDA, GINETTE, LISE: Le diable? voyons donc! Ecoutez, faut être de son temps! Les clubs, c'est pas la fin du monde! C'est pas pire qu'ailleurs. Pis c'est ben l'fun! C'est ben l'fun, les clubs!

LES AUTRES FEMMES: Ah ! Jeunesses aveugles! Jeunesses aveugles! Vous allez vous pardre, pauvres jeunesses, vous allez vous pardre, pis vous allez v'nir brailler dans nos bras, après! Mais y s'ra trop tard! Y s'ra trop tard! Attention! Faites attention à ces endroits maudits! On s'en aperçoit pas toujours quand on tombe, pis quand on se r'lève, y est trop tard!

LISE PAQUETTE: Trop tard! Y'est trop tard! Mon Dieu, y est trop tard!

GERMAINE LAUZON: J'espère au moins que vous allez vous en confesser, Angéline Sauvé!

ROSE OUIMET: J'vous vois aller communier tous les dimanches matin.... Communier avec un pareil péché sur la conscience!

GABRIELLE JODOIN: Un péché mortel!

GERMAINE, ROSE, GABRIELLE: On nous l'a assez répété: 'Mettre le pied dans un club, c'est dejà faire un péché mortel.'

ANGELINE SAUVE: Assez! Farmez-vous pis écoutez-moé!

LES FEMMES: Jamais! Vous avez pas d'excuses!

ANGELINE SAUVE: Rhéauna, écoute-moé, toé! On est des vieilles amies, on reste ensemble depuis 35 ans! J't'aime ben mais un moment donné j'ai l'goût d'voir d'autre monde! Tu sais comment j'sus faite! J'aime ça avoir du fun! J'ai été élevée dans les sous-bassements d'églises, pis j'veux connaître d'autre chose! On peut aller dans les clubs sans faire de mal! Ça fait quatre ans que j'fais ça, pis j'ai jamais rien faite de pas correct! Le monde qui travaillent là, sont pas pires que nous autres! J'ai envie d'connaître du monde! J'ai jamais ri de ma vie, Rhéauna!

RHEAUNA BIBEAU: Y a d'autres places que les clubs pour rire! T'es t'après te pardre, Angéline! Dis-moé qu'tu y retourneras pus!

ANGELINE SAUVE: 'Coute Rhéauna, j'peux pas! J'aime ça aller là, comprends-tu, j'aime ça!

RHEAUNA BIBEAU: Y faut qu'tu m'promettes, sans ça, j'te parle pus jamais! Choisis! C'est l'club, ou c'est moé! Si tu savais la peine que tu me fais! Une amie d'toujours! Une coureuse de clubs! Mais que c'est qu'tu dois avoir l'air, Angéline! Pour que c'est que l'monde doivent te prendre en t'voyant rentrer là? Pis surtout où Pierrette travaille! Y a pas plus trou! Y faut pus qu'tu r'tournes là jamais, Angéline! M'entends-tu? Sinon c'est fini entre nous deux! Tu devrais avoir honte!

ANGELINE SAUVE: Y faut pas m'demander de pus y r'tourner, Rhéauna! Mais réponds-moé donc!

RHEAUNA BIBEAU: J'te parle pus tant qu'tu promettras pas!

(L'éclairage redevient normal. Angéline s'assoit dans un coin, Pierrette Guérin vient la rejoindre.)

ANGELINE SAUVE: Que c'est que t'avais d'affaire à v'nir icitte, toé, à soir?

PIERRETTE GUERIN: Laisse-les donc parler. Y'aiment ça s'faire des drames à noirceur. Y savent ben dans l'fond qu'tu fais rien de mal au club. Dans cinq menutes, y y penseront plus!

ANGELINE SAUVE: Tu penses ça, toé? Pis Rhéauna, elle, que c'est qu't'en fais? Tu penses qu'à va m'pardonner ça d'même? Pis madame de Courval qui s'occupe des loisirs de la paroisse, pis qui est présidente de la Supplique à Notre-Dame du Perpétuel Secours![48] Tu penses qu'à va continuer à me parler? Pis tes soeurs qui peuvent pas te sentir justement parce que tu travailles dans un club! J'te dis qu'y'a pus rien à faire! Rien! Rien!

GERMAINE LAUZON: Pierrette!

PIERRETTE GUERIN: Ecoute, Germaine, Angéline a ben d'la peine, ça fait que c'est pas le temps de nous chicaner! Chus v'nue pour vous voir pis pour coller des timbres, pis j'veux rester! J'ai pas la lèpre! Laisse-nous tranquilles, toutes les deux, on va rester dans not'coin! Après la soirée, si tu veux, j'reviendrai pus jamais... Mais j'peux pas laisser Angéline tu-seule!

ANGELINE SAUVE: Tu peux t'en aller, si tu veux, Pierrette...

PIERRETTE GUERIN: Non, j'veux rester!

ANGELINE SAUVE: Bon, ben c'est moé qui va partir, d'abord!

LISETTE DE COURVAL: Si elles pourraient s'en aller toutes les deux!

(Angéline se lève.)

ANGELINE SAUVE, *à Rhéauna*: T'en viens-tu? *(Rhéauna Bibeau ne répond pas.)* Bon, c'est correct. J'vas laisser la porte débarrée... *(Elle se dirige vers la porte. Noir. Projecteur sur Angéline Sauvé.)* C'est facile de juger le monde. C'est facile de juger le monde mais y faut connaître les deux côtés d'la médaille! Le monde que j'ai rencontré dans c'te club-là, c'est mes meilleurs amis! Y'a jamais personne qui a été fin comme ça avec moé, avant! Même pas Rhéauna! Avec eux-autres, j'ai du fun; avec eux-autres, j'ris ! J'ai été élevée dans des salles paroissiales par des soeurs qui faisaient c'qu'y pouvaient mais qui connaissaient rien, les pauvres! J'ai appris à rire à cinquante-cinq ans! Comprenez-vous? J'ai appris à rire à cinquante-cinq ans! Pis par hasard! Parce que Pierrette m'a emmenée dans son club, un soir! J'voulais pas y aller! A l'a été obligée de me tirer par la queue de manteau! Mais sitôt que j'ai été rendue là, par exemple, j'ai compris c'que c'était que d'avoir passé toute une vie sans avoir de fun! Tout le monde peut pas avoir du fun dans les clubs, mais moé j'aime ça! C'est ben sûr que c'est pas vrai que j'prends juste un coke quand j'vas là! C'est ben sûr que j'prends d'la boésson! J'en prends pas gros mais ça me rend heureuse pareil! J'fais de mal à parsonne, j'me paye deux heures de plaisir par semaine! Mais y fallait que ça m'arrive un jour! J'le savais que j'finirais par me faire poigner! J'le savais! Que c'est que j'vas faire, mon Dieu, que c'est que j'vas faire! *(Un temps.)* Bonyeu! On devrait pourtant avoir le droit d'avoir un peu de fun, dans'vie! *(Un temps.)* J'me sus toujours dit que si j'me faisais prendre, j'arrêterais d'aller au club... mais j'sais pas si j'vas être capable! Pis Rhéauna acceptera jamais ça! *(Un temps.)* Après toute, Rhéauna vaut mieux que Pierrette. *(Long soupir.)* Fini les vacances!

(Elle sort. Projecteur sur Yvette Longpré.)

YVETTE LONGPRE: C'était la fête de ma belle-soeur Fleur-Ange, la semaine passée. Y y'ont faite un beau party. On était une grosse gang. D'abord, y'avait sa famille à elle, hein! Son mari, Oscar David, elle, Fleur-Ange David, pis leurs sept s'enfants: Raymonde, Claude, Lisette, Fernand, Réal, Micheline, pis Yves. Y'avait les parents de son mari: Aurèle David, pis sa dame Ozéa David. Y'avait ensuite la mère de ma belle-soeur, Blanche Tremblay. Son père était pas là, y'est mort... Ensuite, y'avait les autres invités: Antonio Fournier, pis sa femme Rita; Germaine Gervais était là, Wilfrid Gervais, Armand Gervais, Georges-Albert Gervais, Louis Thibault, Rose Campeau, Daniel Lemoyne, pis sa femme Rose-Aimée, Roger Joly, Hormidas Guay, Simonne Laflamme, Napoléon Gauvin, Anne-Marie Turgeon, Conrad Joannette, Léa Liasse, Jeannette Landreville, Nina Laplante, Robertine Portelance, Gilberte Morrissette, Laura Cadieux,[49] Rodolphe Quintal, Willie Sanregret, Lilianne Beaupré, Virginie Latour, Alexandre Thibodeau, Ovila Gariépy, Roméo Bacon, pis sa femme Juliette; Mimi Bleau, Pit Cadieux, Ludger Champagne, Rosaire Rouleau, Roger Chabot, Antonio Simard, Alexandrine Smith, Philémon Langlois, Eliane Meunier, Marcel Morel, Grégoire Cinq-Mars, Thodore Fortier, Hermine Héroux, pis nous autres, mon mari Euclide, pis moé. Bon, ben, c't'a peu près toute, j'pense...

(Les lumières s'allument.)

GERMAINE LAUZON: Bon, ben, on va continuer, là, hein?

ROSE OUIMET: Allons-y gaiement!

DES-NEIGES VERRETTE: On n'a pas mal de faite, hein? R'gardez, j'ai déjà toute ça de collé...

MARIE-ANGE BROUILLETTE : A part de c'que vous avez volé...[50]

LISETTE DE COURVAL: Passez-moé dons des timbres, madame Lauzon.

GERMAINE LAUZON: Ah! oui... certain... T'nez, en v'là en masse!

RHEAUNA BIBEAU: Angéline! Angéline! C'est pas possible!

LINDA LAUZON, *à Pierrette*: Allô, ma tante!

PIERRETTE GUERIN: Salut, comment ça va?

LINDA LAUZON: Ah! ça va pas ben ben... J'me chicane toujours avec ma mère, pis chus ben tannée! On est toujours après s'astiner pour rien. Eh! si j'pouvais donc m'en aller!

GERMAINE LAUZON: Les retraites vont commencer ben vite, hein?[51]

ROSE OUIMET: Ben oui! Y'ont dit ça, à messe, dimanche passé.

MARIE-ANGE BROUILLETTE : J'espère que ça s'ra pas le même prêtre que l'année passée, qui va v'nir...

GERMAINE LAUZON: Moé aussi! J'l'ai pas aimé, lui! Y'était ennuyant à mort!

PIERRETTE GUERIN: Entéka, y'a rien qui t'empêche de partir! Tu pourrais v'nir rester avec moé...

LINDA LAUZON: Vous y pensez pas! Des plans pour qu'y veulent pus jamais me voir!

LISETTE DE COURVAL: Non, ce n'est pas le même qui va venir, cette année...

DES-NEIGES VERRETTE: Non? Qui c'est, d'abord?

LISETTE DE COURVAL: Un dénommé monsieur l'abbé Rochon. Il paraît qu'il est formidable! L'abbé Gagné m'a justement dit l'autre jour que c'était un de ses meilleurs amis...

ROSE OUIMET, *à Gabrielle*: La v'là qui r'commence avec son abbé Gagné! On n'a pour toute la nuit, certain! On dirait quasiment qu'est en amour avec! Monsieur l'abbé Gagné par icitte, monsieur l'abbé Gagné par là... Ben moé l'abbé Gagné, là, j'l'aime pas ben ben...

GABRIELLE JODOIN: Ni moé non plus ! Y'est un peu trop à'mode. C'est ben beau de s'occuper des loisirs d'la paroisse, mais faut quand même pas oublier qu'on est prêtre! Homme de Dieu!

LISETTE DE COURVAL: Ah! oui, c'est un saint homme... Vous devriez le connaître, madame Dubuc, vous l'aimeriez ben gros... Quand il perle, là, c'est comme si ça serait le bon Dieu lui-même qui nous perlerait !

THERESE DUBUC: Faudrait pas exagérer...

LISETTE DE COURVAL: J'vous le dis! Les enfants l'adorent... Hon! Ça me fait penser... Les enfants d'la paroisse organisent une soirée récréative pour dans un mois. J'espère que vous allez toutes venir, ce sera une soirée formidable! Ça fait déjà pas mal longtemps qu'ils se pratiquent, aux loisirs...

DES-NEIGES VERRETTE: Que c'est qui va y avoir, au juste?

LISETTE DE COURVAL: Ah! ça va être bien bon. Y va y avoir toutes sortes de numéros. Le petit garçon de madame Gladu va chanter...

ROSE OUIMET: Encore? Y me tanne, lui. Chus ben tannée de l'entendre! A part de ça, depuis qu'y'a passé à'télévision, là, sa mère porte pus à terre! A se prend pour une vraie vedette!

LISETTE DE COURVAL: Mais il chante si bien, le petit Raymond!

ROSE OUIMET: Ouais... Moé, j'trouve qu'y'a un peu trop l'air d'une fille avec sa p'tite bouche en trou de cul de poule...[52]

GABRIELLE JODOIN: Rose!

LISETTE DE COURVAL: Diane Aubin va donner une démonstration de nage aquatique...[53] On va faire la fête à côté de la piscine municipale, ça va être de toute beauté...

ROSE OUIMET: Pis, y va-tu y avoir des prix de présence?

LISETTE DE COURVAL: Bien oui, hein, vous pensez bien! Et puis la soirée va se terminer par un grand bingo!

LES AUTRES FEMMES, *moins les quatre jeunes*: Un bingo!

OLIVINE DUBUC: Bingo!

(Noir. Quand les lumières reviennent, les neuf femmes sont debout au bord de la scène.)

LISETTE DE COURVAL: Ode au bingo!

OLIVINE DUBUC: Bingo!

(Pendant que Rose, Germaine, Gabrielle, Thérèse et Marie-Ange récitent 'l'ode au bingo', les quatre autres femmes crient des numéros de bingo en contrepoint, d'une façon très rythmée).

GERMAINE, ROSE, GABRIELLE, THERESE ET MARIE-ANGE: Moé, l'aime ça le bingo! Moé, j'adore le bingo! Moé, y'a rien au monde que j'aime plus que le bingo! Presque toutes les mois, on en prépare un dans' paroisse! J'me prépare deux jours d'avance, chus t'énarvée, chus pas tenable, j'pense rien qu'à ça. Pis quand le grand jour arrive, j't'assez excité que chus pas capable de rien faire dans'maison! Pis là, là, quand le soir arrive, j'me mets sur mon trente-six, pis y'a pas un ouragan qui m'empêcherait d'aller chez celle qu'on va jouer! Moé, j'aime ça, le bingo! Moé, c'est ben simple, j'adore ça, le bingo! Moé, y'a rien au monde que j'aime plus que le bingo! Quand on arrive, on se déshabille pis on rentre tu-suite dans l'appartement ousqu'on va jouer. Des fois, c'est le salon que la femme a vidé, des fois, aussi, c'est la cuisine, pis même, des fois, c'est une chambre à coucher. Là, on s'installe aux tables, on distribue les cartes, on met nos pitounes gratis, pis la partie commence! *(Les femmes qui crient des numéros continuent seules quelques secondes.)* Là, c'est ben simple, j'viens folle! Mon Dieu, que c'est donc excitant, c't'affaire-là! Chus toute à l'envers, j'ai chaud, j'comprends les numéros de travers, j'mets mes pitounes à mauvaise place, j'fais répéter celle qui crie les numéros, chus dans toutes mes états! Moé, j'aime ça, le bingo! Moé, c'est ben simple, j'adore ça, le bingo! Moé, y' rien au monde que j'aime plus que le bingo! La partie achève! J'ai trois chances! Deux par en haut, pis une de travers! C'est le B 14 qui me manque! C'est le B 14 qui me faut! C'est B 14 que je veux! Le B14! Le B 14! Je r'garde les autres... Verrat, y'ont autant de chances que moé! Que c'est que j'vas faire! Y faut que je gagne! Y faut que j'gagne! Y faut que j'gagne!

LISETTE DE COURVAL: B 14![54]

LES CINQ FEMMES: Bingo! bingo! J'ai gagné! J'le savais! J'avais ben que trop de chances! J'ai gagné! Que c'est que j'gagne, donc?

LISETTE DE COURVAL: Le mois passé, c'était le mois des chiens de plâtre pour t'nir les portes, c'mois icitte, c'est le mois des lampes torchères!

LES NEUF FEMMES: Moé, j'aime ça, le bingo! Moé, c'est ben simple, j'adore ça, le bingo! Moé, y'a rien au monde que j'aime plus que le bingo! C'est donc de valeur qu'y'en aye pas plus souvent! J's'rais tellement plus heureuse! Vive les chiens de plâtre! Vive les lampes torchères! Vive le bingo!

(Eclairage général.)

ROSE OUIMET: Ouan, ben moé, j'commence à avoir soif!

GERMAINE LAUZON: Mon Dieu, c'est vrai, les liqueurs! Linda, passe donc les cokes!

OLIVINE DUBUC: Coke... coke... oui... oui... coke...

THERESE DUBUC: T'nez-vous donc tranquille, madame Dubuc, vous allez en avoir comme tout le monde, du coke! Mais vous avez besoin de boire proprement, par exemple! Pas de renvoyage comme l'aut'fois, là!

ROSE OUIMET: Moé, a m'énarve avec sa belle-mère, elle, c'est ben simple...

GABRIELLE JODOIN: Rose, prends sur toé! Y'a déjà eu assez de chicane comme c'est là! Tu veux d'aut'drames?

GERMAINE LAUZON: Ben oui, reste tranquille, un peu! Pis colle! Tu fais rien!

(Projecteur sur le frigidaire. La scène qui suit doit se passer 'dans la porte du réfrigérateur'.)

LISE PAQUETTE, *à Linda*: Y faut que j'te parle, Linda...

LINDA LAUZON: Oui, j'sais, tu me l'as déjà dit au restaurant... Mais c'est pas ben ben l'temps...

LISE PAQUETTTE: Ça s'ra pas long. Y faut absolument que j'le dise à quelqu'un. T'es ma meilleure amie, Linda, ça fait que j'veux que tu sois la première à savoir... J'peux pus le cacher, j'ai trop de peine... Linda, j'vas avoir un p'tit!

LINDA LAUZON: Quoi! Viens-tu folle! Est-tu sûre?

LISE PAQUETTE: Ben oui. C'est le docteur qui me l'a dit!

LINDA LAUZON: Mais que c'est que tu vas faire?

LISE PAQUETTE: J'le sais ben pas! Si tu savais comme chus découragée! J'ai encore rien dit à mes parents, tu comprends. J'ai trop peur de me faire tuer par mon père! Quand le docteur m'a dit ça, c'est ben simple, j'aurais pu me sacrer en bas du balcon...

PIERRETTE GUERIN: Ecoute, Lise...

LINDA LAUZON: Vous avez entendu?

PIERRETTE GUERIN: Oui. T'es ben amanchée là ma fille. Mais... j'pourrais p't'être t'aider...

LISE PAQUETTE: Ah! oui? Comment ça?

PIERRETTE GUERIN: Ben, j'connais un docteur...

LINDA LAUZON: Vous y pensez pas, ma tante!

PIERRETTE GUERIN: Voyons, y'a pas de danger... Y'en fait deux-trois par semaine, c'te docteur-là!

LISE PAQUETTE: Faut dire que j'y avais déjà pensé... Mais je connaissais pas personne...[55] pis j'avais peur d'essayer tu-seule.

PIERRETTE GUERIN: Fais jamais ça! Ça, c'est dangereux! Mais avec mon docteur... Si tu veux, j'peux toute arranger. Dans une semaine d'icitte, tout s'rait arrangé!

LINDA LAUZON: Lise, t'as pas envie d'accepter! Ça s'rait un vrai crime!

LISE PAQUETTE: Que c'est que tu veux que je fasse d'autre? Y'a pas d'aut'moyen de m'en sortir! Pis chus quand même pas pour le laisser v'nir, c't'enfant-là! Tu vois c'que Manon Bélair est devenue? Elle aussi, c'était une fille-mère. Astheur est pris avec un p'tit sur les bras pis a'n'arrache sans bon sens!

LINDA LAUZON: Le père, y peut pas te marier?

LISE PAQUETTE: T'sais ben qu'y m'a laissé tomber, hein? Y'est disparu dans'brume, ça pas été long! Les belles promesses qu'y m'avait faites! On était donc pour être heureux, ensemble! Y faisait d'l'argent comme de l'eau, ça fait que moé, la folle, j'voyais pus clair! Des cadeaux par icitte, des cadeaux par là, y finissait pus! Ah! j'en ai ben profité, un temps. Mais maudit, y fallait que ça arrive! Y fallait que ça arrive! Maudite marde! J'ai jamais de chance, jamais! Y faut toujours que j'reçoive un siau de marde su'à tête! Mais j'veux tellement sortir de ma crasse! Chus t'écoeurée de travailler au Kresge![56] J'veux arriver à queq'chose, dans'vie, vous comprenez, j'veux arriver à queq'chose! J'veux avoir un char, un beau logement, du beau linge! J'ai quasiment rien que des uniformes de restaurant à me mettre sur le dos, bonyeu! J'ai toujours été pauvre, j'ai toujours tiré le diable par la queue, pis j'veux que ça change! J'sais que chus cheap, mais j'veux m'en sortir! Chus v'nue au monde par la porte d'en arrière, mais m'as donc sortir par la porte d'en avant![57] Pis y'a rien qui va m'en empêcher! Y'a rien qui va m'arrêter! Tu sauras me dire plus tard que j'avais raison, Linda! Attends deux-trois ans, pis tu vas voir que Lise Paquette a va devenir quelqu'un ! Des cennes, a va n'avoir, O.K.?

LINDA LAUZON: Tu commences mal!

LISE PAQUETTE: C'est justement, j'ai faite une erreur pis j'veux la réparer! J'vas recommencer en neuf, après! Vous Pierrette, vous devriez comprendre ça?

PIERRETTE GUERIN: Oui, j'te comprends. J'sais c'que c'est de vouloir gagner ben d'l'argent. Prends moé, par exemple, à ton âge, chus partie de chez nous pour faire de l'argent. Mais j'ai pas commencé par travailler dans les quinze cennes, par exemple. Ah! non, chus rentrée au club tu-suite! Là, y'avait d'l'argent à faire! Pis ça s'ra pas long que j'vas avoir le gros mâgot, moé aussi! Johnny me l'a promis...

ROSE, GERMAINE, GABRIELLE: Maudit Johnny! Maudit Johnny!

GINETTE MENARD: Que c'est qui se passe icitte, donc?

LISE PAQUETTE: Rien, rien. *(A Pierrette.)* On en reparlera...

GINETTE MENARD: De quoi, donc?

LISE PAQUETTE: Ah! Laisse faire!

GINETTE MENARD: Tu veux rien me dire?

LISE PAQUETTE: Laisse-moé donc tranquille, toé, colleuse!

PIERRETTE GUERIN: Viens là-bas, on va continuer à jaser...

GERMAINE LAUZON: Ça arrive pas, ces liqueurs-là?

LINDA LAUZON: Me v'là, me v'là... *(Les lumières se rallument.)*

GABRIELLE JODOIN: Combien tu l'as payé, donc, ton p'tit costume bleu, Rose?

ROSE OUIMET: Quel, donc?

GABRIELLE JODOIN: T'sais ben, le p'tit costume bleu avec du braidage blanc autour du collet.

ROSE OUIMET: Ah! c'ui-là... J'l'ai payé $9.98.

GABRIELLE JODOIN: Me semblait ben, aussi! Imagine-toé donc que j'l'ai vu, chez Reitman's, aujourd'hui, à $14.98...

ROSE OUIMET: Es-tu folle! J'l'avais ben dit, hein, que j'le payais pas cher...

GABRIELLE JODOIN: Mon étronne, toé! T'es donc bonne pour trouver des bargains!

LISETTE DE COURVAL: Ma fille Micheline a changé d'emploi, dernièrement.

Elle travaille maintenant sur les machines F.B.I.[58]

MARIE-ANGE BROUILLETTE: Ah! oui? Y paraît que c'est mortel pour les nerfs, ces machines-là! Les filles qui travaillent là-dessus sont obligées de changer au bout de six mois. La fille de ma belle-soeur Simonne a faite une dépression narveuse, là-dessus. Simonne m'a appelé, justement, aujourd'hui pour me conter ça...

ROSE OUIMET: Mon Dieu, ça me fait penser, Linda, t'es demandée au téléphone!

(Linda se précipite sur le téléphone.)

LINDA LAUZON: Allô, Robert? Ça fait-tu longtemps que t'attends?

GINETTE MENARD: Dis-moi-lé donc!

LISE PAQUETTE: Non! Es-tu achalante! Arrête donc de coller après moé comme une sangsue! Laisse-moé parler à Pierrette, un peu! Envoye, chenaille!

GINETTE MENARD: Bon, c'est correct, j'ai compris! T'es ben contente de m'avoir quand y'a personne, mais aussitôt qu'y'arrive quelqu'un, par exemple...

LINDA LAUZON: Ecoute, Robert... ben oui, ça fait cinq fois que j'te dis qu'y viennent juste de m'avertir! C'est pas de ma faute!

THERESE DUBUC: T'nez, cachez ça, madame Dubuc!

ROSE OUIMET, *à Ginette Ménard qui distribue les cokes*: Comment ça va, chez vous, Ginette?

GINETTE MENARD: Ah! c'est toujours pareil... Y se battent à coeur de jour... C'est pas nouveau. La mère continue à boire... Le père se fâche... Ça fait des chicanes à pus finir...

ROSE OUIMET: Pauv'p'tite... Pis ta soeur?

GINETTE MENARD: Suzanne? C'est toujours la smatte d'la famille! Sont toutes pâmés devant elle! Y'a rien qu'elle qui compte. 'Ça c't'une bonne fille. Tu devrais faire comme elle, Ginette. A l'a réussi, dans la vie, elle.' Moé, j'compte pas. Ils l'ont toujours aimée plus que moé. J'le sais. Pis astheur qu'est rendue maîtresse d'école, vous comprenez, c'est pus des maudites farces!

ROSE OUIMET: Ben non, voyons, Ginette, pour moé, t'exagères un peu.

GINETTE MENARD: J'sais c'que j'dis ! Ma mère s'est jamais occupée de moé! C'est toujours Suzanne la plus belle, Suzanne la plus fine. J'ai mon voyage d'entendre ça à coeur de jour! Même Lise s'occupe pus de moé!

LINDA LAUZON, *au téléphone*: Ah! pis sacre-moé patience! Si tu veux rien comprendre, que c'est que tu veux que j'te dise? Quand tu s'ras plus de bonne humeur, tu me rappelleras! *(Elle raccroche.)* Vous auriez pas pu me le dire avant que j'étais demandée au téléphone, non? Y m'a lâché un paquet de bêtises à cause de vous, ma tante!

ROSE OUIMET: Est ben bête! Non, mais est ben bête, c't'enfant-là!

(Projecteur sur Pierrette Guérin.)

PIERRETTE GUERIN: Quand chus partie de chez nous, j'étais en amour par-dessus la tête. J'voyais pus clair. Y'avait rien que Johnny qui comptait pour moé. Y m'a faite pardre dix ans de ma vie, le crisse! J'ai rien que trente ans pis j'me sens comme si j'en arais soixante! Y m'en a tu fait faire, des affaires, c'gars-là! Moé, la niaiseuse, j'l'écoutais! Envoye donc! J'ai travaillé pour lui, au club, pendant dix ans! J'étais belle, j'attirais la clientèle. Tant que ça duré, ça allait ben... Mais là... Bâtard, que chus tannée! J'me crisserais en bas d'un pont, c'est pas mêlant! Tout ce qui me reste à faire, c'est de me soûler. Pis c'est c'que j'fais depuis vendredi. Pauv'Lise, a s'lamente parce qu'est enceinte, pis qu'est mal pris! Mais bonyeu, est jeune, elle, j'vas y donner l'adresse de mon docteur, pis toute va s'arranger, a va pouvoir toute recommencer en neuf. Pas moé! Pas moé! Chus trop vieille! Une fille qui a faite la vie pendant dix ans, ça poigne pus! Chus finie! Pis essayez donc d'expliquer ça à mes soeurs. Comprendront rien! J'le sais pas c'que j'vas devenir, j'le sais pas pantoute!

LISE PAQUETTE, *à l'autre bout de la cuisine*: J'le sais pas c'que j'vas devenir, j'le sais pas pantoute! Se faire avorter, c'est pas une petite affaire! J'ai entendu assez d'histoires là-dessus! Pis c'est pire quand on fait ça nous-autres mêmes, ça fait que chus mieux d'aller voir le docteur à Pierrette! Ah! pourquoi que ça m'arrive toujours à moé, ces affaires-là! Est chanceuse, elle, Pierrette, a travaille dans le même club depuis dix ans, a fait d'l'argent comme de l'eau, pis est en amour. Ah! que j'l'envie donc! Même si sa famille l'aime pas, au moins est heureuse de son bord!

PIERRETTE GUERIN: Y m'a laissé tomber comme une roche! Tiens, fini, n-i, ni! Veux pus te voir! T'es trop vieille, astheur, t'es trop laide! Fais tes bagages, pis débarrasse! Pus besoin de toé! Ben l'écoeurant, y m'a pas laissé une cenne! Pas une maudite cenne noire! Après toute c'que j'ai faite pour lui pendant dix ans! Dix ans! Dix ans pour rien! C'est pas assez pour se tuer, ça, vous pensez? Que c'est que j'vas d'venir, moé, hein? Que c'est que j'vas d'venir? Une p'tite waitress cheap du Kresge comme Lise? Ah! non, marci ben! Le Kresge, c'est bon pour les débutantes pis les mères de famille, pas pour les filles comme moé! Je le sais pas c'que j'vas d'venir, je le sais pas pantoute! Pis chus t'obligée de faire la smatte, icitte! Chus pas pour dire à Linda pis à Lise que chus finie! *(Silence.)* Ouais... Y me reste pus rien que la boisson, astheur... Une chance que j'aime ça...

LISE PAQUETTE, *à plusieurs reprises pendant le monologue de Pierrette:* J'ai peur, bonyeu, j'ai peur! *(Elle s'approche de Pierrette et se jette dans ses bras.)* Es-tu sûre que ça va ben aller, Pierrette? Si tu savais comme j'ai peur!

PIERRETTE GUERIN, *en riant:* Ben oui, ben oui, toute va s'arranger, tu vas voir, toute va s'arranger... *(L'éclairage redevient normal.)*

MARIE-ANGE BROUILLETTE , *à Des-Neiges*: On n'est même pus en sécurité aux vues! L'aut'jour, chus t'allée voir une vieille vue d'Eddie Constantine.[59] Mon mari était resté à la maison. Au beau milieu d'la vue, v'là t'y pas un espèce de vieux écœurant qui vient s'asseoir à côté de moé, pis qui commence à me tâter! J'étais assez gênée, c'est ben simple! Mais ça fait rien, j'me sus levée, pis j'y ai sacré un coup de sacoche en pleine face!

DES-NEIGES VERRETTE: Vous avez donc ben faite! Moé, j'emporte toujours une épingle à chapeau avec moé quand j'vas aux vues. On sait jamais c'qui peut arriver. Pis le premier qui viendrait essayer de me tâter... Mais j'ai jamais eu à m'en servir.

ROSE OUIMET: Sont pas mal chauds, tes cokes, Germaine.

GERMAINE LAUZON: Quand est-ce que tu vas arrêter de critiquer, hein, quand est-ce que tu vas arrêter?

LISE PAQUETTE: Linda, as-tu un crayon pis un papier?

LINDA LAUZON: J'te le dis, Lise, fais pas ça!

LISE PAQUETTE: J'sais c'que j'ai à faire! Chus décidée pis y'a rien qui va me faire changer d'idée!

RHEAUNA BIBEAU, *à Thérèse*: Que c'est que vous faites là, donc?

THERESE DUBUC: Chut! Pas si fort! Vous devriez faire pareil! Deux-trois livrets, ça paraît pas.

RHEAUNA BIBEAU: Chus pas une voleuse!

THERESE DUBUC: Voyons donc, mademoiselle Bibeau, y'est pas question de voler! A les a eus pour rien, ces timbres-là! Pis a n'a un million! Un million!

RHEAUNA BIBEAU: Tant que vous voudrez! A nous a invitées pour venir coller ses timbres, on est toujours ben pas pour en profiter pour y voler!

GERMAINE LAUZON, *à Rose*: De quoi y parlent, ces deux-là, donc? J'aime pas les messes basses! *(Elle s'approche de Rhéauna et de Thérèse.)*

THERESE DUBUC, *la voyant venir:* Heu... ben oui... vous ajoutez deux tasses d'eau, pis vous brassez.

RHEAUNA BIBEAU: Quoi? *(Apercevant Germaine.)* Ah! Oui! A me donnait une recette!

GERMAINE LAUZON: Une recette de quoi, donc?

RHEAUNA BIBEAU: Des beignes!

THERESE DUBUC: Une poudigne au chocolat!

GERMAINE LAUZON: Ben, entendez-vous, c't'une poudigne, ou bedonc des beignes! *(Elle revient vers Rose.)* J'te dis, Rose, qu'y se passe des choses pas correctes, icitte, à soir.

ROSE OUIMET, *qui vient de cacher quelques livrets dans son sac à main*: Ben non, ben non... C'est des idées que tu te fais...

GERMAINE LAUZON: Pis j'trouve que Linda reste un peu trop longtemps avec sa tante Pierrette! Linda, viens icitte...

LINDA LAUZON: Une menute, moman...

GERMAINE LAUZON: J't'ai dit de v'nir icitte! C'est pas pour demain, c'est pour aujourd'hui!

LINDA LAUZON: O.K. Enarvez-vous pas de même pour rien! Oui, que c'est qu'y'a, là?

GABRIELLE JODOIN: Reste avec nous autres, un peu... Tu te tiens pas mal trop avec ta tante...

LINDA LAUZON: Pis? Que c'est que ça peut ben faire?

GERMAINE LAUZON: Mais que c'est qu'a l'a à tant jaser avec ton amie Lise, donc?

LINDA LAUZON: Ah... rien...

GERMAINE LAUZON: Réponds donc comme du monde, quand on te parle!

GABRIELLE JODOIN: Lise a écrit quelque chose, tout à l'heure.

LINDA LAUZON: C'tait une adresse...

GERMAINE LAUZON: Dis-moé pas qu'a l'a pris l'adresse de Pierrette, toujours! Si jamais j'apprends que t'as été chez ta tante, toé, tu vas avoir affaire à moé, tu m'as compris?

LINDA LAUZON: Laissez-moé donc tranquille! Chus t'assez vieille pour savoir c'que j'ai à faire!

(Elle retourne auprès de Pierrette.)

ROSE OUIMET: C'est peut-être pas de mes affaires, Germaine, mais...

GERMAINE LAUZON: Quoi, donc, que c'est qu'y'a encore!

ROSE OUIMET: Ta fille Linda est sur une pente ben dangereuse...

GERMAINE LAUZON: J'le sais ben que trop ben! Mais fais-toé s'en pas, Rose, j'vas y voir! Pis j'te dis qu'a va revenir dans le droit chemin, ça prendra pas gouttinette! Pis la Pierrette, là, c'est la dernière fois qu'a met les pieds icitte! M'as la sacrer dehors, frette, net, sec, les cheveux coupés en balai!

MARIE-ANGE BROUILLETTE : Vous avez pas remarqué que la fille de madame Bergeron a engraissé depuis quequ'temps?

LISETTE DE COURVAL: Oui, j'ai remarqué ça...

THERESE DUBUC, *insinuante*: C'est drôle, hein, a l'engraisse rien que du ventre.

ROSE OUIMET: Faut croire que les érables ont coulé plus de bonne heure c't'année!

MARIE-ANGE BROUILLETTE : A l'essaye de le cacher, à part de ça. Mais ça commence à paraitre un peu trop!

THERESE DUBUC: J'comprends donc! J'sais pas qui c'est qui y'a fait ça, par exemple, hein?

LISETTE DE COURVAL: Ça doit être son beau-père...

GERMAINE LAUZON: Ça me surprendrait pas pantoute. Y court assez après elle depuis qu'y'a marié sa mère!

THERESE DUBUC: Ça doit pas être beau à voir dans c'te maison-là! Pauvre Monique, est ben jeune...

ROSE OUIMET: Ah ben, y faut dire qu'a l'a pas mal couru après pareil! Pour s'habiller comme a s'habille, ça prend une pas grand-chose! Moé, l'été passé, c'est ben simple, a me gênait! Pourtant chus pas scrupuleuse! J'sais pas si vous vous rappelez de ses shorts rouges... y'étaient short all right! J'l'ai toujours dit qu'à tournerait mal, Monique Bergeron! Ça l'a le yable au corps, c'te fille-là! Une vraie possédée! D'ailleurs, est rousse. Non, y'ont beau dire, dans les vues françaises que les filles-mères font pitié, moé, j'trouve pas!

(Lise Paquette fait un geste pour se lever.)

PIERRETTE GUERIN: Non, prends sur toé, Lise!

ROSE OUIMET: Ecoutez donc, on se fait pas prendre de même! Ah! j'parle pas de celles qui se font violer, là, ça, c'est pas la même chose; mais les filles ordinaires qui attrapent un p'tit, là, ben j'les plains pas pantoute! C'est ben de valeur! J'vous dis que j'voudrais pas que ma Carmen m'arrive ammanchée de même, parce qu'a passerait par le châssis, ça s'rait pas long! Mais y'a pas de danger que ça y'arrive, est ben que trop demoiselle pour ça! Non, pour moé, là, les filles-mères, c'est des bon-riennes pis des vicieuses qui courent après les hommes! Mon mari appelle ça des agace-pissettes, lui!

LISE PAQUETTE: Si a se farme pas tu-suite, j'la tue!

GINETTE MENARD: Pourquoi ? Moé, j'trouve qu'a l'a pas mal raison!

LISE PAQUETTE: Ah ! toé, va t'en, va t'en avant que j't'étrippe!

PIERRETTE GUERIN: Tu y vas un peu fort, Rose!

ROSE OUIMET: On sait ben, toé, tu dois t'être habituée d'en voir, des affaires de même! Y'a pus rien qui doit te surprendre! Tu dois trouver ça normal! Ben pas nous autres! Y'a quand même moyen d'éviter...

PIERRETTE GUERIN, *en riant:* Oui, c'est vrai, j'en connais quequ's'uns. Les pilules anti-contraceptives, par exemple...[60]

ROSE OUIMET: Y'a pas moyen de te parler, toé! C'est pas c'que j'voulais dire! Tu sauras que chus pas pour l'amour libre, moé! Chus catholique! Reste donc dans ton monde pis laisse-nous donc tranquilles! Maudite guidoune!

LISETTE DE COURVAL: J'trouve quand même que vous exagérez, madame Ouimet. Des fois, les filles qui se font prendre, ce ne sont pas toujours de leur faute.

ROSE OUIMET: Vous, vous croyez toute c'qu'on vous dit dans les vues françaises.

LISETTE DE COURVAL: Que c'est que vous avez contre les vues françaises, donc?

ROSE OUIMET: J'ai rien contre, mais j'aime mieux les vues anglaises, c'est toute! Les vues françaises, c'est trop réaliste, trop exagéré! Y faut pas tout croire c'qu'y disent! Dans les vues, les filles-mères font toujours pitié sans bon sens, pis c'est jamais de leur faute. Vous en connaissez, vous, des cas de même? Moé, j'en connais pas! Une vue, c't'une vue, pis la vie, c'est la vie!

LISE PAQUETTE: M'a la tuer, la calvaire! Grosse maudite sans dessine! Ça se parmet de juger le monde, pis ça pas plus de tête... Ben sa Carmen, là, hein, j'la connais sa Carmen, pis j'vous dis que ça vaut pas cher la varge! Qu'a regarde donc dans sa propre maison avant de chier su'à tête du monde!

(Projecteur sur Rose Ouimet.)

ROSE OUIMET: Oui, la vie, c'est la vie, pis y'a pas une crisse de vue française qui va arriver à décrire ça! Ah! c'est facile pour une actrice de faire pitié dans les vues! J'cré ben! Quand à l'a fini de travailler, le soir, à rentre dans sa grosse maison de cent mille piasses, pis à se couche dans son lit deux fois gros comme ma chambre à coucher! Mais quand on se réveille, nous autres, le matin... *(Silence.)* Quand moé j'me réveille, le matin, y'est toujours là qui me r'garde... Y m'attend. Tous les matins que le bonyeu emmène, y se réveille avant moé, pis y m'attend! Pis tous les soirs que le bonyeu emmène, y se couche avant moé, pis y m'attend! Y'est toujours là, y'est toujours après moé, collé après moé comme une sangsue! Maudit cul! Ah! ça, y le disent pas dans les vues, par exemple! Ah! non, c'est des choses qui se disent pas, ça! Qu'une femme soye obligée d'endurer un cochon toute sa vie parce qu'à l'a eu le malheur d'y dire 'oui' une fois, c'est pas assez intéressant, ça! Ben bonyeu, c'est ben plus triste que ben des vues! Parce que ça dure toute une vie, ça! *(Silence.)* J'l'ai-tu assez r'gretté, mais j'l'ai-tu assez r'gretté. J'arais jamais dû me marier! J'arais dû crier 'non' à pleins poumons, pis rester vieille fille! Au moins, j'arais eu la paix! C'est vrai que j'étais ignorante dans ce temps-là pis que je savais pas c'qui m'attendait! Moé, l'épaisse, j'pensais rien qu'à 'la Sainte Union du Marriage'! Faut-tu être bête pour élever ses enfants dans l'ignorance de même, mais faut-tu être bête! Ben, moé, ma Carmen, à s'f'ra pas poigner de même, ok? Parce que moé, ma Carmen, ça fait longtemps que j'y ai dit c'qu'valent les hommes! Ça, a pourra pas dire que j'l'ai pas avartie! *(Au bord des larmes.)* Pis a finira pas comme moé, à quarante-quatre ans, avec une p'tit gars de quatre ans sur les bras pis un écœurant de mari qui veut rien comprendre, pis qui demande son dû deux fois par jour, trois cent soixante-cinq jours par année! Quand t'arrive à quarante ans pis que tu t'aparçois que t'as rien en arrière de toé, pis que t'as rien en avant de toé, ça te donne envie de toute crisser là, pis de toute recommencer en neuf! Mais les femmes, y peuvent pas faire ça... Les femmes, sont poignées à'gorge, pis y vont rester de même jusqu'au boute![61]

(Eclairage général.)

GABRIELLE JODOIN: En tout cas, les vues françaises, moé, j'aime ça! Eh ! qu'y'ont donc le tour de faire des belles vues tristes, eux-autres! J'vous dis qu'y'ont pas de misère à me faire brailler! Pis y faut dire que les Français sont ben plus beaux que les Canadiens! Des vraies pièces d'hommes!

GERMAINE LAUZON: Ah! ben non par exemple, là j't'arrête! Là, t'as menti!

MARIE-ANGE BROUILLETTE: Les Français, c'est toute des p'tits bas-culs qui me viennent même pas à l'épaule! Pis y sont ben trop efféminés! Y'ont toute l'air de vraies femmes!

GABRIELLE JODOIN: J'vous demande ben pardon! Y'en a qui sont hommes! Pis autrement hommes que nos pauvres maris!

GERMAINE LAUZON: Ah! J'cré ben, si tu prends nos maris comme exemple! On mélange pas les torchons pis les sarviettes![62] Nos maris, c'est ben sûr qu'y font durs, mais prends nos acteurs, là, sont aussi beaux pis aussi bons que n'importe quel Français de France!

GABRIELLE JODOIN: En tout cas, moé, Jean Marais,[63] j'y f'rais pas mal! Ça, c't'un homme!

OLIVINE DUBUC: Coke... coke... encore... coke...

THERESE DUBUC: Taisez-vous donc, madame Dubuc!

OLIVINE DUBUC: Coke! Coke!

ROSE OUIMET: Ah! faites-là taire un peu, on s'entend pus coller! Donnes-y donc un coke, Germaine, ça va la boucher pour quequ'temps!

GERMAINE LAUZON: Ben, j'pense que j'en ai pus!

ROSE OUIMET: Bonyeu, t'en avais pas acheté gros! Tu ménages! Tu ménages!

RHEAUNA BIBEAU, *en volant des timbres*: Après toute, y m'en manque juste trois pour avoir mon porte-poussière chromé. *(Entre Angéline Sauvé.)*

ANGELINE SAUVE: Bonsoir... *(A Rhéauna.)* Chus rev'nue...

LES AUTRES, *sèchement*: Bonsoir...

ANGELINE SAUVE: J'ai été voir l'abbé de Castelneau...

PIERRETTE GUERIN: A m'a même pas regardée!

DES-NEIGES VERRETTE: Que c'est qu'à peut ben vouloir à mademoiselle Bibeau, donc?

MARIE-ANGE BROUILLETTE: Moé, chus certaine qu'a vient y demander pardon. Après toute, mademoiselle Sauvé, c't'une bonne personne, a sait comprendre le bon sens. Vous allez voir, tout va s'arranger pour le mieux.

GERMAINE LAUZON: En attendant, j'vas aller voir à combien de livrets qu'on est rendu.

(Les femmes se dressent sur leurs chaises.
Gabrielle Jodoin hésite, puis...)

GABRIELLE JODOIN: Hon! Germaine, j'ai oublié de te dire ça! J't'ai trouvé une corsetière! Une dame Angélina Giroux! Viens icitte, que j't'en parle!

RHEAUNA BIBEAU: J'savais que tu m'reviendrais, Angéline! Chus ben contente. Tu vas voir, on va prier ensemble, pis le bon Dieu va oublier ça ben vite! C'est pas un fou, t'sais, le bon Dieu!

LISE PAQUETTE: C'est ben ça, Pierrette, y sont raccordées!

PIERRETTE GUERIN: J'ai mon hostie de voyage!

ANGELINE SAUVE: J'vas quand même aller dire bonsoir à Pierrette, y expliquer...

RHEAUNA BIBEAU: Non, tu s'rais mieux de pus y parler pantoute! Reste avec moé, laisse-là faire, elle! C'est fini, c't'histoire-là!

ANGELINE SAUVE: Bon, comme tu voudras.

PIERRETTE GUERIN: Ça y'est. A l'a gagné! J'ai pus rien à faire icitte, moé, chus t'écœurée quequ'chose de rare! J'vas crisser mon camp!

GERMAINE LAUZON: T'es ben smatte, Gaby. J'commençais à désespérer, tu comprends. C'est pas n'importe qui qui peut me faire des corsets. J'vas aller la voir, la semaine prochaine. *(Elle se dirige vers la caisse aux livrets. Les femmes la suivent toutes du regard.)* Bonyeu, y'en a pas gros! Ousqu'y sont toutes, donc, les livrets? Y'en a rien qu'une dizaine, dans le fond! Y sont peut-être... non, la table est vide! *(Silence. Germaine Lauzon regarde toutes les femmes.)* Que c'est qui se passe icitte, donc?

LES AUTRES: Ben... heu... j'sais pas... franchement...

(Elles font semblant de chercher les livrets.
Germaine se poste devant la porte.)

GERMAINE LAUZON: Où sont mes timbres?

ROSE OUIMET: Ben, voyons, Germaine, cherche un peu!

GERMAINE LAUZON: Y sont pas dans la caisse, pis y sont pas sur la table! J'veux savoir où sont mes timbres!

OLIVINE DUBUC, *sortant des timbres cachés dans ses vêtements*: Timbres? Timbres... timbres... *(Elle rit.)*

THERESE DUBUC: Madamc Dubuc, cachez ça... Maudit, madame Dubuc!

MARIE-ANGE BROUILLETTE: Bonne Sainte-Anne!

DES-NEIGES VERRETTE: Priez pour nous!

GERMAINE LAUZON: Mais a n'a plein son linge! Mais que c'est ça, a n'a partout! Tiens, pis tiens... Thérèse... c'est pas vous, toujours.

THERESE DUBUC: Ben non, voyons , j'vous jure que j'savais pas!

GERMAINE LAUZON: Montrez-moé vot'sacoche!

THERESE DUBUC: Voyons donc, Germaine, si vous avez pas plus confiance en moé que ça.

ROSE OUIMET: Germaine, t'exagères!

GERMAINE LAUZON: Toé aussi, Rose, j'veux voir ta sacoche! J'veux toute voir vos sacoches! Toute la gang!

DES-NEIGES VERRETTE: J'refuse! C'est la première fois qu'on me manque de respect de même!

YVETTE LONGPRE: Oui, certain!

LISETTE DE COURVAL: Je ne remettrai plus jamais les pieds ici!

(Germaine Lauzon s'empare du sac de Thérèse et l'ouvre. Elle en sort plusieurs livrets.)

GERMAINE LAUZON: Hein? Hein? J'savais ben! j'suppose que c'est pareil dans les autres sacoches! Mes maudites vaches, par exemple! Vous sortirez pas d'icitte, vivantes! M'as toutes vous assommer!

PIERRETTE GUERIN: M'as t'aider, Germaine! Toute une gang de maudites voleuses! Pis ça vient lever le nez sur moé!

GERMAINE LAUZON: Montrez-moé toutes vos sacoches. *(Elle arrache le sac à Rose.)* Tiens... pis tiens! *(Elle prend un autre sac.)* Encore icitte. Pis tiens, encore! Vous aussi, mademoiselle Bibeau? Y'en a rien que trois, mais y'en a pareil!

ANGELINE SAUVE: Hon! Rhéauna! Toé aussi!

GERMAINE LAUZON: Toute! Toute la gang! Vous êtes toutes des écœurantes de voleuses!

MARIE-ANGE BROUILLETTE: Vous les méritez pas, ces timbres-là!

DES-NEIGES VERRETTE: Pourquoi vous plus qu'une autre, hein?

ROSE OUIMET: Tu nous a fait assez baver avec ton million de timbres!

GERMAINE LAUZON: Mais, c'est à moé ces timbres-là!

LISETTE DE COURVAL: Ils devraient être à tout le monde!

LES AUTRES: Oui, à tout le monde!

GERMAINE LAUZON: Mais sont à moé! Donnez-moé-les!

LES AUTRES: Jamais !

MARIE-ANGE BROUILLETTE: Y'en reste encore ben dans les caisses, servons-nous!

DES-NEIGES VERRETTE: Oui, certain!

YVETTE LONGPRE: J'vas remplir ma sacoche.

GERMAINE LAUZON: Arrêtez! Touchez-y pas!

THERESE DUBUC: T'nez, madame Dubuc, en v'là. T'nez, encore.

MARIE-ANGE BROUILLETTE: V'nez, mademoiselle Verrette, y'en a en masse, icitte. Aidez-moé.

PIERRETTE GUERIN: Lâchez ça tu-suite!

GERMAINE LAUZON: Mes timbres! Mes timbres!

ROSE OUIMET: Viens m'aider, Gaby, j'en ai trop pris!

GERMAINE LAUZON: Mes timbres! Mes timbres!

(Une grande bataille s'ensuit. Les femmes volent le plus de timbres qu'elles peuvent. Pierrette et Germaine essaient de les arrêter. Linda et Lise restent assises dans un coin et regardent le spectacle sans bouger. On entend des cris, quelques femmes se mettent à se battre.)

MARIE-ANGE BROUILLETTE: C'est à moé, ceux-là!

ROSE OUIMET: Vous avez ben menti, sont à moé!

LISETTE DE COURVAL, *à Gaby*: Voulez-vous ben m'lâcher! Voulez-vous ben m'lâcher!

(On commence à se lancer des livrets de timbres par la tête. Tout le monde pige à qui mieux mieux dans les caisses, on lance des timbres un peu partout, par la porte, par la fenêtre. Olivine Dubuc essaie de se promener avec sa chaise roulante et hurle le 'O Canada'. Quelques femmes sortent avec leur bagage de timbres. Rose et Gabrielle restent un peu plus longtemps que les autres.)

GERMAINE LAUZON: Mes soeurs! Mes propres soeurs! *(Gabrielle et Rose sortent. Il ne reste plus dans la cuisine que Germaine, Linda et Pierrette. Germaine s'écroule sur une chaise.)* Mes timbres! Mes timbres!

(Pierrette passe ses bras autour des épaules de Germaine.)

PIERRETTE GUERIN: Pleure pas, Germaine![64]

GERMAINE LAUZON: Parle-moé pas! Va-t'en! T'es pas mieux que les autres!

PIERRETTE GUERIN: Mais...

GERMAINE LAUZON: Va-t'en, j'veux pus te voir!

PIERRETTE GUERIN: Mais, j't'ai défendue! Chus t'avec toé, Germaine!

GERMAINE LAUZON: Va-t'en, laisse-moé tranquille! Parle-moé pus! J'veux pus voir parsonne!

(Pierrette sort lentement. Linda se dirige elle aussi vers la porte.)

LINDA LAUZON: Ça va être une vraie job, toute nettoyer ça!

GERMAINE LAUZON: Mon dieu! Mon dieu! Mes timbres! Y me reste pus rien! Rien! Rien! Ma belle maison neuve! Mes beaux meubles! Rien! Mes timbres! Mes timbres!

(Elle s'écroule devant une chaise et commence à ramasser les timbres qui traînent. Elle pleure à chaudes larmes. On entend toutes les autres à l'extérieur qui chantent le 'O Canada'.[65] *A mesure que l'hymne avance, Germaine retrouve son 'courage' et elle finit le 'O Canada' avec les autres, debout à l'attention, les larmes aux yeux. Une pluie de timbres tombe lentement du plafond.)*

RIDEAU

NOTES TO THE PLAY

1. The four huge boxes and their potential for causing trouble are reminiscent of Pandora's box in Classical mythology. See Richard Chadbourne, 'Michel Tremblay's "Adult Fairy Tales": The Theater as Realistic Fantasy. Once upon a time, in East Montreal...' *Quebec Studies* 10 (1990) p. 63.

2. Tremblay, stressing that 'Les charnières sont toujours dans les premières répliques', gives this opening line as one example: 'Le premier mot que j'aie écrit en québécois de ma vie, la première réplique de *Les Belles-Soeurs*, c'est "Misère moman, qu'est-cé ça?"' (Roch Turbide, 'Michel Tremblay: Du texte à la représentation', *Voix et images* 7 [1982], p. 216).

3. This explanation for the setting of the play seems awkward and unnecessary. The description of the bingo sessions in Act II, p. 41 makes it clear that it is likely that such gatherings of family and neighbours may take place in a kitchen or even in a bedroom as readily as in a 'salon'. It may be, though, that Linda's comment reflects Germaine's social pretentions and also shows how these are passed from mother to daughter.

4. The local cinema. The rue Amherst and the square Amherst are located near the Parc Lafontaine in francophone East Montreal.

5. Robert and Linda evidently both work in one of Montreal's shoe factories.

6. c'est pus des farces!: here 'You're talking real money'.

7. après ma journée à shop: after a day's work (in the factory).

8. The telephone serves in the play to underline the thematics of (failed) communication. Linda and Robert fail to 'connect' both here and later on. Germaine's telephone conversation with Rose is essentially a monologue.

9. être en (beau) verrat: 'to be cross, put-out, annoyed'. See also glossary, p. 83; 'verrat', literally 'the male pig, the boar' (in both France and Quebec), figures also in Quebec French in a variety of affective, often strongly negative expressions, including use as a swear-word. Tremblay's entertaining account of his frustration as a child with the dialogue form of the Comtesse de Ségur's children's story *L'Auberge de l'ange gardien* and the ensuing backchat with his mother flags both the literal and the affective meanings:

> 'C'est quand même pas toi qui vas montrer à la comtesse de Ségur comment écrire des livres, verrat!' Elle porte une main a sa bouche, l'autre à son coeur. 'Ça y est, y m'a faite sacrer un matin de Noël!' 'Grand-moman Tremblay a dit, l'autre jour, que 'verrat' c'tait pas un sacre! Un verrat, c'est un cochon, pis un cochon, ça peut pas être un sacre!' (*AC*, p. 39)

10. The youthful Tremblay's sleep, unlike that of Germaine's Henri, was unaffected by the 'loud' décor of his

> chambre au plafond rouge sang et aux murs couverts d'un papier peint en carreauté écossais agressif – mes amis ne pouvaient pas comprendre que je puisse dormir dans des couleurs aussi criardes; je me contentais de répondre que je ne dormais pas les yeux ouverts. (*DC*, p. 191)

11. The character's name neatly encapsulates the ambivalencies of her situation, the first names, Marie-Ange, linking her to an ideal of holy motherhood, the surname Brouillette suggesting her resentment against life in general and, on this occasion, against Germaine and her good fortune in particular.

12. embolie: i.e. 'abolie', an example of the malapropisms scattered through the *belles-soeurs*' speech.

13. a va 'se prélasser dans la soie et dans le velours'!: 'she's lounging in luxury'. The lexical register of the French moves up a notch here (as indicated by Tremblay's quotation marks) to deride Germaine's pretentions.

14. Lisette de Courval's 'aristocratic' surname suggests the social and cultural pretentions of the character, as established here by her would-be elevated 'poetic' diction. Tremblay sees her as a caricature. 'Elle est très drôle, elle est très ridicule, mais elle n'a aucune espèce d'humanité' (*Voix et images* 7 [1982], p. 216).

15. The first name Des-Neiges is a modification of Denise. See Louis Hémon, *Maria Chapdelaine* (LGF, Grasset 1954) pp. 54-5:

> Au pays de Québec l'orthographe des noms et leur application sont devenues des choses incertaines. Une population dispersée dans un vaste pays demi-sauvage, illettrée pour la majeure part et n'ayant pour conseillers que ses prêtres, s'est accoutumé à ne considérer des noms que leur son, sans s'embarrasser de ce que peut être leur aspect écrit ou leur genre. Naturellement la prononciation a varié de bouche en bouche et de famille en famille, et lorsqu'une circonstance solennelle force enfin à avoir recours à l'écriture, chacun prétend épeler son nom de baptême à sa manière, sans admettre un seul instant qu'il puisse y avoir pour chacun de ces noms un canon impérieux. Des emprunts faits à d'autres langues ont encore accentué l'incertitude en ce qui concerne l'orthographe ou le sexe. On signe Denise, ou Denije ou Deneije; Conrad ou Courade; des hommes s'appellent Herménégilde, Aglaé, Edwige...

16. Léandre Bergeron's *Dictionnaire de la langue québécoise* (Montreal: VLB, 1980) p. 524, lists Yvette as a 'nom donné à une femme qui joue le rôle traditionnel de femme au foyer à l'ombre de son mari'.

17. Rose is playing here on the literal and figurative meanings of 'serin', literally 'a canary', figuratively 'a dumbcluck'. In their translation of the play, Martin Bowman and Bill Findlay, carried along by Rose's vulgarity, take the image further: 'ROSE (*laughing*). The Canary Islands! That'd be jist the place for a honeymoon. The cocks sit on the nest all day there.' (*The Guid Sisters*, p. 9).

18. The Italian community in Quebec trebled in size in the 1950s, from 34,165 (1951) to 108,552 (1961). See John A. Dickinson and Brian Young, *A Short History of Quebec*, p. 264. See also, Introduction p. xxiv and n. 61.

19. 'Pue/pudeur': note the possible word-play.

20. John Van Burek and Bill Glassco's translation (p. 19) renders 'fou raide' euphemistically: 'without getting an...without getting all worked up! Goddam sex'. An explicit rendering 'hard-on' gives a better sense of the shock impact of this line. In 1971, an interviewer observed to Tremblay of the characters of *Les Belles-Soeurs*: 'C'est nous-autres, mais c'est différent. Dans bien des milieux populaires, jamais à ma connaissance le mot "cul" n'est prononcé. Caché! Tabou!'; to which Tremblay responded: 'C'est pour cela que dans *Les Belles-Soeurs*, quand [Rose] dit "Maudit cul" le monde frémit dans la salle' (*Nord* 1 [Autumn 1971], p. 65).

21. Le chapelet: the daily prayers said on the rosary. In Quebec these were commonly recited by the family together until relatively recent times. The radio presentation underlines the institutional preservation of a devotional ritual which has lost its quality of personal and communal commitment.

22. neuvaine: 'novena'. An old form of prayer traditionally repeated once every day for nine days. The novena is an act of supplication, often addressed to a saint, based on the belief that 'persevering in prayer' (*Acts* I, 14) will be a means of obtaining what one asks, hence Rose's question: 'Que c'est qu'a peut ben vouloir à sainte Thérèse, donc elle?'. The nine-fold repetition may be extended further to a series of weeks or months, thus Germaine's exchange with Rose, p. 12 where Germaine explains: 'ma neuvaine, c'tait neuf semaines!'

23. This hauling of the aged grandmother up three flights of stairs has been instanced as one of the 'absurd' elements in the play. Her falls, here and later, are developed as comic by-play, but they may perhaps also be understood, along with Monsieur Dubé's fall from the window or Rosaire Baril's death, as symbolically signalling the imminent collapse of the old order in its various sexual, social and political manifestations.

24. Tremblay gives the character the Christian name of his paternal grandmother, Olivine Tremblay.

25. mnasse: i.e. 'menasse' = 'mélasse' (molasses).

26. y faut ben gagner son ciel!: 'We all have our cross to bear!'

27. cours classique: Raymond is an academic high-flier who is attending, no doubt as a scholarship-holder, one of the élite *écoles classiques* which until the 1960s provided the only route into higher education in Quebec. See Introduction, p. x and its accompanying note 25.

28. Birds (canaries, sparrows) in cages are a leitmotif of the play. See Introduction, pp. xxv-xxvi.

29. The bar (*la taverne*) is the man's traditional space in Quebec, as the kitchen is the woman's.

30. Bruno's name is a departure from a traditional religiously-based choice of name.

31. on nous prend pour la banque de Jos Violon: a popular Quebec expression, meaning: 'they think we're made of money'.

32. 'pleurer comme une Madeleine': a proverbial expression, current both in France and in Quebec, meaning to 'weep buckets', like the sinner Mary Magdalene weeping her sins.

33. Fernande Saint-Martin's editorial in the first number of the women's magazine *Châtelaine* (vol. I, no. 1 [October 1960] p. 3) highlighted the following objectives:

> Il importe que la femme cultive avec une perfection toujours plus grande l'élégance et la beauté, ainsi que les divers arts ménagers qui perpétuent dans notre vie quotidienne les plus belles traditions françaises. D'autre part, les beaux-arts et la politique, l'éducation, la science ou les problèmes sociaux ne sont plus aujourd'hui une chasse gardée du sexe fort; il est bon aussi que 'l'honnête femme' ait 'des lumières sur tout', puisque son sort et et celui de ses enfants sont liés au destin du monde.

The magazine assumed a more radical feminist image in the late 1960s and 70s under the editorship of Francine Montpetit but, in 1985, directives from the publishers in Toronto imposed a return to its former traditional and consumerist approach. See Marie José Des Rivières, *'Châtelaine' et la littérature (1960-1975)* (Montréal: l'Hexagone, 1992) and Collectif Clio, *L'histoire des femmes au Québec depuis quatre siècles*, pp. 416, 440-41, 468, 481, 572.

34. Another malapropism, comically illustrating the linguistic naïvety of the *belles-soeurs*.

35. exiprès: i.e. 'exprès'. The addition of *i* gives extra (comic) articulatory force.

36. The description of the wedding cake recalls Flaubert's celebrated description of Emma Bovary's wedding cake, the one 'romantic' item at her wedding meal *(Madame Bovary*, Part I, Ch. 4). See also Introduction, p. xx. The Longpré confection, with only two out of six tiers actual cake, underlines both the basic economics upon which such fantasy will founder and the importance, nonetheless, for the participants of the social pretence.

37. la voix à Duplessis: Maurice Duplessis, Prime Minister of Quebec, 1936-39 and 1944-59. For a discussion of Duplessis' Quebec, see Introduction, pp. xi-xv.

38. Rose confuses 'étole' (stole) with 'étoile'.

39. 'Péter plus haut que son trou [que son cul]': an idiom, current in France as well as in Quebec, which the Oxford/Hachette dictionary renders (very politely!) as: 'to be too big for one's boots'.

40. une avis, un tourne-avis... un grand crochet tout croche...: Repetition and redundancy provide a comic indication of Yvette's linguistic limitations.

41. Note the higher register of language for the journalist, marked by euphemism ('la chose horrible') and the polite use of the conditional.

42. 'La Presse': continues as the most broadly based francophone daily in Montreal, set between the tabloid *Journal de Montréal* on the one hand and the intellectuals' newspaper, *Le Devoir*, on the other.

43. 'Être sur ses trente-six': to be dressed up to the nines, to be very smart, very well turned-out. In France, the expression is normally 'être sur son trente-et-un'.

44. 'Les livres de Magali': a Mills and Boone type romance series.

45. The name Angéline Sauvé points towards the paradoxes and ironies of the scenario of sin and salvation in which this character, 'angelic' church-goer, fallen 'angel', 'lost soul', 'saved' sinner, will become embroiled.

46. It is difficult to understand, in realistic terms, why the arrival of the two aging spinsters should induce Linda to return to the party. In dramatic and thematic terms her return is necessary for the further exploration in Act II of the situation of the younger, unmarried women.

47. The curly-haired child film-star, Shirley Temple, was a household name in the 1930s and 40s. She made her first appearance in 1932, at the age of four, and subsequently starred in 49 films, including, notably, *Bright Eyes* (1934), in which she sang 'The Good Ship Lollipop'. Tremblay refers (*VA*, p. 100) to:

> la monstrueuse Shirley Temple que je n'ai jamais pu supporter et dont ma mère disait toujours: 'est tellement belle que j'la mordrais jusqu'au sang'.

48. Lisette de Courval's role as a leader of good works in the parish stands in ironic contrast to her lack of any charitableness of spirit.

49. Laura Cadieux and her husband Pit Cadieux both appear in Tremblay's short novel *C't'à ton tour, Laura Cadieux* (Montréal: Leméac, 1973). The other personages are limited to their mention here in *Les Belles-Soeurs*.

50. On the phonetic and thematic interplay of 'coller' and 'voler', see Introduction, p. xxxix.

51. Les retraites: the annual parish retreat where members of the church and the clergy spend some time together in a meditative environment.

52. Martial Dassylva (*La Presse*, 16 June 1973) tracing the changing reception of *Les Belles-Soeurs*, notes:

> Quelques petites choses avaient changé au pays de Québec et on venait de se rendre compte que Paris n'était pas la France, que la bouche en cul-de-poule n'était qu'une torture inutile et que la France éternelle et séculaire n'était qu'une invention de la Société du Bon Parler français.

The Société du Bon Parler français au Canada was founded in 1902 as a defense against anglicisation and had as its objective 'l'étude, la conservation et le perfectionnement de la langue française, écrite et parlée au Canada'.

53. nage aquatique: the tautology is a further example of linguistic ineptitude among the *belles-soeurs*.

54. It seems entirely appropriate that it should be Lisette de Courval who calls the winning number.

55. je connaissais pas personne: the redundancy of the double negative helps to underline both Lise's desperation and her lack of linguistic sophistication.

56. Kresge: a cheap chainstore, now no longer in existence. Tremblay based the character in part on his cousin Lise 'qui travaillait au Kresge [...] et qui nous rapportait qu'on lui commandait des sandwiches au fromage en anglais et qu'elle rapportait des sandwiches au jambon en français (*VA*, p. 140). The character's role as 'fallen woman' may have suggested the surname Paquette. This is a common surname in Quebec, but it may also recall Paquette la Chantefleurie, the 'fallen woman' who is Esmeralda's mother in Victor Hugo's *Notre-Dame de Paris*, part of Tremblay's youthful reading (see Introduction, p. xiii).

57. An example of what Tremblay calls his 'phrases marteaux':

> Ces phrases, c'est ma façon, mes plus gros trucs, mais il arrive souvent qu'à la représentation, Brassard me les coupe. Il pense que cela peut être efficace à la lecture, mais que quand du monde intelligent t'interprète, il y a des choses que tu n'as pas besoin de dire. Les coupures qu'il fait à mes textes sont d'ailleurs toujours à ce niveau-là.

(Roch Turbide, 'Michel Tremblay: Du texte à la représentation', *Voix et Images*, 7 [1982], p. 220).

58. Lisette de Courval inadvertently reveals her lack of general knowledge, confusing F.B.I. (Federal Bureau of Investigation) with I.B.M. (International Business Machines).

59. Eddie Constantine (1917-93), French actor, singer and film-star, who came to popularity in the 1950s in a series of films based on Peter Cheyney's detective stories.

60. anti-contraceptives: the prefixes cancel each other out. Pierrette, for all the intelligence she showed at school, gets entangled in the same linguistic knots as the other *belles-soeurs*.

61. This monologue was added to the 1965 version of the play to provide a second monologue in the definitive 1968 version for the creator of the role, Denise Filiatrault. In *Nord* 1 (Autumn 1971), p. 65, Tremblay stresses the electrifying effect of Rose's explicitness on an audience unused to the public discussion of sexual matters:

> Quand elle dit 'Maudit cul' le monde frémit dans la salle. Rose Ouimet [...] est la première qui s'avance en avant de la scène devant deux mille personnes et puis qui dit: *'mon mari me viole deux fois par jours, pis ce qu'y me fait est pas agréable!'* C'est la première femme qui ose le dire. Y faut le dire.

62. 'On ne mélange pas les torchons avec les sarviettes!': a proverb, current also in France, meaning: 'there's absolutely no comparison!'

63. Jean Marais (1913-98), French actor and film-star, celebrated for his many leading roles as dashing lover, hero and righter of wrongs.

64. *Pleure pas, Germaine* is the title of a novel by Claude Jasmin (Montréal: Editions Parti pris, 1965). In Jasmin's book Germaine, the long-suffering wife of the drifting and disorientated narrator, is the positive symbol of Quebec, courageous and smiling even in adversity. Tremblay's depiction of his Germaine is an ironic reprise of this trope, stressing only the loss, with no hope of salvation or even of mutual consolation.

65. 'O Canada' is the Canadian national anthem. The music was composed by Calixa Lavallée (1842-91) of Verchères, Quebec, who had been a Northern army bandsman in the American Civil War. The English words were written by Robert Stanley Weir, the French words by Sir Adolphe-Basile Routhier. The French version was first sung in public at the Saint-Jean-Baptiste Day celebrations on the Plains of Abraham (Quebec City) in 1880. For the music and for the words in English and French, see Appendix II, pp. 75-7.

APPENDIX I

The Language of the Play[1]

Les Belles-Soeurs challenged its first Quebec audiences by transposing to the serious stage the distinctive intonations and raw vocabulary of *joual*, the language of the Montreal street.[2] In 1973 this socio-cultural challenge assumed a more specifically linguistic form as a Paris audience confronted the particularities of *joual* within the wider phonetic and lexical unfamiliarities of Quebec French. But the linguistic difficulties of the text are not limited to their oral rendering on stage.[3] The written text, through which Tremblay made his linguistic intentions plain, also challenges the reader not only with its sometimes unfamiliar vocabulary but also with variations of spelling and punctuation designed to transcribe for the eye some of the characteristic phenomena of working-class Montreal speech.[4] Tremblay's aim is above all a theatrical one and his notations therefore are neither totally consistent nor fully comprehensive. Rather they are designed to suggest a perceived poverty of linguistic performance which is the main element of identification for the particular social group to which the *belles-soeurs* belong and a major factor in its continuing socio-cultural deprivation. In the same spirit this note has no pretensions to be an in-depth linguistic analysis of Quebec French and its *joual* variety but aims merely to facilitate the reading and understanding of the text of *Les Belles-Soeurs* by focusing on some main linguistic features, noting those that are highlighted by Tremblay and contextualising his choice within the range of social and situational variation available to the general Quebec population.[5]

As oral language the *joual* of the *belles-soeurs* displays many of the features of oral Metropolitan French, e.g. deletion of unaccented vowels and consonants, omission of *ne* in negations, introduction of non-standard liaisons, but it does so with far greater consistency and intensity than its Metropolitan counterpart. The omission of *ne*, for instance, is a well-nigh categorical feature. In addition the speech of Tremblay's women exhibits idiosyncratic Quebec characteristics explicable in terms of the origins of the Quebec colonists and the historical evolution of Quebec society. The seventeenth-century settlers in New France came with their various local speech differences from the north-western regions of France: Normandy, Brittany and the Paris basin.[6] With infrequent contact from the mother country these soon converged amongst the settler population into a broadly-based Canadian-French variety. A century later the British conquest of 1759, definitively breaking the links with France, effected an even clearer divergence in linguistic development.[7] Though a francophone elite, educated by the priesthood, was still able to adhere to norms of linguistic correctness established in France, the uneducated agricultural and backwoods population, isolated in its remote communities, tended to perpetuate the pronunciation and lexis of its rural forbears. With industrialisation and migration from the land these speech patterns transferred to the city as the language of the under-class attracting the criticism and derision of the educated bourgeoisie.

The distinctive features of Quebec French and of its Montreal variety *joual* can be summarised under the four headings of phonology, morphology, syntax and lexis. This note indicates some major variations from Metropolitan French and the ways in which some of these variations, particularly those that serve as markers of social class, are rendered by Tremblay in his written text.

Phonology

Variations in pronunciation and intonation vis-à-vis Metropolitan French include the following.

1. Many vowels have a more fronted realisation in Quebec French. In the case of nasal vowels this is such a generalised Quebec feature that Tremblay has not found it necessary to display it orthographically, though other playwrights on occasion have subsequently done so. Dominic Champagne for example in his play *La Répétition* (1990) regularly transcribes *dans* as *dins*. Tremblay, however, is at pains to indicate the still more extensive fronting characteristic of *joual*, in particular the fronting of *a* in his transcriptions of *patate>pétate* (p. 15), *magasinage>mégasinage* (p. 7), *tâter>têter* (p. 14), of *e* in *stéréo>stirio* (p. 51) and of *ou* in *tout de suite> tu-suite, toute(s)-seule(s)>tu-seule(s)*.

2. The weakening of unstressed vowels is more marked in Quebec French and in *joual* than in Metropolitan French. Glides are commonly deleted (*bien>ben, puis>pis*) as is unstressed *e*, a feature rendered in Tremblay's script by a proliferation of apostrophes: *J'pense que j'vas pouvoir toute prendre c'q'y'a d'dans!* (p. 4); *j'sais c'qu'j'dis* (p. 45); *Que c'est que j'vas d'venir, moé, hein? Une p'tite waitress cheap?* (p. 46); and by his transcriptions of phono-morphological modifications: *je suis> j'sus* (*tu sais comment j'sus faite* [p. 37])>*chus*; *je m'en vais t'aider>je m'en vas t'aider* (see Morphology, point 3)>*m'as t'aider* (p. 53). In parallel, high vowels in certain pre-tonic contexts lose the tense articulation of Metropolitan French. *Pinotte* (p. 3, from English *peanut*) and the transcription *minute>menute* (p. 48) are examples of this vocalic relaxation.

3. In counterpoint, vowel lengthening is a common feature in Quebec French and in many cases may produce diphthongal variants, particularly in familiar speech.[8] Such lengthening in combination with the weakening and deletion of unaccented vowels gives Quebec French its distinctive intonation pattern of two stresses, initial and final (compare final stress only in Metropolitan French).[9] Again Tremblay's spelling does not attempt to represent such a widespread phenomenon except for the odd notation, e.g. *maison mal-famée>maison mal farmée* (p. 24). Instead he concentrates on vowel lengthening as a stylistic marker characteristic of *joual*, focusing on the particular phenomenon of the lowering and opening of *e* to *a* before pre-consonantal *r*: *énarvé*, *sarvice*, *farmez*, *pardre*, *marde*, *parsonne*, *avartie*, *sarviettes*. Additional attention is comically drawn to this socially marked feature by the misguided attempt of social climber Lisette de Courval to 'correct' *parler* to *perler* and Marie-Ange Brouillette's exasperated mimicry in response: 'Chus pas t'obligée de me forcer pour bien *perler*' (p. 8).

4. Perhaps the single most characteristic marker of *joual* is the pronunciation of *moi* and *toi*, rendered orthographically by the spellings *moé*, *toé*. This pronunciation, current in France by the sixteenth century (*le roé Francoé*, i.e. François 1er) has been maintained as an aspect of popular register in Quebec, whereas in France it was gradually superseded in the two hundred years up until the French Revolution by the popular pronunciation [**wa**], now consecrated as standard pronunciation in Metropolitan French.[10] Associated phonological developments and variations in the prounciation of *oi* over the centuries lie behind other Quebec particularities. The tendency as early as 1300 to reduce *oé* to *é* gave forms and spellings still surviving in Quebec, *boésson* (p. 39), *dret* (from *droit*) (p. 31), *frette* (from *froid*) (p. 48), *je cré bien* (from *croire>crère*) (p. 51), *creyable* (p. 4). These older pronunciations, surviving as a result of marginalisation from the Metropolitan mainstream, attract a negative evaluation by a Quebec social and educational establishment looking to France for standards of linguistic correctness. It is entirely suitable for Tremblay's theatrical purposes that his working-class characters should use them.

5. As in Metropolitan French, unaccented consonants are frequently deleted, especially the liquid consonants *r* and *l* in final position or in clusters. Tremblay indicates this as a particularly widespread phenomenon of the *belles-soeurs*' speech: *not'soeur* (pp. 11, 18), *aut'chose* (p. 16), *leu'toucher* (p. 26), *prends su-toé* (p. 28); *pus*, *quequ'chose*, *quequ'un*,[11] *quequ'temps*, *quequ'minutes*. Deletion of the *l* of the definite article is a constant feature of *joual* after the prepositions *à*, *dans* and *sur*: *sur'es épaules* (p. 4); *sentir sa grosse main su'a mienne* (p. 24, double deletion of *r* and *l*); and is further accompanied by vowel merging: *à la porte>à a porte>à porte* (p. 2), *à mode* (p. 41), *à télévision* (p. 42), *à messe* (p. 40).

The same pattern obtains by analogy in *à soir* and in *dans'cuisine* (p. 2), *dans'paroisse* (p. 41). The deletion of *l* in the personal pronouns *il* and *elle* is another widespread phenomenon as shown in Tremblay's transcriptions *y* and *a* (see below, Morphology, point 5).[12]

6. Conversely the retention of final *t* is a sociolinguistic marker of joual. Thus Tremblay consistently transcribes *tout* as *toute*, 'après *toute*' (p. 3), 'J'vas *toute* prendre ça' (p. 5); the past participle *fait* as *faite*, 'vous avez bien *faite*!' (p. 15); *bout* as *boute*, 'on vous entend crier à l'aut'*boute* de la maison' (p. 11), 'chus rendue au *boute*' (p. 12). Cuirs, the non-standard addition of linking *t* (on analogy perhaps with *t* liaison in the singular, e.g. *aime-t-il*) are also a constant feature: *chus t'allée voir les voisines* (p. 3); *chus pas t'obligée de me forcer pour bien perler* (p. 8); *chus t'énarvée* (p. 41); *chus t'écoeurée de travailler au Kresge* (p. 43); *t'es t'après à te pardre* (p. 37); *J'les aurait étripés* (p. 15). Lisette de Courval, despite her pretentions to speak correctly, involuntarily follows the same pattern: *Moi quand je suis t'allée en Europe* (p. 7). Velours (the addition of non-standard linking [*s* or *z*], by analogy with [*z*] liaison in plural contexts) are similarly a frequent phenomenon: *J'leu s'ai donné chacun une bonne fessée* (p. 15); *huit z'erreurs* (p. 17), *dix-sept s'opérations* (p. 30), *sept s'enfants* (p. 39). The pronouncing of final *t* or *s* can also serve to differentiate masculine and feminine: *pourrite* (p. 32) (compare *pourri/pourrie*), *les ceuses* (p. 6, compare *ceux/celles*).

7. Two further distinctive features of Quebec French not specifically indicated in Tremblay's script are the affrication of *t* and *d* before *i* and *u* (*petit>petsit*; *lundi>lundzi; constitution>constsitsution*) and the pronunciation of *r* as a front rolled [**r**], instead of Metropolitan French uvular [**R**].[13]

Morphology

In the matter of grammatical forms the *joual* text of *Les Belles-Soeurs* displays the following departures from Metropolitan French.

1. *Avoir* is used as the auxiliary verb for all verbs in the perfect tense: *j'ai resté surpris* (p. 2); *j'ai déjà sorti avec* (p. 17).

2. Instead of present tense vocalic alternation of some verb stems as in Metropolitan French, various processes of analogical reformation obtain: *éteindez donc le radio* (p. 12), *assisez-vous* (p. 29).

3. The first person singular of the verb *aller* appears as *vas* (not *vais*): *je vas répondre*; *je vas y [lui] téléphoner*. This corresponds to the analogical aligning of the first person and second person singular of a number of verbs in sixteenth-century French. The seventeenth-century French grammarian Vaugelas defended this aligning for the verb *aller* but from the seventeenth century on it was considered vulgar or dialectal in France. Molière uses it in his plays for the speech of the servants. Similarly in

Tremblay's play it acts as a marker of an uneducated social class.

4. The conditional of *avoir* appears in its older form *arais*, now archaic in educated French: *j'arais dû crier 'non'* (p. 50); *j'arais jamais pensé ça de toé, Angéline!* (p. 36).

5. The colloquial handling of pronouns mirrors and extends that of Metropolitan French. Subject pronouns have reduced variants according to context. *Je* is phonetically modified or may even disappear (see Phonology, point 2). *Tu*, before a vowel, is reduced to *t'*. *Il* /*ils* is generally reduced to *y*. *Elle* is reduced to *a* before a consonant: *a m'a conté son histoire* (p. 16) and to *al* (transcribed by Tremblay as *a l'*) before a verb beginning with a vowel (or before the indirect pronoun *y*): *a l'a quatre-vingt-treize ans* (p. 13); *a l'agit comme un bébé* (p. 13). *Elle* before the pronoun *en* and a verb beginning with a vowel loses its *l* and reduces to *a*, while *en*, reducing from nasal vowel to nasal consonant, forms a liaison with the verb: *elle en arrache sans bon sens*>*a'n'arrache sans bon sens* (p. 43); *elle en a plein son linge [...] elle en a partout*>*a n'a plein son linge [...] a n'a partout* (p. 53). (This is confusing at first for the foreign reader who sees what appears to be a negation.) *Elles* is replaced by the masculine form *y*. The singular indirect object pronoun *lui* reduces to *y*: *vous n'avez pas peur d'y faire mal* (p. 19). It retains, however, its stressed forms *lui* and *elle*: *que c'est qu'a peut ben vouloir à sainte Thérèse,donc elle?* (p. 10); *elle, a l'a la grosse étoile de vison* (p. 21); *a l'a réussi dans la vie, elle* (p. 45). The stressed forms of the plural are frequently reinforced by *autres*, *eux-autres* serving both as the stressed masculine pronoun (*Avec eux-autres j'ai du fun*, Angéline referring to the people who frequent Pierrette's club, p. 39) and the stressed feminine pronoun (*Mon Dieu, que j'ai donc honte d'eux autres!* Lise de Courval of the other *belles-soeurs*, p. 27).

6. Genders vary from those of Metropolitan French: *un espèce* (p. 2), *le radio* (pp. 10, 12), *une habit* (p. 31). English borrowings are often feminine: *une job*, *la gang*.

7. *Le monde*, in the sense of 'people' attracts a plural agreement: *c'est du monde qui sont pas ben propres! D'ailleurs, en Urope, le monde se lavent pas!* (p. 9); *Pour que c'est que l' monde doivent te prendre* (p. 38).

Syntax

The following differences from Metropolitan French sentence structure (some of them also found in regional and popular French) can be observed in *Les Belles-Soeurs*.

1. The conditional is used instead of the imperfect in conditional *si* clauses: *si j'arais de l'argent* (p. 20); *si j'arais pensée une chose pareille!* (p. 36); *comme si j'en arais soixante (ans)* (p. 46); *si Linda s'rait là [...] a pourroit m'aider* (p. 13).

2. The particle *tu* is used to mark interrogation or emphasis (cf. the use of *ti* in popular French from the sixteenth century onwards): *je peux-tu y dire?* (p. 18); *c'tu assez beau, hein?* (p. 5); *c'tu effrayant!* (p. 12) – both with vowel deletion in the verb; *J'ai-tu l'air de quequ'un qui a déjà gagné quequ'chose!* (p. 17); *ça se peux-tu?* (p. 28); *j'en ai-tu arraché* (p. 30); *j'l'ai-tu assez r'gretté* (p. 50).

3. Elsewhere, as in lower register Metropolitan French, interrogative forms such as *Quand c'est que vous voudriez que je sorte?* (p. 16); *Qui c'est qui vient à part ça?* (p. 17); *Que c'est qu'y disait?* (p. 2) avoid inversion.

4. Word-order in imperative clauses may differ from the standard sequence of educated French, maintaining instead the word-order of the declarative clause: *Parlez-moé s'en pas* (p. 14) [*ne m'en parlez pas*]; *promets-moé-lé* (p. 31) [*promets-le-moi*]; *donnez-moé-les* (p. 54) [*donnez-les-moi*].

5. *Que* is used as a universal (and sometimes redundant) complementiser: *j'y ai donné du vieux linge que* [*dont*] *j'avais pu besoin* (p. 16); *J' parle comme que j'peux* (p. 8); *commère comme que t' es* (p. 11); *ç'a'rait été ben que trop cher* (p. 19).

Lexis

Quebec French vocabulary offers several departures from Metropolitan French usage, some of them accepted by the whole population, some of them more extensively employed by the urban, working-class group to which the *belles-soeurs* belong. This section deals briefly with the different lexical categories that distinguish Quebec French and its *joual* variety. Details of the English (and, if appropriate, the French) equivalent of Quebec vocabulary in Tremblay's play are provided in the separate Glossary, pp. 80-3.

1. Quebec French retains as part of normal usage a range of expressions that are either archaic in Metropolitan France, eg. *icitte* (*ici*), *itou* (*aussi*), *pantoute* (*pas du tout*), *astheur* (*à cette heure*), or that now have a different meaning there, e.g.*catin* (QF *child's doll,* MF *prostitute*), *portique* (QF *hall*, MF *portico*), *châssis* (QF *window*, MF *window frame*).

2. 'Correct' usage in Quebec also accepts a range of 'canadianismes de bon aloi', authorised by the Quebec Government's Office de la langue française and often relating to the specificities of the Canadian environment, e.g. *poudrerie* (*tempête de neige*) or to the maritime or agricultural origins of the population.Thus Des-neiges Verrette is 'la mieux *grayée* (*greyée*) en fait de brosses, dans la paroisse' (p. 22) from *greyer* (*équiper*) *un navire*.

3. Quebec French also includes a number of Amerindian or Inuit words mainly relating to the flora and fauna of the different regions of the province. These fall outside the *belles-soeurs*' purview.

4. On the other hand their borrowings from English, especially American English, overt and covert, are frequent: *c'est le fun, chum, cheap, cute* (p. 14), *ma shape* (p. 20), *le club, une grosse gang* (p. 39), *du braidage* (p. 44), *des bargains* (p. 44), *ses shorts rouges - y étaient short, all right!* (p. 49), *smatte* (p. 20), *lâchez-moé lousse!* (p. 26), *élévateur* (p. 28), *poudigne* (p. 48).

5. Anti-anglicisms, not present in Metropolitan French, appear in Quebec French as a defensive reaction against the pervasiveness of English. They include *Arrêt* instead of *Stop* at road junctions, *chien chaud* instead of *hot-dog*, *fin de semaine* instead of *weekend*. The *belles-soeurs* make no use of them in the play. This is no doubt a matter of chance but could perhaps also be construed as one further indication of the *belles-soeurs*' flagging sense of their francophone identity.

6. Religious swear-words (*sacres*) are an ubiquitous element in Quebec French, reflecting the history of a settler society where physical survival long took precedence over formal education and where a strong Catholic Church enforced strict codes of behaviour. The *sacre* was the transgressive outlet for the forceful expression of inarticulate emotion, an affective passe-partout, as Gilles Charest puts it, for an often uneducated population.[14] Alongside euphemisms of a type found across Christendom such as *bonyeu* (p. 10), *bonyenne* (p. 13), *mon doux* (p. 10), *sapré* (*saprée folle*) (pp. 15-16), Quebec possesses an exceptionally wide range of blasphematory expressions based particularly on the Mass: *calice*, *ciboire*, *hostie* (often abbreviated to *stie*), *tabernacle* (always pronounced *tabarnak*) as well as a secondary layer of religious allusions: *baptême*, *viarge* (*vierge*), etc. Central to the whole process *Christ* naturally stands as the most used of all the *sacres*. Its effect, as a result, is the weakest, at least when used alone. However a further feature is the multiple linking of *sacres*, e.g. *hostie de christ de tabernacle*, to reinforce the emphatic expression of frustration, surprise or admiration. Another idiosyncrasy is the inventive relexification of several of the *sacres*, and particularly of *Christ* into a myriad derivative verbs, nouns and adjectives.[15]

Les Belles-Soeurs provides just a small, relatively restrained range of indicative examples,[16] characteristic especially of Pierrette, the woman who has lost her reputation and transgressed all the behavioural precepts of Church and family. Her despair at her abandonment by 'le maudit Johnny' can only be voiced by recourse to a 'forbidden' vocabulary: *me sacrer en bas du balcon* (p. 43); *il m'a faite pardre dix ans de ma vie, le crisse* (p. 46), *J'me crisserais en bas d'un pont* (p. 46). In the same way her sister Rose has only the *sacre* to articulate her misery in a married life that bears no resemblance to *une crisse de vue française* (p. 50), and which she dreams vainly of leaving (*toute crisser là* [p. 51]). Meanwhile, through a remark made by Germaine as she loses her temper with Linda, Tremblay flags up the norm of 'proper' language, whereby the emotional effectiveness of the swearing as a release for the pent-up emotion of the speaker is shown as an inverse function of its offensiveness to the listener: 'Hein, c'est ça, tu veux me faire sacrer devant le monde? Ben crisse, tu vas avoir réussi!' (p. 24). Public swearing by the women, contravening a cultural taboo which tolerates swearing by males but rejects female swearing as contrary to woman's role as moral exemplar, is designed on the aesthetic level to strike the members of the bourgeois theatre audience with the full force of its social unacceptability, reinforcing yet again their sense of the low linguistic register in which the *belles-soeurs* remain trapped.

Bibliography

More detailed information on Quebec French, language in Canada, and suggestions for further reading can be found in the works listed below. The prefaces of the dictionaries are also worth consulting for interesting insights into the varying descriptive, prescriptive and proscriptive ambitions of the different compilers and their attitudes on the one hand towards Metropolitan French, on the other towards Quebec French and its variants.

Ball, Rodney, *The French Speaking World. A Practical Introduction to Sociolinguistic Issues* (London and New York: Routledge, 1997). Chapter 6, pp. 100-116: 'Local Varieties of French outside France' (pp. 108-11, 'North America: Quebec').

Blanc, Michel, 'French in Canada' in Sanders, Carol, ed. *French Today. Language in its Social Context* (Cambridge, New York, Melbourne: Cambridge University Presss, 1993), pp. 239-56.

Charest, Gilles, *Le Livre des sacres et des blasphèmes québécois* (Montréal: L'Aurore, 1974).

Corbett, Neil, ed., *Langue et identité. Le français et les francophones d'Amérique du Nord* (Québec: Presses de l'Université Laval, 1990).

Dumas, Denis, *Nos Façons de parler* (Sillery: Presses de l'Université du Québec, 1987).

Edwards, John, ed., *Language in Canada* (Cambridge: Cambridge University Press, 1998).

Gauvin, Lise, 'Littérature et langue parlée au Québec', *Études françaises* 10 (1974), 80-109.

Labsade, Françoise Tétu de, *Le Québec. Un pays, une culture* (Montréal: Boréal, 1990). Chapter I, 3, pp. 83-109, 'La langue'.

Ostigny, Luc and Tousignant, Claude, *Le français québécois, normes et usages* (Montréal: Guérin Universitaire, 1993).

Walker, Douglas C, *The Pronunciation of Canadian French* (Ottawa: University of Ottawa Press. 1984).

Dictionaries

Bergeron, Léandre, *Dictionnaire de la langue québécoise* (Montréal: VLB and Léandre Bergeron, 1980).

Boulanger, Jean-Claude, *Dictionnaire québécois d'aujourd'hui. Langue française, histoire, géographie, culture générale*. Saint-Laurent, Québec: DicoRobert, 1992.

Desruisseaux, Pierre, *Dictionnaire des expressions québécoises. Nouvelle édition revue et augmentée* (Bibliothèque québécoise, 1990).

Dulong, Gaston, *Dictionnaire des canadianismes*. (Larousse, Canada, 1989).

Notes

1. I am indebted to Marie-Anne Hintze, my colleague in the French Department of the University of Leeds, for her help and advice in the preparation of this linguistic note. Any imperfections are entirely my own.

2. The term *joual* is an elastic one, that sometimes coalesces with the broader notion of *le québécois*, but that remains essentially focussed on the specific variety of working-class Montreal speech. For more details on *joual* as a socio-cultural phenomenon, see also Introduction, pp. v-ix.

3. Even for a Québécois cast, the specificities of *joual* can be challenging on the practical level. According to the actress Rita Lafontaine:

> le joual ne m'avait pas dérangée, pas plus qu'il ne faisait problème aux autres comédiens de l'époque. La puissance de l'écriture et des personnages submergeait toutes les réserves qu'on aurait pu avoir vis-à-vis du joual. Ce n'était pourtant pas mon langage, le joual. [...] J'avais eu un peu de difficulté à me le mettre en bouche, je m'en souviens, parce que je ne suis pas une Montréalaise, moi, je viens de Trois-Rivières.
> (Lorraine Camerlain, 'Au fil des ans et des textes. Entretien avec Rita Lafontaine', *Cahiers de théâtre. Jeu* 47 [June 1988], p 76)

4. In an early interview Tremblay recognises the difficulty of *reading* joual:

> Je s'rais pas capable de décrire Montréal en rendant ça beau et en te flanquant des beaux grands dialogues en joual. D'abord, le joual est laid à lire. Ça sert à rien d'écrire des romans joual au complet non plus, parce que je respecte trop le lecteur éventuel pour lui faire endurer du joual. Quand un lecteur qui lit du théâtre sait qu'il va lire du joual d'avance, pis y l'accepte au départ, il s'habitue en le lisant tout haut, mais je n'écrirais pas de roman comme ça parce que c'est pas agréable, – je suis typographe – c'est plein d'élisions. Ton oeil accroche tout le temps après des apostrophes pis c'est ben fatigant à lire.
> (Rachel Cloutier, Marie Laberge, Rodrigue Gignac, 'Entrevue avec Michel Tremblay', *Nord* 1 [Autumn 1971], p. 70-1)

5. The use of phonetic symbols has generally been avoided since the aim of this note is to provide the non-specialist with some readily accessible explanation of Tremblay's own transcriptions of the phonological specificities of the *belles-soeurs*' speech.

6. The French population that settled Acadia, subsequently Nova Scotia, and that is now concentrated in New Brunswick, came largely from south of the Loire, especially Poitou, and their French has undergone a separate development as another Canadian-French variety.

7. In particular there was no longer a French administrative and military élite travelling to and fro across the Atlantic according to their tours of duty and thus maintaining a continuous link with developments in France.

8. Denis Dumas, *Nos Façons de parler* (Sillery: Presses de l'Université du Québec, 1987), p. 131, stresses the social context of this use of diphthongs:

> Dans toutes les formes du discours officiel – parole en public, informations à la télévision ou à la radio, discours politiques, etc. – le style de prononciation qui est pratiqué ne les utilise pas, et une fois mis dans la situation de devoir produire ces discours officiels, les locuteurs s'interdisent avec une facilité relative (et un succès variable) de transformer les voyelles longues en diphtongues. Ils bloquent alors volontairement le phénomène comme ils le font aussi dans plusieurs formes de la parole chantée (hymne national, chants religieux ou folkloriques, etc.) sauf peut-être dans la chanson populaire, qui est souvent assez proche de la langue parlée courante dans plusieurs de ses caractéristiques.

9. A flavour of the intonations of the spoken language in Quebec, its greater marking than in Metropolitan French of strong and weak accentuation, and the variety of its registers, from quasi-Metropolitan French at one extreme to *joual* at the other, can be obtained via Radio-Canada newscasts and other Quebec programmes transmitted on TV5, the dedicated international francophone channel funded by Belgium, France, Canada and Switzerland for the maintenance and development of international francophone links. The channel is available on cable and satellite. For an analogous linguistic effect for a speaker of Standard English, see an extract from Martin Bowman and Bill Findlay's latest, unpublished Scots version of *Les Belles-Soeurs* (Appendix III, pp. 78-9) I am most grateful to the two translators for their permission to use this passage.

10. As Dumas neatly puts it: 'Moé et toé même s'ils ont [...] leurs lettres de noblesse, pour ainsi dire, sont aujourd'hui mal jugées comme étant anciennes, vulgaires, etc. [...] la prononciation en moé et toé est [...] devenue le symbole et le bouc émissaire du mauvais goût, de l'absence de l'éducation, de la vulgarité, etc. sans doute parce qu'ils s'éloignent passablement de la prononciation admise... et d'autant plus qu'ils ont une haute fréquence dans le discours.' (op.cit., p. 212).

11. But note the retention of *l* when the pronoun is stressed: 'Lise Paquette a va devenir quelqu'un!' (p. 44).

12. Note also the deletion of unstressed *e* and of *l* in *celui>c'ui*: *Combien tu l'as payé donc, ton p'tit costume bleu, Rose?* [...] *Ah! c'ui-là... J'l'ai payé $9.98* (p. 44).

13. Tremblay recalls the mother of his childhood playmate Daniel Paradis reprimanding her son 'si par malheur [il] attrapait une de nos expressions ou se mettait à rouler les 'r' comme nous'. (*DC*, p. 13).

14. Gilles Charest, *Le livre des sacres et des blasphèmes québécois* (Montréal: L'Aurore, 1974), distinguishes three levels of swearing: the *juron* ('Jurer [...] c'est dire maudit, sacrifice, baptême'); the *sacre* ('Sacrer, c'est employer les termes religieux (Christ, calice, ciboire, tabernacle, calvaire et sacrement) et leurs combinaisons'); the *blasphème* ('Blasphèmer, c'est employer les sacres en les faisant précéder d'un maudit, maudit christ, maudit tabernacle, etc.'). He also notes that these distinctions in an increasingly secularised society have tended to collapse:

> Entre jurer, sacrer et blasphémer, il y a une gradation du plus petit au plus gros, une différence de niveau que seule une éducation catholique et québécoise peut expliquer. [Mais] les différences [...] se perdent en même temps que se perd la crainte du péché.
> (Quoted by Françoise Tétu de Labsade, *Le Québec, un pays, une culture*, [p. 92])

15. Charest, ibid., p. 40, supplies the following list for *Christ*: *crisseur (euse), déconcrisseur(euse), crissage, décrissage, déconcrissage, crissaillage, décrissaillage, décrissable décocrissable, crisser, déconcrisser, reconcrisser, crissailler, décrissailler, contre-crisser*.

16. Tremblay's nuanced attitude with regard to *les sacres*, both at the beginning of his writing career and subsequently, emerges in his interview in *Séquences* 88 (April 1977), 7:

> Dans mes premières pièces, les 'sacres' sont très calculés, très dosés. Dans les 'Belles-Soeurs', on fait beaucoup de verbes avec les 'sacres'. Mais il n'y a qu'un 'sacre' volontaire: 'chrisse'. Les autres sont aussi inconscients que le reste. Ils faisaient partie du langage. [...] Mais depuis, les 'sacres' se sont systématisés au théâtre et au cinéma. J'ai rarement retrouvé chez les autres [auteurs] un égal souci de dosage du 'sacre' à l'intérieur d'une pièce ou d'un film.

APPENDIX II

O Canada!

2 O Canada! Where pines and maples grow,
Great prairies spread and lordly rivers flow,
How dear to us thy broad domain
From east to western sea!
Thou land of hope for all who toil,
Thou True North strong and free!
We stand on guard; we stand on guard for thee.
We stand on guard; we stand on guard for thee.

3 O Canada! Beneath thy shining skies
May stalwart sons and gentle maidens rise,
To keep thee steadfast through the years
From east to western sea,
Our own beloved native land,
Our True North strong and free!
(Chorus)

4 Ruler Supreme, who hearest humble prayer,
Hold our Dominion in Thy loving care.
Help us to find, O God in Thee
A lasting rich reward,
As waiting for the better day
We ever stand on guard.
(Chorus)

2

Sous l'oeil de Dieu, près du fleuve géant,
Le Canadien grandit en espérant.
Il est né d'une race fière,
Béni fut son berceau,
Le ciel a marqué sa carrière
Dans ce monde nouveau.
Toujours guidé par sa lumière,
Il gardera l'honneur de son drapeau,
Il gardera l'honneur de son drapeau.

3

De son patron, précurseur du vrai Dieu,
Il porte au front l'auréole de feu.
Ennemi de la tyrannie
Mais plein de loyauté
Il veut garder dans l'harmonie
Sa fière liberté;
Et par l'effort de son génie,
Sur notre sol asseoir la vérité,
Sur notre sol asseoir la vérité.

4

Amour sacré du trône et de l'autel,
Remplis nos coeurs de ton souffle immortel!
Parmi les races étrangères,
Notre guide est la loi.
Sachons être un peuple de frères,
Sous le joug de la foi,
Et répétons, comme nos pères,
Le cri vainqueur: 'Pour le Christ et le roi.'
Le cri vainqueur: 'Pour le Christ et le roi.'

APPENDIX III

Extract from *The Guid Sisters*

I am indebted to Martin Bowman and Bill Findlay for their permission to include this extract from the unpublished, revised version of their translation of *The Guid Sisters*. (For Tremblay's text, see above, pp. 6-7)

MARIE-ANGE BROUILLETTE: Yu'll no catch me winnin something like thon. Nae danger. Ah bide in a shite-house an that's whaur ah'll be till the day ah dee. A mull-yin stamps! Thon's a haill hoosefu. If ah dinnae keep a grip oan masel, ahm gaunnae start screamin. Typical! The wans wi aw the luck are the wans at least deserves it. Whit's thon Mme Lauzon ivir done tae deserve aw this? Nothin! Not a bloody thing! What makes her sae special? Ah'm iviry bit as good as she is! Thae competitions shouldnae be allowed. The priest wis right the ither day. They should be abolished. Why should she win a mullyin stamps an no me? Whey? It's no fair. Ah've goat bairns tae keep clean tae, and ah work as hard as she dis, wiping thur erses moarnin, noon an nicht. In fact, ma bairns are a damnsight cleaner nor hers. Whey d'ye think ah'm aw skin an bone? Acause ah work ma guts oot, that's whey. But look at her. She's as fat as a pig. And noo ah've goat tae live ben the waw fae her and her braw, free hoose. Ah tell ye, it maks me boke. It really maks me boke. No jist that, ah'll have tae pit up wi her bumming her load. She's jist the type, the big-heidit bitch. It's aw ah'll be hearing fae noo oan. Nae wunner ah'm scunnert. Ah'm no gaunnae spend ma life in this shite-hole while Lady Muck here plays the madam. It's no fair. Ah'm scunnert sweatin ma guts oot fur nothin. Ma life is nothin. Nothin. Ah'm seek scunnert bein hard up. Ah'm seek tae daith o this empty scunnering life.

(During this monologue, Gabrielle Jodoin, Rose Ouimet, Yvette Longpré and Lisette de Courval have made their entry. They have sat down in the kitchen without paying attention to Marie-Ange. The five women stand up and turn towards the audience. The lighting changes.)

THE FIVE WOMEN *(together)*: This empty, scunnering life! Monday!

LISETTE DE COURVAL: When the sun has begun to caress with its rays the wee flowers in the fields and the wee birds have opened wide their wee beaks to offer up to heaven their wee prayers...

THE OTHERS: Ah drag masel up fur tae make the breakfast. Coffee, toast, ham an eggss. Ah'm vernear dementit jist getting the rest ae thum up oot thur stinkers. The bairns leave fur the school. Ma man goes tae his work.

MARIE-ANGE BROUILLLETTE: No mine. He's oan the dole. He steys in his bed.

THE FIVE WOMEN: Then ah works like a daft yin till denner time. Ah waash froacks, skirts, soacks, jerseys, breeks, knickers, brassieres... The haill loat. Ah scrub thum. Ah wring thum oot. Ma hands are rid raw. Ah'm cheesed aff. Ah curse an swear. At denner time the bairns came hame. They eat like pigs. They turn the hoose upside doon. Then they clear oot. In the efternin ah hing oot the waashin. Hit's the worse. Ah hate it. Eftir that, ah make the tea. They aw come hame. They're crabbit. Thur's aye a rammy. Then at night we watch the telly. Tuesday.

LISETTE DE COURVAL: When the sun has begun to caress...

THE OTHERS: Ah drag maasel up fur tae make the breakfast. Ayeways the same bloody thing. Coffee, toast, ham an eggs. Ah pu thum oot thur beds an hunt them oot the door. Then it's the ironin. An work, ah work, ah work. It's denner-time afore ah ken where ah am an the bairns are bawlin fur thur denner isnae ready. Ah open a tin ae luncheon meat an make pieces. Ah work aw efternin. Tea-time comes. Thur's aye a rammy. Then at night we watch the telly. Wednesday... Message day. Ah'm oan ma feet aw day. Ah brek ma bag humping bags ae messages. Ah gets hoame deadbeat but ah've goat tae make the tea. When the rest ae thum gets hame ah'm waashed oot. Ma man starts cursin. The bairns start bawling. Then at night we watc the telly. Thursday, then Friday... It's the same thing. Ah slave. Ah skivvy. Ah caw ma guts oot fur a pack of getts. Then Seturday tae cap it aw, ah've goat the bairns oan ma back aw day. Then at night we watch the telly. Sunday we go oan the bus fur tea at the mither-in-law's. Ah cannae lit the bairns oot ma sight.... Ah huv tae kid oan ah'm laughin at the faither-in-law's jokes. Ha-bloody-ha! Ah huv tae no choke oan the auld bitch's cookin. They aye rub in ma face at her's better nor mines. Then at night, we watch the telly. Ah's seek ae this empty, scunnerin life! This empty, scunnering life! This empty...

(The lighting returns to normal. They sit down abruptly.)

GLOSSARY

(MF: Metropolitan French QF: Quebec French)

achaler annoy, bother, nag, irritate, hassle; **achalle-moi donc pas!** lay off!

achalant irritating, wearing, 'a pain', a nuisance

am(m)ancher to be stuck, in a tight spot, caught out

en arracher experience a lot of difficulty, put up with; **a n'arrache sans bon sens** she's a lot to put up with

astheur (MF *à cette heure*) now

s'astiner persist in ; talk endlessly; **on est toujours après s'astiner pour rien**: we're always arguing over nothing at all

ayoye! heave! up we come! (expressing effort)

bâtard used as a general swear-word

baver bore; **tu nous a fait assez baver avec ton million de timbres**: you've bored us silly, with your million stamps

beding! bedang! (*onomat.*) boing! boing!

bedonc, ou bedonc (MF *ou bien*) or else

ben (*bien*) very

boésson *n.f.* (MF *boisson*) drink

bon, comme un bon/une bonne very hard, really hard: **travailler comme un bon/une bonne, se forcer comme un bon/une bonne; j'hais comme une bonne:** I really hate it

bon-rien, bon-rienne no-good, useless (person)

bonyenne! bonyeu! my goodness! my god!

bougraise *n.f.* slut

brailler (MF *howl* of children) cry (including adults)

brassière *n.f.* (MF *soutien-gorge*) bra

caduc (MF *obsolete*, *null and void*) off-colour, poorly

câlisse! (from *calice*) [*lit*] chalice; used as a swear-word

(la) calvaire! [*lit*] calvary; used as swear-word

can(n)eçons *n.m.pl.*(MF *caleçons*) underpants

casque, en avoir plein le casque to have had it up to here, to have had enough

cataloye *n.m.* catalogue

catin *n.f.* (in MF *prostitute*) child's doll

cenne *n.f.* cent; **y m'pas laissé une cenne.**

Pas une maudite cenne noire not one red cent
char *n.m.(*MF *voiture*) car
châssis *n.f.(*MF *fenêtre*) window
chaudron *n.m.*(MF *marmite*) saucepan
checqué dressed up to the nines
chenailler to leave quickly;
envoye, chenaille! go on, push off
chiâler complain, whine
chicane *n.f.* bickering, argy-bargy
se chicaner bicker, argue, squabble, quarrel
à coeur de jour all the time, all day long
correct alright, OK
courailleur/se womaniser/man-hunter/eater; loose woman
créyable believable; **pas creyable** unbelievable;
je cré ben (*je crois bien*) I think so
crisse *(interjection or n.)* *as interjection, swear word* Christ!;
as n.:**Y m'a fait pardre dix ans de ma vie, le crisse** He wasted ten years of my life, the bastard/ the bugger;
une crisse de vue a bloody film;
as v. **crisser; j'me crisserais en bas d'un pont** I'd throw myself off a bridge;
j'ai envie de tout crisser là; crisser mon camp get the hell out
croche (*lit.*) bent; (*fig.*) dishonest, improper, rude
avoir la tête croche have a dirty mind

débarrer unlock (door)
se désâmer wear oneself out
dessin/e: sans dessin/e (*adj*) ignorant; (*n.)* nitwit, idiot
doux: mon doux! (MF *mon Dieu!*) my goodness! good heavens!
dret, drette (MF *droit*) straight

écoeurant disgusting (person); **un vieux écoeurant** a dirty old man;
des écoeurantes de voleuses dirty thieves
en écoeurant very, ever so
c'est beau/bon en écoeurant
éfouerré slumped, all in a heap
élévateur *n.m.*(MF *ascenseur*) lift; (American) elevator
émit(t)e *n.f.* limit
s'énarver (MF *énerver*) get worked up
ennuyant (MF *ennuyeux*) boring;
ennuyant à mort! a deadly bore!
entéka (MF *en tout cas*) in any case
envoye donc (MF *vas-y*) **envoyez donc** go on! get away!
étriper beat the living daylights out of someone; belt someone
étriver tease; have someone on
exiprès (MF *exprès*) on purpose

fatiquer (MF *fatiguer*) get tired, get worn down;
je fatiquais it was getting me down, getting on my nerves;
fatiquant tiring
follerie *n.f.* rubbish, nonsense
frette (MF *froid*) cold;
frette, net, sec in a flash

galerie *n.f.* balcony
garrocher throw
se garrocher hurl oneself on, after
goutinette/goût de tinette **ne pas prendre goutinette** to do something quickly

greyer/grayer (*lit.*) fit (ship); (*fig.*) prepare; equip
guidoune *n.f.* whore

hostie n.f. (*lit.*) Host (at the Mass); *as swear-word* a helluva...;
j'ai mon hostie de voyage well, I never (*surprise*); I'm fed up to the back teeth; I've had it up to here (*annoyance*)

icitte (MF *ici*) here
itou (MF *aussi*, *également*) also

jaser (MF *médire*; *jacasser* [oiseaux]) chat, talk

lavier *n.m.* (MF *évier*) sink
liqueur *n.f.* (MF *boisson gazeuse*) soft drink
lousse (*adj.*) loose;
lâchez-moé lousse let go of me; lay off!

mag(h)aner spoil, wear out
marde *n.f.*(MF *merde*) shit;
maudite marde! holy shit!
maudire **je la maudirais en bas de la galerie** I'd chuck her off the balcony
maudit (*adj*) damned, bloody;
(*n.*) **le petit maudit/la petite maudite** the little bugger/bitch;
maudit verrat de bâtard Christ All Bloody Mighty;
être en maudit be cross
mêlant complicated;
c'est pas mêlant, c'est pas ben ben mêlant it's clear, easy, certain; it's quite straightforward; there's no two ways about it; that's all there is to it!
ménager skimp, be stingy
misère! good grief!
avoir de la misère à faire q.ch. to have difficulty doing something
menasse/m'nasse *n.f.*(MF *mélasse*) molasses
se monter get carried away (*fig*)

niaiser waste one's time
niaiseux/euse nit-wit
nono/nounoune stupid

ouache! (MF *ouais!*) exclamation of disgust

pantoute (MF *pas du tout*) not at all
papier **je vous en passe un papier** I assure you, I'm telling you straight
patente *n.f.* thingy, whatsit;
toute la patente the whole shebang, the whole lot
pétate *n.f.* (MF *patate*) potato
piasse *n.f.* (from MF *pièce*) dollar
pinotte *n.f.* peanut
pitoune *n.f.* counter
placoter chatter, gossip, natter
poigner catch (*lit. and fig.*)
être poigné/se faire poigner get caught
les femmes sont poignées à gorge they've got us women by the throat;
une fille qui a faite la vie pendant dix ans, ça poigne plus a girl who's lived it up for ten years is finished
portique *n.m.* hall
poudingue *n.f.* pudding

pour que c'est faire (MF *pourquoi*) why
pourri/tte spoiled rotten (child); **sa petite pourrite** his little sweetie pie
pourde *n.f.* (MF *poudre*) powder

quasiment roughly, about, nearly
quinze-cennes (*n.m.*) (five and) dime store, cut-price store

r'poigner start again; **la chicane va se r'poigner** they're going to start arguing again
revirer à l'envers turn upside down
ruelle *n.f.* backstreet

sacoche (*n.f.*) handbag
sacrer **sacrez-moi donc patience!** give me strength! **sacrer quelqu'un dehors** throw someone out; **sacrer le camp** leave, get out; **se sacrer en bas du balcon** throw oneself off the balcony; **se sacrer de** not to care; **je m'en sacre** I couldn't care less
sans bon sens very; **a disait qu'a l'avait payé ça cher sans bon sens** it was frightfully expensive
sapré/e softened form of **sacré/e**; **Ça prend-tu une saprée folle!** how daft can you get!
shop *n.f.* workshop, factory
en s'il vous plaît very, a lot
siau *n.m.* (MF *seau*) bucket
sma(r)t/smatte smart, clever; **la smatte de la famille** the brain-box of the family; **t'es donc smatte** clever clogs!; **faire la smatte** show off
strapeur/se *n.* strap-maker

tanné/e fed up
téter (MF *tâter*) try, taste **téter des liqueurs** go off for a drink
torcher wipe, scrub, clean up

valeur **être de valeur** to be a pity
varge *n.f.* (MF *verge*) measure of length for materials; **ça vaut pas cher la varge** she's no better than she should be
verrat *n.m.* a scoundrel; (*as expletive*) damn! (*as adjective*) **ses verrats de timbre** her damned/dratted stamps
en verrat very
en (beau) verrat angry, cross, put-out
v'lon (MF *voilà*) here they are!
voyage; avoir son voyage well, I never! what! (*amazement*); to have had enough (*frustration*); **j'ai mon verrat de voyage** it makes me sick! for crying out loud!
vrai (*as adv.*) **vous restez haut vrai** you're a long way up (in Germaine's third floor flat); **Ça doit être plat vrai** that must be awfully boring
vue *n.f.* **(animée)** film, movie; **aller aux vues** to go to the pictures

yable *n.m.* (MF *diable*) devil
y(u)eule *n.f.* (MF *gueule*) throat; **farme ta yeule**: shut your face, your gob

CPSIA information can be obtained
at www.ICGtesting.com
Printed in the USA
LVHW050711221121
704088LV00008B/396

9 781853 995507